CONNECT YOUSELF WITH JESUS AND HIS WORD

HOLY BIBLE

CLICK

BIBLE STUDY/CHRISTIAN
EDUCATION LESSONS FOR
YOUTH AND YOUNG ADULTES

TEACHER

BOOK 2

Includes:

52 Lessons and teaching resources for each lesson

I0108483

Click - Connecting With Christ and His Word, #2

Published by: Mesoamerica Region Discipleship Ministries

Monte Cyr - Discipleship Ministries Coordinator

www.discipleship.MesoamericaRegion.org

www.NdiResources.MesoamericaRegion.org

Copyright © 2022 - All rights reserved

ISBN: 978-1-63580-322-8

Reproduction of this material is permitted only for local church use.

All of the scripture verses quoted are from the NIV Bible unless otherwise stated.

Spanish Editor - Patricia Picavea

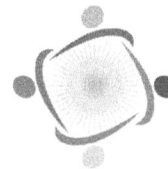

NAZARENE DISCIPLESHIP
INTERNATIONAL
MESOAMERICA REGION

Table of Contents T

Unit Four • Creation Managers

Unit Five • Relationship life

Unit Six • Different concepts in the light of the Bible

Unit Seven • Special dates

Presentation

We begin another year and continue the extraordinary work of teaching; work that, with the help of God, will help you challenge the adolescents and young people that God has entrusted to you so that they may be saints in all their ways of life.

This isn't an easy task; today's adolescents and young people belong to a generation that doesn't accept absolutes, nor does it want advice, a generation that doesn't want rules and where everyone does, acts and thinks as they see fit. Unfortunately, this philosophy of life is creeping into the church and subtly creeping into its teachings. What will you do in the face of this challenge?

We believe that no matter how much time passes, or how much human thinking changes, the Bible and its teachings don't change. Jesus said, "Heaven and earth will pass away, but my words will never pass away" (Luke 21:33). The Word of God is the only thing that lasts forever and gives us direction in our daily lives.

Therefore, there's no other solution but to teach, teach and teach the Word of God without getting tired. What a challenge to teach the Word of God as the only truth when the world and even many Christians say the opposite!

Understanding the challenge that lies ahead, we have given ourselves the task of developing this Click book with the purpose of helping you present the Word of God in a dynamic, current and relevant way for the lives of today's adolescents and young people. In this book, we address different topics in light of the Bible that will help you put clear principles into the life of each adolescent and young person.

Never stop teaching the Word of God in a serious, constant and consistent way. Nothing should change the principles that were established by our God and Lord. Your obligation as a disciple of Christ is to teach what you have received to those who will follow you, thus forming new disciples. We hope that this book will help you fulfill this commandment inherited from the Lord.

Click was written by people from different countries who bring a great wealth to the study, while giving light, seriousness and biblical foundations to the topics covered.

This year with Click we will study: Challenges of the Christian life, living salvation, being and making disciples, stewards of creation, life relationships, and different concepts in light of the Bible. Within the 52 lessons, you'll find a unit on Special Dates to use on appropriate occasions. We include a lesson for Palm Sunday, Easter, Pentecost, Christmas and New Years that you can use on the Sunday corresponding to each celebration.

We want you to enjoy using the material as much as we enjoyed making it, and that through it you can fully fulfill the ministry that God has entrusted to you. Click! and continue your work of making disciples in the image of Christ.

Patricia Picavea
Editor in Chef

Aids
A

for the teacher

Teaching is one of the Spirit-given gifts mentioned by the apostle Paul in Ephesians 4:11. In verse 12 of the same chapter, the apostle says that this is one of the gifts that helps "perfect the saints" so that they can do the ministry entrusted to them. This gift is important for the edification of the church.

For this reason, we should not underestimate it. On the contrary, we should use it with the help of God and the best of our abilities to fulfill the objective of "Perfect the saints" (Ephesians 4:12) so that they live a life that pleases the Lord always and in all respects (1 Peter 1:15).

Teaching is not just transmitting knowledge, or telling stories, or relating experiences. When we talk about teaching, we're talking about transforming, about producing changes in the lives of students, about preparing them for what they will have to live on a day-to-day basis.

It's with this understanding that we prepared this book. We wholeheartedly want to help you teach the Word of God to your students in a practical, up-to-date and dynamic way, leaving a mark on them that no one can erase.

Lesson Preparation:

Understanding that what you are venturing into is a ministry focused on adolescents and young people, ask God to give you grace to come into their lives. Pray that through each lesson, you'll reach the hearts of your students and make God's message clear to them. Here is a guide to preparing the lesson:

1. Find a place and time where, with this book and your Bible, you can read and reflect on the lesson.

2. It is advisable to have different versions of the Bible and a Bible dictionary. They are resources that will be of great help to you in the teaching ministry.

3. Start by reading the lesson objective carefully, so that throughout the lesson you know where you want to go.

4. Memorize the verse from the "Memorize Verse" section. This will help you use it in the lesson and motivate students to memorize it as well.

5. Read the section "Navigate" as many times as necessary to get to know the subject in depth. This will give you more security when teaching the lesson.

6. Look in the Bible and read each Bible verse that is indicated. Practice reading, especially those passages that have words that are difficult to pronounce.

7. Make sure you understand exactly what the passage is adding to the lesson. If you're in doubt about anything, check with your pastor before using it.

8. Although the book contains the development of the lesson, it's good that you make your own summary to guide you in class. Write on a piece of paper the name of the lesson, the main points, and develop a summary as you study the lesson. Highlight the Bible quotes that you will read in class. All this will give you more security when teaching the lesson.

9. The book is designed for two age groups: Adolescents or Teens 12-17 and Youth 18-23. Therefore, read the introductory dynamic in the "Connect" section for the group you're in charge of. Practice to make sure you understand it and can do it. Check if you need to bring any additional materials to class.

10. Do all the activities in the "Review/Application". This will help you know the activity well so you can help your students carry it out. We provide the answers to the activities.

11. Don't forget to check the "Challenge" section. Remember that this is a practice assignment for the week. It's the challenge that you want them to go away with. Don't forget to ask them at the start of the next class (Attention) how this activity went. This will help you get to know your students better and help them in their spiritual growth.

Lesson Presentation:

1. Be the first to class and set up the space creatively. From time to time, try to change the location of the chairs, the desk, the white/blackboard and the decorations. Find a way to create a conducive and pleasant environment. And start on time.

2. Welcome your students personally. This will help you create a pleasant study environment. Get to know each other's names, find ways to remember new people's names, etc.

3. Begin the class with prayer, asking for the Lord's guidance and direction.

4. Start with the introductory Dynamics; this will help them get into the subject.

5. Write the title of point 1 and start explaining it. Continue like this with the following points. This is very helpful for your students to follow you in the development of the topic.

6. Use the board as a teaching resource to write down conclusions, important words, biblical quotes, make diagrams, etc.

7. As the lesson progresses, lead the class through the activities in the "Review/Application" section.

8. Encourage all the students to participate in the class with their opinions, questions and suggestions. Don't criticize, but on the contrary, be attentive and always guide them to answers in the Word of God.

9. Explain the challenge for the week and encourage everyone to follow through on it.

10. Encourage the class to invite their friends who don't know the Lord to attend the next class.

11. End the class with prayer; you can ask a student to pray.

Other suggestions

1. You can offer a simple prize for those who:
   - Memorize the memory verses.
   - Are punctual and faithful in their attendance.

2. At the end of the book, we're including a unit called Special Dates. These lessons are counted as part of the 52 lessons of the year. You should share them on the appropriate dates. The lessons are:
   - Palm Sunday.
   - Easter Sunday.
   - Day of Pentecost (50 days after Easter Sunday).
   - Christmas
   - The New Year.

3. Don't stop using the introductory dynamics which will help you:
   - Capture the students' attention.
   - Get the group involved.
   - Get the class to relate to the topic of the day.
   - Motivate them to arrive early to participate in them.
   - Make the class more dynamic.

4. Decorate the classroom according to the age of the students. If you don't know what they like, ask the class for suggestions and decorate it together.

5. Take time to teach the memory verse. Include the text in the lesson so that the student understands its meaning; this will help his memorization. To facilitate memorization, you can do some of the following activities:

   a. Divide the group into equal teams. Provide each team with general interest magazines, no matter how old or new. Each group must cut out words to form the verse and paste them on a sheet of paper. After about five minutes, remove the magazines. Have everyone finish and stick the sheets on the classroom wall. Looking up the words will help them memorize it.

   b. Ask them to sit in a circle. Everyone should choose a different fruit (eg apple, grape, banana, etc.). Start reciting the verse, and part way through, mention the name of any fruit, for example, apple, and the one who chose that fruit continues the verse until they finish or until you mention another fruit, for example, banana. Then the one who has chosen that fruit must continue saying the text where the previous one ended. Doing it several times will help the group memorize it.

   c. Divide the class into two or three groups of three or four people each. Write the biblical text on pieces of paper. Each word must go on a different piece of paper. Make as many verse sets as groups formed. Put the words of the verse in a bag and place the bags (1 per team) at the far end of the room. Then ask the students (one from each group) one by one to walk to the bag corresponding to their group and take out a piece of paper with a word from the text and place it in the order that it should go according to the text. Then another will pass and so on until they put together the complete text.

      The groups must do this simultaneously. The group that finishes first and says the text from memory without reading it wins. If someone finishes first and they don't all know it by heart, give the second-place group a chance.

   d. Have the group sit in a circle. Give a small ball or a lemon to one of the young people. Then play a song or sing yourself. The idea is that the young people will pass the lemon or the ball while the song is playing. When it stops, whoever has the ball or the lemon must repeat the text from memory. Doing it several times will help the group memorize it.

   e. Divide the class into two or three groups. Give each group a lemon or an orange or a tangerine. The group must peel the fruit and distribute it to their group, and before eating their portion, each one must say the text. At the end, all group members must say the memoria verse at the same time. Repeating it and listening to it several times will help them memorize it.

In God's Hands

Objective: To understand that God cares about all people and that they should obey Him at all stages of life.

Memory verse: "Keep me safe, my God, for in you I take refuge." Psalm 16:1

Attention! At one point in the session, ask the group about what they have done as responsible disciples.

Accept

Connect | Navigate

Introductory Activity (12-17 years).

- Supplies: Paper and a pencil

- Instructions: Give each participant the required materials and write on the whiteboard the following questions: How does it feel to be safe? What person in your life makes you feel truly safe? Why do you think you feel safe with that person?

    Note: Give enough time for participants to answer these questions and then let some of them share their answers.

    At the end, tell the group that the people who make us feel safe are the ones who love us or bring us closer as friends or family members.

Introductory Activity (18-23 years).

- Supplies: A bandana and a chair per person.

- Instructions: The group will form pairs. Let each person choose a partner with whom he or she feels comfortable interacting with. Using the bandana, blindfold one member of each pair. Place the chairs randomly around the room. In each pair, those that are not blindfolded must guide their partners between chairs using only their voice and without touching them. At the end of the activity, ask the person who was blindfolded: Did you feel safe being guided by your partner? Why did you choose the partner in particular to be your guide? Why do you feel safer with this person than with the other people in your group?

Connect | Navigate

Now let me ask you, Do you feel safe with God? Do you believe that God cares about you? If we're not sure that God cares about us, or that our lives are in His hands, then that's the root of the problem.

How is my relationship with God? We only trust the people we think love us.

1. God knows you and is with you

In Psalm 139:1-18, it says that God knows everything about us. According to this passage, is God interested in the life of each person?

Ask the group to mention some of the verses in the passage that make them think that God is interested in the life of each person.

Of course God is interested in each person's life! Like the psalmist, we also should exclaim: "How wonderful is the love that God has for me! It's so amazing to know it! I will never be able to understand it fully, but it is real" (Psalm 136:6, paraphrased).

There are hundreds of Bible verses that teach us that God loves us and we can live our lives trusting in Him. The Bible tells us that God is our Rock, our refuge, and just like a hen looks after her chicks, God takes care of us. Many other metaphors in the Bible invite us to recognize God as our protector, loving Father, and friend to whom we can run for safety... God loves me!

Love is the attribute of God from which everything else flows. God's love is much more than just a personality trait. The Bible tells us that God doesn't merely show us love, but God IS love.

The next question that we should ask ourselves is: "Do I think of Him as love?"

There's a story about a young man who abandoned his parents. As things began to go downhill for him, he wasn't brave enough to confront his troubles. When he returned home, his father gave him a letter, but the young man ignored it and packed it up with the rest of his things. This young man lived in extreme poverty. He felt so guilty, and he couldn't even open the letter that his father had given him for fear of finding words of rebuke or contempt because of the words he had said to his parents before he left. One day, after a very long time and after becoming very sick, he decided to finally read the letter that he had packed away like a treasure. The letter said: "I will always love you, come home."

God is just like this father in the story. In His Word, the Bible, He has left us so many words of love, but they have no value unless we discover them for ourselves. The invitation that God gives us is the same that the father gave to his son: "Let us then approach God's throne of grace with confidence, so that we may receive mercy and find grace to help us in our time of need" (Hebrews 4:16).

2. God wants you to seek Him

Just like the activity at the beginning when you chose the person that you trust the most, we can trust God the more that we know Him. How do we get to know people more? Only by spending time with them. How can you spend more time with God?

It's important to have time with God daily: "Listen to my words, Lord, consider my lament. Hear my cry for help, my King and my God, for to you I pray. In the morning, Lord, you hear my voice; in the morning I lay my requests before you and wait expectantly" (Psalm 5:1-3).

Remember that knowing God means so much more than just an intellectual knowledge; it involves relationship.

God desires that you encounter Him, because He has always been waiting for you, "He has constantly been knocking at your door" (Revelation 3:20, paraphrased).

Who doesn't want to be in the hands of someone who loves them? The people who love us don't want anything bad to happen to us. The Bible tells us that God wants only good things for His children, just like the prophet Isaiah says: "You will keep in perfect peace those whose minds are steadfast because they trust in you" (Isaiah 26:3).

3. God loves you, and He wants you to walk in His ways

Ask the youth if they have ever wrestled to live under one of God's commandments? Have you ever felt that the Christian life is a restrictive life?

Perhaps, all of us who have been Christians from a young age at some point felt that way, but as we grew up, we realized we had misinterpreted the Christian Life and above all, we had misinterpreted the attributes of God. In this stage of my life, I've learned that we obtain true freedom in this life when we're under the loving care of God.

Just as every discipline that parents impose on their children is because they love them and want to protect them from wrong actions, God also disciplines us because He wants the best for us, His children. Sometimes we think that God is like a controlling father, limiting and old-fashioned. We resist obeying Him because we don't see beyond the rules. We're not able to see His love and His protection for us at the moment.

What's interesting is that God still gives us the ability to choose, and we can see that in His Word.

God wants us to obey Him from our own free will, as a response to the trust we have in Him, as His love is revealed in our lives. He shows us that although we have free will, we should discern and be able to differentiate what's good for us and what isn't. But He always encourages us to take the better way, and the better way is obedience.

Do you know why Jesus was able to resist all of the temptations in His life? Jesus resisted temptation because He knew God and could trust Him (His Father), who He was (the Father's beloved Son), and what His purpose on earth was (to complete His Father's mission).

Do we have this clarity today? Do we have this passion to please God, this conviction that there's no one better that we can give our present and future to with complete trust?

Jesus didn't give in to his natural desires that tempted Him to do something that displeased His Father. And this is the attitude that we should imitate today as well.

We can grow only if we decide to live in obedience. Jesus chose the path of obedience. It was His life's purpose, which kept Him firm even in the most difficult times, just as we read of His experience in the Garden of Gethsemane: "Then Jesus went with His disciples to a place called Gethsemane, and He said to them, "Sit here while I go over there and pray." He took Peter and the two sons of Zebedee along with Him, and He began to be sorrowful and troubled. Then He said to them, "My soul is overwhelmed with sorrow to the point of death. Stay here and keep watch with me." Going a little farther, He fell with His face to the ground and prayed, "My Father, if it is possible, may this cup be taken from me. Yet not as I will, but as you will" (Matthew 26:36-39).

Remember that God loves each one of us with an eternal and unique love. He desires to have a continuous relationship with each one of His children to reveal to them His will. We can give our lives into His hands, rest in His word, not be afraid, and obey Him. Only in God's hands are we really truly safe!

Review/Application:

Start an informal conversation among your class with the following questions:

1. Do you obey your parents in everything? Why or why not?

2. Is there something you want to do that your parents won't let you do?

3. Why do you think your parents put restrictions or limits on you, or deny you the chance of participating in something that you really want to do?

4. How do you apply this to God?

Challenge:

Try to have a time each day to have your appointment with God. Take your Bible, a notebook, pencil and if you want, music whose lyrics exalt the name of God for who He is.

During this time, read a passage from the Bible. Think about what that Word meant to those who heard it and also what it means to you today. Put your comments, feelings or application in your notebook and then pray, thanking God for his love and for speaking to you.

Don't worry if it lasts two minutes or an hour. If you do it daily, you'll see how you'll enjoy this time more and more!

Created by Design

Objective: To understand that human beings were created in the image of God and His likeness, and this makes them responsible before their Creator.

Memory Verse: "So God created mankind in His own image, in the image of God He created them; male and female He created them" (Genesis 1:27).

Attention!
You could start the session by asking about the group's devotional life. If they still haven't started, encourage them in this area.

Accept

Connect / Navigate

Introductory Activity (12-17 years).

- Supplies: Large pictures from calendars or magazines that show different landscapes. Also, containers with paint, trash or liquids. Make sure that they are things that will leave a stain.

- Instructions: Hang the pictures around the room so that your group can look at them and comment on the beauty of the pictures. (Be sure to cover the spaces around these pictures to protect them.) Then, ask someone to throw one of the containers at the pictures and stain them. Then, ask the group what they think about what just happened and how they feel about doing it.

    Finally, explain to them that God created a beautiful world, and put man and woman in charge of His greatest creation so that they would enjoy and look after it, but sin came into the world and changed everything.

Introductory Activity (18-23 years).

- Supplies: Make three human silhouettes in different colors but the same size. Make a crown the same size as the silhouette's head. Write the word "body" in one silhouette, "soul" in the second, and "Spirit" in the third one.

- Instructions: Ask for two volunteers to organize the silhouettes in order according to their own criteria. Ask them to explain to the group the criteria that they used to organize them and let the others give their opinion too. Finally, explain to them that it doesn't matter what order you put them in because as human beings, we are a whole. Put the three silhouettes together and the crown on top of its head. These silhouettes are interrelated, and together they represent the human being created in the image of God.

Connect / Navigate

Humans can't create something out of nothing. They're only capable of creating with materials that already exist. A carpenter can create a piece of furniture using wood; a cook can bake using flour, butter, eggs, etc. But out of nothing, God created everything perfectly. He gave the word and it was done!

The Bible teaches us that the universe and life were created by God, and it was He who created the heavens and the earth. He created the heavens and blessed the living beings. He formed man and woman in His image and likeness. In the book of Genesis, the phrase "and God saw that it was good" is repeated six times, showing how pleased God was with His creation (Genesis 1:10, 12, 18, 21, 25, and 31).

1. Man and woman were created in the image of God

"Image of God" is a phrase used in the Bible story of creation (Genesis 1:26-28). Mankind was created in the image of God, and this makes them the only creatures with personal dignity (Genesis 1:26a). A Dictionary of the Bible & Christian Doctrine in Everyday English (Eby, et al, 2004) notes: "Only humans were enough like God to enjoy fellowship with Him. The image of God is what makes people different from other creatures." They're a bodily and spiritual being, and their spirit and physical material form one unique nature. They're not two united, but one unique nature. The biblical story illustrates how God formed man from the dust and made him a living being (Genesis 2:7). To understand this concept better, we often split each part of man's nature into categories, but we need to remember that it's just a way of studying it, because humans are inseparable in nature.

In the early Church, there were a few streams of thought that said that the body was something bad, and for this reason, instead of looking after it, the believers punished it because they believed that sin was in the body. However, the body is part of the dignity of the "image of God" precisely because it is brought to life by the spiritual soul. On the other hand, the temple of the Spirit is the whole person (1 Corinthians 6:19). Therefore, it's not right for humans to despise their body, but on the contrary, their body is good and worthy of honor because it was created by God. Through the body, humans interact with the outside world. Our body is a gift from God that we must look after responsibly and treat wisely, because it doesn't belong to us.

The soul is the repository of emotions, desires, and affections. Through the soul, humans become aware of themselves. In the Bible, the word "soul" references human life (Matthew 16:25-26). But it also describes the deepest parts of humans (Matthew 26:38; John 12:27) and is valuable (Matthew 10:28), which is what makes it part of the image of God: "Soul" is the spiritual component in humans.

Frequently, the term "spirit" refers to humans as a whole (Galatians 6:18; 2 Timothy 4:22). This affirms the inseparability of human nature, and although occasionally it refers to emotions just like the term "soul" does (Luke 1:47; John 11:33; 1 Corinthians 4:21), it also refers to the core of reflection, reason, will, and intentions (Matthew 26:4; Luke 1:80; Acts 18:25; 1 Corinthians 2:11; 2 Corinthians 2:13). The apostle Paul says that the person's spirit is what relates with God (Romans 8:15-16; 1 Corinthians 6:17).

Unlike other beings, humans have privileges and responsibilities for which they'll have to give an account to their Creator.

Men and women are not a product of change, as material determinism says. Human life is not just a mound of molecules that play the laws of physics and chemistry. But neither are we fallen angels, superhumans or demigods as many myths have proposed throughout history.

Exalting humans to the level of God or degradation to the lowest level isn't a Christian approach. The radical dignity of all humans, believers or not, has its ultimate foundation in God because they are created in His image. The image of God is seen in us as we reflect Him in intellectual, emotional, and moral ways as we fulfill His will.

This means:

- Humans must always be treated as a person, regardless of gender, race or skin color; and no one should ever be treated as an object or superior being.

- There must be a fundamental respect for life. The human body shouldn't be understood as just a set of organs and functions, like animals, but as the physical expression of a person.

- We're the ones God described as "...whom I created for my glory, whom I formed and made." (Isaiah 43:6) The authentic purpose of creation isn't found in humans, but in God Himself.

"Humans are sacred beings." It's interesting that the person who coined this phrase wasn't a believer but a pagan philosopher called Seneca. He wanted to censor and prohibit the use of humans as public spectacles where they had to face beasts or other people in gladiator matches. It's important to affirm the value of every human being and condemn all forms of violence, degradation, or abuse of his or her dignity.

2. Both were put in charge of administering what God created

Humans were created in the image of God with the privilege of sharing with Him the responsibility of taking care of creation. The love and careful attention of God sustains each living thing, God clothes the grass of the field (Luke 12:28), and He's even concerned about the life of a sparrow (Matthew 10:29).

God placed man and woman in the garden so that they would work and cultivate the ground. God, as Lord, commands us to "lord" over it in His name, because we were created in His image and given the ability to do it. The idea of "Christian stewardship" is born from this teaching, which is the correct way to use and administer what God has given us. As beings created in the image of God, we possess the ability that He has given us to explore, conceive, and bring to life new possibilities in the creation order. We are called to praise our Creator with His creation (Psalm 148) and take part with God as active participants in the development and care of creation.

What does the psalmist mean in Psalm 8:6-8? In God's plan, man and woman are called to "subdue" the earth (Genesis 1:28). God is the owner of everything, but he delegates responsibilities to human beings, making them the administrators and governors of the earth itself. Human beings are responsible for what they do with their body. God wants them to glorify Him in their bodies (1 Corinthians 6:20).

Ask the group: Why is it important to understand that God created man and woman in His image?

Note: It's because it puts human beings over creation. Therefore, human beings are responsible for bearing witness to God and must announce the news of the magnificent existence of the living God, the creator of the world. Also, speaking of human beings as made in the image of God brings us closer to Him, to His perfect plans and purposes. We have the moral duty to conserve and cultivate what has been entrusted to us by our Creator. Every creature, every living thing, speaks of the Creator and gives glory to Him. That is to say, every created thing contributes to reflecting His perfection and divine beauty. Human beings are destined to speak of God in a deeper way. Human beings must give honor to the Creator by offering, in thanksgiving and praise, all that they have received from Him (Psalm 8: 4-7).

Review/Application:

Match the questions to the Bible verses and give the answers.

1. What were the instructions God gave Adam on how to care for the planet?
2. What was God's plan in creating male and female?
3. The authentic purpose of creation is not found in human beings, but in God himself.

A. Genesis 1:27
B. Genesis 2:15
C. Isaiah 43:7

ANSWERS

1. B *Let him cultivate and care for it.*
2. A *That men and women are made in the image of God.*
3. C *The human being is the glory of God.*

Challenge:

What things could you do this week that would help show God's image to those around you?

What's up with your emotions?

Objective: To understand that emotions are part of the image of God in human beings.

Memory Verse: "Above all else, guard your heart, for everything you do flows from it." Proverbs 4:23

Attention! x

Talk about the different activities they completed, showing the image of God.

Accept

Connect | Navigate

Introductory Activity (12-17 years).

- Supplies: Sheets of paper, pencils, and a container.

- Instructions: Each person will take a piece of paper and write the name of an emotion on it, fold the paper, and put it in the container. Then, one by one, they'll go to the front of the group, take one of the papers and show the emotion that is on their paper by only using gestures. Everyone else will guess which emotion he or she is acting out.

- This activity will help you know which emotions are most prominent in your group, and also which facial or bodily expressions they associate with an emotion. Many of them have the same universal representation.

Introductory Activity (18-23 years).

- Supplies: Chalkboard and chalk or whiteboard and whiteboard markers

- Instructions: Open a round table discussion, a space to dialogue. Ask the following questions: What are emotions? What are they for? What characteristics does an emotion have? How do we show our emotions as Christians? (Feel free to add more questions to enrich the discussion). The group will participate by giving their opinions, meanwhile one person will write on the whiteboard the most frequent answers.

- The activity will help the group think about the concept of emotions.

Connect | Navigate

As Christians, we rarely talk about emotions. It's easier for us to focus on rationality or free will. But what are emotions? What do they have to do with our lives as Christians? Emotions are part of every human being. To think about someone without emotions is to think about some kind of robot. As God's creation, we know that we were created perfectly. Our body, mind, heart, and spirit play a marvelous role within ourselves.

1. Emotions: What do I want to express?

When we try to define what emotions are, we often become confused. Are they something that I feel? Are they a reaction to some kind of situation or person? It's difficult to grasp the concept, mainly because emotions are interwoven with other aspects such as: feelings, character, and conduct.

The English term "emotion" comes from a Latin phrase meaning the impulse that induces an action. Emotions are much more than just feelings. From a psychological view, emotions are a means of expression. As human beings, our emotions tell our emotional and internal state: feelings, needs, desires, dislikes, or even objectives. Emotions accompany words and actions, sometimes alone, to express what each person is experiencing internally.

The ways in which emotions are expressed are connected strongly to physical reactions like trembling, blushing, sweating, a fast heartbeat, and also conduct like facial expressions, actions, and gestures. We can see that emotions are reflected physically as well as in behaviors; in this way, we can identify the emotions both we and others experience.

Refer to the opening activity and the emotions the group identified. Then, remind the group that fear, surprise, disgust, anger, joy, and sadness are some of the major emotions.

These reflect what is happening inside of us, and many times direct our actions, show us how we evaluate or judge various situations that we go through, and occasionally help us make decisions and adapt. These emotions prevent us from taking unnecessary risks, and act in a positive way (for example, during a robbery we're able to stay calm and avoid getting hurt). But if we're paralyzed by fear, we won't even try to do what's necessary in a situation. Then our emotions could be a negative factor (for example, when we see an accident, we can become afraid and won't help those in need).

2. Created in His image: Is God emotional?

According to Genesis 1:26-27, Adam and Eve were created in God's image, but what happened when Adam and Eve sinned? Was the image of God lost in human beings? Let the group share their opinion.

The Bible tells us that on many occasions, God the Father showed His emotions. In Genesis 6:6, we see God as being sad, an emotion that showed His regret for having created human beings. In Zephaniah 3:17, God spoke through the prophet and mentioned His reason for being joyful. In these two passages, we can see God experiencing emotions, just like human beings experience emotions.

In Jesus Christ, we can perceive different emotions. He's our biggest point of comparison, because He is God incarnate. In Mark 3:5, we read that Jesus felt anger and sorrow for the Pharisees because these men didn't believe Him and tried to corner Him, which was saddening.

There are moments or difficult situations, like the loss of a loved one, where it's understandable to be sad and cry. Crying is a way of relief that God Himself put in us. In John 11:33-36, we see Jesus moved and hurt to see the suffering of others and the loss of a friend. Verse 35 tells us that Jesus wept. What might be seen as a sign of weakness might simply be a way to externalize pain and be beneficial to our emotional health.

Nevertheless, as we cope with emotions, there's an appropriate way to manage them. God's purposes were never changed by His emotions, because if He had, He would have destroyed humanity in more ways than the flood. On the other hand, if Jesus was paralyzed by His emotions, he wouldn't have died for our sins.

3. My emotions with God

Many psychologists have come to the conclusion that emotions are neither good nor bad. On many occasions, the emotions that we express depend on the circumstances we have gone through. For example: Two people go to an amusement park. One of them is afraid of rollercoasters because in the past they saw one breakdown and create a tragedy. This person perceives danger and this produces fear. On the other hand, the other person had fun on rollercoasters with family and friends. For that person, rollercoasters produce excitement.

Before God came and changed us, perhaps we felt out of control in every aspect of our lives. Therefore, we couldn't manage our emotions well, and we would become upset and lash out in anger. Maybe when we loved something or someone, we might have reacted too excitedly without thinking of the consequences. God doesn't want us to be negatively driven by our emotions (2 Timothy 1:7). As Christians, we aren't alone, and we're strong and capable in God and through the Holy Spirit. God asks that our lives be driven by one emotion in particular: Joy (1 Thessalonians 5:16). This joy is anchored in Him. On the other hand, He disapproves of lingering anger (James 1:19-20). Overall, our joy should be found in God, who wants us to rejoice in Him. We are to "Worship the Lord with gladness; come before him with joyful songs" (Psalm 100:2). To feel anger, sadness, surprise, disgust, and fear is normal but always in a controlled way. These emotions will be fleeting but our joy is in God and is everlasting.

Review/Application:

Give them a few minutes to answer the following questions. They can do this individually, in pairs or in groups.

What are emotions and what are they for? *(These are means of expression, which indicate what is inside of us, such as desires, feelings, needs, dislikes, etc.)*

Name the basic categories of emotions: *(Fear, surprise, anger, disgust, joy and anger.)*

Why do we say that God is emotional? Quote some texts that mention the emotions of God. *(Because the Father and Jesus Christ showed their emotions in different circumstances: Genesis 6:6 - God was sad and sorry for the creation of man. John 11:35 - Jesus wept at the loss of his friend.)*

How can we make good use of our emotions? *(Let God take control of them and let us be guided by what God is telling us, showing fear, anger, joy, etc., but in due measure. Not letting emotions control us.)*

What emotion should prevail in us and why? *(Happiness and joy because Jesus, who is the Christ, has redeemed us, and walking and serving in obedience to Him brings lasting joy.)*

Challenge:

We know that emotions are born in us, either to express what we perceive of ourselves or of other people. Let's make a daily list in the week ahead about the emotions that we have experienced in the day. Let's observe how many of them are negative and how many are positive. And let's repeat the memory verse: "Above all else, guard your heart, for everything you do flows from it" Proverbs 4:23. Let's pray asking God to keep our hearts and allow life to come out of it, to come out of the wonderful things that God constantly does in our lives.

Flesh vs. Spirit

Attention! Ask the group how they managed their emotions during the week. Talk about any new emotions that they discovered in the past days. *Accept*

Objective: To understand the constant battle between the flesh and the Spirit in their life, and the answer that Christ gives us.

Memory Verse: "Therefore, there's now no condemnation for those who are in Christ Jesus, because through Christ Jesus the law of the Spirit who gives life has set you free from the law of sin and death." Romans 8:1-2

Connect | Navigate

Introductory Activity (12-17 years).

- Supplies: One balloon per person, string, a blackboard/ whiteboard, whiteboard markers or chalk and two sheets of letter sized paper.

- Instructions: Before starting the session, cut up the sheets of paper into 10 equal pieces (you'll have 20 in total). On 10 of the pieces, write the letter F (flesh) and on the other 10 write the letter S (Spirit). Fold them as small as you can and put a piece of paper in each balloon. Blow up the balloons, and with the string, tie the balloons to the ceiling or the walls of the meeting room so they are ready when the group arrives. On the board, draw the following table:

Flesh vs. Spirit

Team No. 1		Team No. 2	
F	S	F	S

Divide the group into two teams, and each team will form a circle. Explain that they'll have a race to search for Bible verses. One person from the team who finds the Bible verse first will be able to choose one of the balloons. Then they'll pop the balloon and read the paper that is inside. According to the letter on the paper, put a point in the "flesh" or "spirit" section of the table. Explain to the group that "F" stands for "Flesh" and "S" for "Spirit". When there are no balloons left, count the points, and the team with the most points in the "Spirit" section of the table wins.

Say: "Throughout our life, there will come a time when we must choose between living according to the Spirit and living according to the flesh, and at that point, it won't be a game, but a personal decision."

Introductory Activity (18-23 years).

- Supplies: 20 red paper circles and 20 green circles (approx. 5cm in diameter), masking tape, markers and a whiteboard

- Instructions: At the end of the introductory activity, draw the following table on the board:

The Face Off

Team No. 1		Team No. 2	
S	F •••••••••	S	F •••••••

In the letter "F" column for each team, place the ten red circles. Divide the group into two teams and ask them to sit together. Explain that the red circles are bad points, and to be able to change them to good points (green), they'll need to look up Bible verses. The first person who finds the Bible verse in each round will remove a red circle from their table and exchange it with you for a green circle and put it in the "S" column.

Play the game for an appropriate amount of time, and at the end, the team with the most number of green points in their "S" column wins.

Say: The sin that lives in us is represented by the red circles that were assigned to each team at the beginning of the game. When we receive Jesus Christ as our Savior and we consecrate our lives to Him, those negative points disappear, and we make space for the work of the Holy Spirit, which is represented by the green circles.

1. The flesh and the Spirit

The word "flesh" comes from the Greek work Sárx. This term means the bodily material of living creatures. A Dictionary of the Bible & Christian Doctrine in Everyday English (Eby, et al, 2004) points out that "It also means the natural life of a creature." It doesn't represent only the physical body that we touch and see but also the "carnality" of humans as we experience weakness and limitations, as well as our rebellion against God (Romans 8:7-9).

A Dictionary of the Bible & Christian Doctrine in Everyday English (Eby, et al, 2004) notes: "The Bible teaches that God created the flesh and called it good." But "People simply live as human beings when they 'live in the flesh' (Galatians 2:19). Flesh becomes sinful when people turn away from God. They make themselves the center of life rather than God. They worship the creature instead of the Creator (Romans 1:25). The New Testament calls this 'life after the flesh' (Romans 8:5, 13; Galatians 5:19-21)."

A Dictionary of the Bible & Christian Doctrine in Everyday English (Eby, et al, 2004) points out that "Spirit is the quality, power, or force that makes a person alive and acting. Spirit cannot be seen, but it's real. This is true of both the Spirit of God and the spirit of people…The spirit of a human refers to his or her capacity to know God. Apart from Christ, the spirit of people is dead in sin. They cannot know God or be fully human until they are born again. Also, God wills that the Christian's spirit be filled with the Holy Spirit. Then the human spirit is set free from all that is opposed to God (John 3:3-8; 1 Corinthians 2:9-16; Galatians 5:16-25; Ephesians 3:14-21; 5:17-20)."

Basically, to live in the Spirit means that although we're still humans, the Spirit of God controls and directs our spirit in such a way that our tendencies and focus will always be on God, loving others, and the values of the kingdom of God.

2. The reason for the fight

The Bible affirms that mankind disobeyed God (Genesis 3), and because of this, sin and its consequences entered the world. In Romans 5:14, Paul says that death still reigns even in those who haven't sinned in an external act of disobedience like Adam and Eve. Therefore, death is the consequence of natural sin, as well as an act of disobedience that happens to all humankind (Romans 5:19).

Christ affirmed that many of the evil tendencies originate in the heart of people (Mark 7:20-23). Paul uses the word "flesh" in a moral sense to refer to the natural fall of mankind (Romans 8:5,8-9). All of these passages and others teach us that this tendency toward sin belongs to the natural fallen human nature, original sin, or inherited depravity. So on the one hand, we need to ask for forgiveness for our acts of disobedience, and on the other hand, we need to be freed from this carnality or tendency toward evil.

The Bible tells us that the blood of Christ is the solution to this double-sided problem. The blood of Christ frees us from the guilt of our actions and grants us forgiveness for them (Jeremiah 31:34). As a church, we affirm that the blood of Christ also has power and authority to free us from this tendency or desire to sin. We have access to that power to live, not by the flesh, but by the Spirit.

3. Life in the Spirit

A Dictionary of the Bible & Christian Doctrine in Everyday English (Eby, et al, 2004) notes: "The Bible says that God created life. God still makes life possible. Life also refers to the activity of people on earth. The Bible teaches that humans may enjoy a special kind of life. This life is salvation. Jesus Christ made salvation possible by giving His life for the sins of the world. This is also called spiritual life…The Holy Spirit presents sinners with the claims of Christ and the Gospel. He draws people to salvation (John 16:7-15). He makes faith possible and completely changes those who believe (2 Thessalonians 2:13; 1 Peter 1:2). Christians are former sinners who have been 'born of the Spirit' (John3:5-8)."

Galatians 2:20 and 5:24 tell us that when people are in Christ, they continue living in their earthly body, but they enter into a new life in the Spirit. Previously, the worries of the "flesh," the world, and the natural life were the priorities and the primary purpose of their existence. In this new life, the things of God have become their primary purpose.

Ask: How can I change this natural tendency to do evil? How can I be victorious in the midst of this struggle? Since it's something that God does in us, what should we do?

Read Romans 12:1-2 and ask: How would we explain what Paul says in our own words? Let the group answer.

The Apostle Paul is talking about consecration. It doesn't mean asking for forgiveness and being free of guilt; it's about believers being freed from sinful tendencies. The Apostle John says, "But if we walk in the light, as he is in the light, we have fellowship with one another, and the blood of Jesus, his Son, purifies us from all sin" (1 John 1:7). We're not talking about growth, but a complete and instantaneous act, that's then reflected through its fruit (Galatians 5:22). The will of God is that we live from victory to victory, and we do this through sanctification (1 Thessalonians 5:23), that liberates us from our carnality (natural tendency to sin). This victory was won by Christ, who by His grace helps us live according to the Spirit (Romans 8:3-4).

"The Holy Spirit is the divine Agent in sanctifying believers. He sets them free from the power of sin. He produces in them the character of Christ. Thus, Christian moral virtues are the 'fruit of the Spirit' (Romans 8:2; 1 Corinthians 6:11; 2 Corinthians 1:21-22; Galatians 5:22-23)" (Eby, et al, 2004). In this new life, we'll discover day by day how to walk under the control of the Holy Spirit, and He'll tell you when an action or attitude isn't in accordance with the values of the kingdom of God.

Review/Application:

Ask your students to form pairs or trios and choose one of the following verses: Galatians 5:16-17; Galatians 5:1; John 8:31-32; 1 Peter 2:16; Matthew 26:41 and rewrite it in their own words. Example: 1 Peter 2:16. Live free but not to steal, participate in evil, or use drugs, but to do the will of God by serving in the way that the Lord guides us.

Challenge:

While we go about our activities during the week I invite us to do a reflection exercise. Write down attitudes that the Spirit warned you are attitudes "according to the flesh" and write what the attitude "in the Spirit" should be. It's good to do this because many times, we don't realize that we act or react according to our flesh and not according to the Spirit.

Tu m'as fait libre !

Objective: To understand that it's Jesus who sets us free from the slavery of sin so that we can live within the boundary of His will.

Memory Verse: "Then you will know the truth, and the truth will set you free." John 8:32

Attention!
A good way to start the session would be by talking about correct and incorrect attitudes that each one had during the past week.

Accept

Connect / Navigate

Introductory Activity (12-17 years).

- Materials: Board, a container, masking tape, a series of cards with the following words written on them: Truth, equality, justice, redemption, independence, joy, privilege, submission, forced labor, condemnation, yoke, tyranny, fear, and humiliation.

- Instructions: Divide the board with a line and write on one side "freedom" and on the other "slavery." Mix up the cards in the container, and ask the group to come to the front one by one, take one of the cards, and stick it on the corresponding side of the board. At the end, each person will share about some words; some will relate with freedom and others with slavery.

  This activity will help us see visually the contrast between freedom and slavery.

Introductory Activity (18-23 years).

- Instructions: Ask the group to think of a time in their lives where they experienced freedom and another time where they felt a lack of freedom.

  Have each person come to the front and explain to the group the times that they chose, explaining the difference between the feelings involved in both situations.

  This exercise will help the group remember the way in which they have used their freedom and circumstances they've found themselves without their freedom. It will also help them to analyze which situation they prefer and why.

Connect / Navigate

Ask: What is freedom? A Dictionary of the Bible & Christian Doctrine in Everyday English (Eby, et al, 2004) notes: "Freedom is the quality of not being limited. People are free to make choices. But they are not completely free of limits. Only God has total freedom. Yet even He has chosen to limit Himself in some ways." This could sound like a series of words without meaning if we take into account that freedom can be a normal part of life today. Although nowadays, certain terms such as "servant" or "slave" are not used, there are people in different parts of the world who don't live in much freedom.

1. The truth will set us free

Read John 8:31-34. What freedom are the Jews referring to? They were referring to freedom of the body, which Jesus referred to as freedom of the soul. It's possible to ask ourselves the question: What is freedom of the soul? How can it be obtained? To teach this truth, Jesus played a word game, using two pairs of words with contrasting / opposite meaning. He used the words "free" vs. "slaves" and "truth" vs. "sin." If we analyze the references to these four words, we can see that Jesus associated them in pairs, that is to say, He connected freedom with the truth, and slavery with sin.

The way that Jesus made the connection between truth and freedom is: "Then you will know the truth, and the truth will set you free." (John 8:32 NIV). So it's valid to ask: What is the truth? Pontius Pilate, the governor, asked this same question. While he questioned Jesus if He was the king of the Jews, it revealed two wonderful principles: first, that Jesus came to this world to give testimony to the truth, and second, that everyone who is on the side of the truth hears His voice (John 18:37). We who have the privilege of being His disciples, rejoice, just like Thomas, of the clearest and the most wonderful answer that Jesus gave to this question: "I am the truth" (John 14:6), so we don't have to continue asking the same question as Pilate, but we can enjoy the bliss of knowing the One who is the truth. The way to freedom is to know the truth, and the truth is Jesus Christ, who sets us free (John 8:36).

2. What do I need to be freed from?

Once we have reflected on the freedom that Jesus wants for us and how we can obtain it, it's important to ask ourselves: What does my soul need to be freed from? Did the Jews ask a similar question? It was definitely something that they couldn't understand, since by their lineage they didn't consider themselves slaves of anybody. However, what Jesus had in mind wasn't physical slavery but slavery to sin. The idea of "practicing sin" means making it a habit. The greatest bond of a human being isn't political or economic slavery but being subjected to the spiritual yoke of rebellion against God, which confines us in prisons of fear, confusion, insecurity and leads us to death.

Christ sets us free from the condemnation of sin (Romans 8:1-2). Rejoicing in freedom, we're exempt from the power of darkness (Colossians 1:13). How wonderful! What Jesus does in our lives by giving us his grace and forgiveness is invaluable. Therefore, the answer to our question "What do I need to be freed from?" is: to be freed from the slavery of sin and death.

3. The limits of my freedom in the Christian life

Jesus has set us free from sin through His blood on the cross and has brought us the benefits of the freedom of the soul. However, we can't use our freedom as an excuse to conduct sinful behaviors, which could open the door for desires that aren't pleasing to God or may lead to those around us stumbling in their faith (1 Corinthians 8:9). It's important to recognize, then, the limits of our freedom found in Christ.

Galatians 5:13 affirms that as followers of Jesus, we have been called to be free; but it also makes the observation and the warning that we must not use this freedom to unleash our carnal desires. This means that although we're not tied up, we will avoid walking in territories where evil reigns. The apostle Peter sums up that acting as free people doesn't mean using our freedom to do evil but to live as servants of God (1 Peter 2:16). Paul invites us to not let ourselves be enslaved anew by the yoke of sin but that we flee from it, and instead he invites us to become "slaves to Christ" (1 Corinthians 7:22). The big difference between this slavery is that it's voluntary. It represents an act of love because Jesus paid a high price for us. Freedom is an active commitment to God.

So how can we use our freedom as servants of God? We're free to walk according to His will. We're free to demonstrate the fruit of what the Spirit of God does in us (Galatians 5:22-23). Above all, we're free to achieve salvation through Christ and to proclaim through our pleasant demeanors the faith we have in Him.

Jesus affirmed that He is the Alpha and the Omega—the beginning and end of everything, including our freedom. We can say that the limit of our freedom found in Christ is everything that doesn't glorify God. The actions we think we need to do in secret, anything that Jesus wouldn't do if He was in our shoes. Jesus Christ is the truth that sets us free from the slavery of sin, to live as His servants, within His will. Let's remember what 2 Corinthians 3:17 says and come into the presence of Jesus, because where the Spirit of the Lord is, there's freedom.

Review/Application:

Give your students some time to answer the following questions individually and then discuss as a class.

1. From what does Christ Jesus free us? (Romans 8:1-2). **From the law of sin and death.**

2. What should we use our freedom for? (1 Peter 2:16). **To serve God.**

3. To what is the sinner a slave? (John 8:34). **To sin.**

4. What yoke must we not subject ourselves to? (Galatians 5:1). **To the yoke of slavery.**

5. What is it that makes us free? (John 8:32). **The truth.**

Challenge:

Have you ever reflected on how far the limits of your freedom go? Try to recognize in your daily life which actions are within God's will and, if so, which aren't.

Who's in charge?

Objective: To understand that the Spirit of God gives us self-control to manage our emotions.

Memory Verse: "For the Spirit God gave us does not make us timid, but gives us power, love and self-discipline." 2 Timothy 1:7

Attention!

Help the group think about some possible limits of freedom in the Christian life.

Accept

Connect | Navigate

Introductory Activity (12-17 years).

- Supplies: A container and various cards with different emotions written on them, e.g. fear, surprise, anger, discouragement, panic, etc.

- Instructions: Fold the cards and put them in the container. Each participant will take a card per turn until all the cards are gone.

  Before you begin the game, choose an uncommon phrase or sentence such as "Your aunt Gladys' dog died."

  The group will form a circle, and each person will take one of the cards and communicate the message to the person on his or her right, in the emotion indicated on the card. Encourage them to be very creative in how they deliver the message. The game ends when all the cards are taken.

  Invite the group to read together 2 Timothy 1:7.

Introductory Activity (18-23 years)

- Supplies: A container and various cards with different emotions written on them, e.g. Fear, surprise, anger, discouragement, panic, etc.

- Instructions: Fold the cards and put them in the container. A volunteer must take a card and act out that emotion. Everyone else in the group will guess the emotion acted out. The person who guesses the emotion first will share a life experience when he or she felt that way. The activity will continue in this way until all of the cards are gone.

  We have all experienced the emotions mentioned in the activity, some at a higher level than others, but none are unfamiliar to us.

  Invite someone to read 2 Timothy 1:7 out loud.

Connect | Navigate

Many times, we confuse emotions with the consequences of acting emotionally. Sometimes we categorize our emotions as something bad, as if they were our enemies that we have to fight against every day. Of course, there are risks when our decisions are exclusively based on how we feel, in the same way that there's a great risk in using reason exclusively.

Emotions are a gift from God and are an essential part of human beings. By design, they're good, because they've been given to us by God. In other terms, emotions are neither good nor bad, but are natural reactions through which our feelings, personality, and intentions of our hearts are expressed. It's here that we need to be careful. Since emotions are part of our own nature, it's uplifting to realize the importance of knowing what they are—how we can recognize them and also enjoy them. Somehow, it's similar to the way in which we learn about our body and satisfy our physiological needs such as hunger, tiredness, going to the bathroom, etc.

1. Looking inside

Talking about our emotions isn't a common practice in our lives. One important reason is because, emotions being natural reactions in a human being, we think that there's nothing we can do about them, and we justify them with expressions like, "that's just how I am," "I'm just hot-headed like that," or "I'm just naturally a nervous person."

Another reason is that since we were little, we've been encouraged not to blindly obey our emotions, but to always analyze well everything we do. So, we act in ways we've been taught but not the way we feel. For example: "Men don't cry." This idea has infiltrated the church, taking us to the extreme of repressing our emotions, for example, "Christians don't cry."

This doesn't mean that we should carried away by our emotions; it means recognizing their role, how they relate to what we believe and learn, how they submit to the will of God, and how they are manifested in our daily life.

The dictionary defines emotion as "a conscious mental reaction (such as anger or fear) subjectively experienced as strong feeling usually directed toward a specific object and typically accompanied by physiological and behavioral changes in the body" (https://www.merriam-webster.com/dictionary/emotion). In other words, emotions are reactions to the events that affect us, reflecting themselves externally through crying, laughing, or anger or internally (as psychological variations) through agitation, rapid heart rate, desire to eat, etc. Emotions allow us to interact with our environment, and through them we approve or disapprove of everything that happens to us.

Especially in the teen-age years, we start the conscious and voluntary process of getting to know ourselves and defining who we are, how we relate to others, who we will be, etc. It's also in this stage that some hormonal changes occur in the body, affecting the way emotions are expressed, which could create some confusion, frustration, stress and even illness. Because of all of these changes, it's important to understand that our emotions are part of God's design (Genesis 1:26-31), and by having a personal relationship with Him, we receive an additional gift from Him, which is the fruit of the Spirit (Galatians 5:22-23). It's precisely the Holy Spirit who gives us the ability to have self-control in using our emotions (2 Timothy 1:7)

2. A spirit of self-control

Self-control is described as a characteristic of the fruit of the Spirit. It isn't solely based on age or gender; it's the product of the Holy Spirit in our life. It's possible to have self-control and act with maturity and in this way assure that our emotions express what is in our heart.

It's worth clarifying that maturity does not mean being trained to control our emotions. Neither does it consist of not saying unpleasant words when we're angry, smiling regularly to appear happy, not smoking, etc. Maturity is, above all, a state of the heart, the result of our relationship with God. From there, it's only the Holy Spirit who can help us in this attitude of the heart that seeks the good of others— a heart focused on pleasing God than being guided by human impulse.

Self-control requires the supernatural action of the Holy Spirit, who helps us to express our joy with pleasure and satisfaction, and restrain anger when there's a situation of injustice. It's the Holy Spirit who gives us power to remove ourselves from situations and places that put us at risk of sinning or when our emotions could get us into trouble. The Holy Spirit creates in us the profound desire to use our emotions for good.

3. Self-control in action

People who have self-control learn to recognize weaknesses and ask for help. When they think about themselves they do it with clarity, humility, and dependency on God (Romans 12:3). For example, in many romantic relationships, people tend to fall in love quickly because someone is interested in them. Perhaps they feel physically attracted or the relationship satisfies their need for social acceptance.

So they may find themselves in a vulnerable situation, which could lead them to make wrong decisions with undesired consequences. They might quickly begin a relationship because it "feels good." However, they should be asking themselves: Am I ready for a relationship? Do I have the emotional maturity to be in a relationship of this kind? Is this the right person who can help me in my relationship with God and with others? Is this the person with whom I'd like to spend the rest of my life?

It's important to not only look for friends who are the same age as us but also adults who can guide us. This attitude will help us to make the right decisions, whether it's about relationships, professions, family, work, etc.

While everything God created is good and was made for us to enjoy with thanksgiving (1 Timothy 4:4), Paul warns us to "not be mastered by anything" (1 Corinthians 6:12). God's grace is necessary in our lives so that we can achieve a supernatural self-control, whatever the innate tendencies of our personality may be. Here, the key word is "master." What is my master? Are my desires of the flesh or of the Spirit? We should always be focused on the desires of the Spirit and on knowing God's will through prayer, reading the Word, serving others, giving a good testimony, completing school tasks, working, helping at home, etc.

Review/Application:

Encourage dialogue among the participants through the following exercise, seeking for them to realize that emotions are a natural part of them, and that it's important to make good use of them (self-control).

We're going to use our short-term memory, through the following exercise:

1. Describe the last time you laughed until your stomach hurt from laughing so hard. What was it that made you laugh so hard and how did you feel after laughing like that?

2. Describe the last time you got angry. What was it that made you angry, and how far did that anger go?

3. How and when was the last time you felt very sad? What helped you make the sadness go away?

4. When was the last time you made a decision that you regretted, because you did it at a time when you didn't stop to think very well about whether it pleased God or about the consequences?

5. What do you think "self-control" means?

Challenge:

Make a personal list of the areas in which you think you're most emotionally vulnerable. Select a specific area and determine an action that during the week will keep you busy, and at the same time, help you develop that seed of self-control that's been given to us by the Holy Spirit.

God's Enemy?

Objective: To understand the importance of not letting themselves be molded by the influences in the world around them.

Memory Verse: "Therefore, anyone who chooses to be a friend of the world becomes an enemy of God." James 4:4b

Attention!
It would be very helpful for everyone to chat for a few moments about self-control and specific present situations.
Accept

Connect | Navigate

Introductory Activity (12-17 years).

- Supplies: Cookies in different shapes (enough for each person to have a different shape) and a cookie mold that's different from the shape of cookies—it can be of any size. The cookie mold could be an ice cube tray, soda caps, etc.

- Instructions: Give a cookie to each person and put the mold in the middle of the room on a table or chair. Have the group to try and fit the cookies in the mold. Then ask them what they would have to do to make their cookie fit in the mold. The answer you are looking for is that they would need to break the cookie. After that, ask them if it's possible to fit the cookie without breaking it, and obviously the answer would be "no." At the end, they can eat their cookie if they wish.

As Christians we have a predetermined form, which is the likeness of Christ. But the world wants us to break this perfect form and mold us to its shape. To fit in the mold of the world, we would have to destroy the image of Christ in us.

Introductory Activity (18-23 years).

- Supplies: Sheets of letter size paper in different colors and a marker.

- Instructions: Cut the sheets of paper in half. Write on each half of the paper one word from today's memory verse. Make two equal sets.

Divide into two groups. The group that organizes the memory verse first is the winner. Once both teams have organized the verse, give them time to memorize it.

Ask the group: "According to the verse, who are God's enemies? And what does it mean for you to be a friend of the world?"

Connect | Navigate

In the New Testament, the word "world" is defined as anything that people say or do when they don't know the will of God; and everything that's against what God desires for His children. As Christians, we must learn to live in a way that rejects any form of friendship with the world around us that takes us away from God. The demands and influences of the world are many, and we could even reach the point where we think that it's impossible to live in a way that we're not molded by the demands of the world. Jesus Christ lived in the world just like us, and in Him we can find guidelines that will help us in our Christian life.

1. We are in the world

In John 17:15-16 we can see a specific request that Jesus gives: "My prayer is not that you take them out of the world but that you protect them from the evil one." Then He continues, "They're not of the world, even as I am not of it" (v.16).

The request was for the disciples that they would not remove themselves from the world while remaining here but would live lives worthy of being called His followers, continuing the work that He had begun. It's important that we also follow this pattern as did the disciples. He left, but before that, he provided us His example and guidelines to follow. In verses 21-23, Jesus says: "I pray that they will all be one, just as you and I are one—as you are in me, Father, and I am in you. And may they be in us so that the world will believe you sent me. I have given them the glory you gave me, so they may be one as we're one. I am in them and you are in me. May they experience such perfect unity that the world will know that you sent me and that you love them as much as you love me." (NLT)

Jesus left his disciples in the world, but they needed to be one with Him and the Father, to be able to make a difference so that the world would believe. It's necessary to recognize the difference between remain and belong. Remain is synonymous with stay or carry on, while belong means to become… or be from. Those who have lived outside of their birth country are able to better understand its implications. To be living in a particular place doesn't mean being from that place. Therefore, although we're in the world, we must learn to live as citizens of the Kingdom.

2. The influences and demands of the world

We've already mentioned that "the world" represents everything that's contrary to what God wants for us. So understanding that what the world asks or demands of us is contrary to what God likes can put us in situations of great pressure when we want to fit into both kingdoms. Remember: you aren't of this world, even if you are in it.

If people go to a country that isn't their own and try to fit in with the culture there and go unnoticed, they might end up doing such strange things that give themselves away even more. They're more of their authentic selves when they don't try and pretend to be someone they are not.

So being from the heavenly kingdom, it's absurd to want to pretend that we're from this world, having the same attitude as it. We are truly authentic when we live as citizens of the Kingdom. We have to admit that the influences and demands around us are very strong, and sometimes it seems that we have no other option but to give in to them. But it helps us to think that all of the pressures we face, Jesus also faced, and He was victorious over them. With His help, we too can be victorious.

3. Practical responses to the world

To reject everything that the world offers us, everything that's against God's will, is to consecrate our lives and transform our minds to the image of Christ.

God wants us to learn to recognize the world's influences that are in our environment and not conform to them, or even feel comfortable in them. To not conform means to reject the influences of the world and adopt a posture of the transformation of our understanding; letting God form our minds from the inside (Romans 12:1-2). As Christians, we must not give in to the influences that want to mold us to the likeness of everything around us, rather, we must attempt to change each day to do the opposite. This must be seen in all areas of our life both internally (thoughts, desires, etc.) and externally (vocabulary, way of dressing, places we attend, etc.).

In James 4:4 it says, "You adulterous people, don't you know that friendship with the world means enmity against God? Therefore, anyone who chooses to be a friend of the world becomes an enemy of God." This passage urges us to make a choice between God and all that's non-Christian. So if we belong to God, we must abandon our friendship with the world, even though we remain in it. But if we engage in any wrong way, welcoming it as a friend, we make ourselves enemies of God, breaking our saving relationship with Him. This is the battle we face while we're in the world but not of it.

The key to success? "Offer your bodies as a living sacrifice, holy and pleasing to God." This is a complete change we go through when we're "transformed by the renewing of your mind" (Romans 12:1-2).

Review/Application:

Ask them to think about the demands or influences of the world that currently affect them. Here are some examples, but let them mention the ones they know.

1. **Pornography.**

2. **Drugs.**

3. **Alcohol.**

4. **Cigarettes.**

5. **Disobedience to parents.**

6. **Sexuality outside of marriage.**

7. **Gambling.**

Think of the things a good friend of God would do. Here are some examples, but let them mention the ones they know.

1. **Healthy entertainment.**

2. **Obedience to God.**

3. **Bible reading.**

4. **Evangelization.**

5. **Services.**

6. **Worship God.**

7. **Good advice.**

Challenge:

An authentic Christian is not one who is carried away by the fashions and demands that the world offers, just to fit into a society to which he does not belong. Our true citizenship is in heaven.

This week look for practical and authentic ways to show that you are a citizen of heaven and not of the world. Do not destroy your form in Christ by trying to fit into a society to which you do not belong.

Rescue Mission

Objective: To confirm or make the decision to recognize Jesus Christ as their personal Savior.

Memory Verse: "For God so loved the world that he gave his one and only Son, that whoever believes in him shall not perish but have eternal life." John 3:16

Attention! Guide the group to think and act in a way that shows they belong to God's kingdom.

Accept

Connect | Navigate

Introductory Activity (12-17 years).

- Supplies: Small pieces of paper, masking tape and pencils

- Instructions: Start the session by giving each person a piece of paper and masking tape. Each person will write down an idea for a penalty that the person who loses the game will receive, and then they'll stick it on the sole of their right shoe without anyone seeing. Then, everyone will sit in a circle, take off their right shoe and put it in the middle. The group leader will also participate, and on their piece of paper they'll write: "eternal death." On the count of three, each participant will grab a shoe at random and put it on as if it was their own (nobody should put their own shoe on). The last person to put a shoe on must complete the penalty that's on the paper. If the penalty is offensive, give the person a different penalty or "forgive" them.

Then, ask each participant to read the penalty on the shoe he or she chooses. Leave your shoe until the end so the last punishment is "eternal death."

Unlike this activity, Adam and Eve's disobedience wasn't a game. They both knew that there were rules in their relationship with God, but they decided to disobey the rules. The consequence of this rebellion was spiritual death, or separation from God. However, even though the punishment was a fair consequence for their disobedience, God provided a plan so that human beings wouldn't have to have that punishment. During this lesson, we'll find out about God's plan to rescue humankind.

Introductory Activity (18-23 years).

- Supplies: Sheets of paper and pencils.

- Instructions: Each person will assume the role of a reporter for "The Red Diary," the most outstanding newspaper in your city.

Before the session, write on sheets of paper different professions (For example: police, banker, football player, housewife, builder, student, pharmacist, etc.). At the beginning of the session, give each person a sheet of paper with a profession on it.

Each person must write a short news piece about their assigned profession—something tragic and funny at the same time. After three minutes, ask each one to read the news out loud, and together the group can choose which story should be the front-page headline.

Every day, we hear about tragic stories that happen all around us. We hear them through different means of communication and from people we know. We could even be part of those stories sometimes. However, none compares to the story of sin and death entering the world, a story which affected us then and continues to affect us.

Even though it's a tragic story, God launched a plan to rescue humankind and give a happy ending to those who accept His help. During this lesson, we'll discover what that plan is.

No story can compare to the one found in the opening verses of Genesis 3: The Fall. Adam and Eve's decision resulted in the spiritual separation of human beings from God, which also gave way to an imminent reality, eternal death.

Disobedience left human incapable of relating to God by their own strength. However, God had mercy and gave them the promise of salvation, which has made it possible for many people throughout history to have the gift of salvation.

1. Christ is the only way to salvation

God's original design implied full communion with people, yet disobedience separated them from God. But even in the midst of that rebellious act, God showed His love for His creation by making a promise (Genesis 3:15). That promise was fulfilled when Jesus Christ came and gave His life as a ransom for those who believe in Him (John 3:16).

But before that time came, God provided a system whereby people could ask God for forgiveness for all their sins by offering an animal as a sacrifice (Leviticus 5). This had to be an animal without any blemish and was offered by a priest, who symbolically prayed for the sins of the people, transferring the sins to the animal. The animal's blood was offered to God as an offering for their sins, recognizing that the wages of sin is death. However, this sacrificial system was only provisional. It was God's way of preparing people for the day when Jesus would sacrifice Himself as the Lamb of God who takes away the sin of the world. Subsequently, the shedding of His blood is sufficient for those who ask forgiveness for their sins, recognize Him as Savior and are born again.

2. Receiving God's Forgiveness

But what does the death and resurrection of Jesus save us from? The consequence of the sin committed by Adam and Eve, and of our own sins, is eternal death, or eternal separation from God. Therefore, if the wages of sin is death, someone has to pay that price; someone has to take our place to bear our punishment. That someone was the Son of God who took our place, serving as a mediator between God and man (1 Timothy 2:5). We didn't deserve it, but God in His great love sent us His Son. That was God's great gift (Ephesians 2:8). To receive this gift, it's necessary to repent of our sins, which means having deep pain for our actions and thoughts that are contrary to God's will, as well as a commitment not to fail Him anymore. When we do, God forgives us (Psalm 103:11-12).

The barrier of sin that once stood between God and us is destroyed by the sacrifice of Jesus (Ephesians 2:13-16). Thanks to His sacrifice, we can be free from sin; we receive eternal life and have communion with God, being adopted as His children (John 1:12). Jesus' death paid for our sins, and His resurrection gives us hope of eternal life with God.

3. A change of life as the result

As a result of receiving forgiveness for our sins, we've been reconciled with God and enjoy eternal life. However, now we have a new way of living (2 Corinthians 5:17). This means a life that pleases and honors God.

Salvation is a gift from God, it's an interior miracle—a spiritual life—that occurs in the life of whoever by faith receives this gift. This new birth requires living according to the design that God prepared for His children. In Ephesians 2:10, we read that "we have been created in Christ Jesus for good works." We can say that although good works don't save us, they do bear witness to our salvation. Our actions are an example of the fruit of repentance that's born in our hearts the moment we ask God for forgiveness (Matthew 3:8), and that must remain consistent with the faithful commitment to please the One who gave His own Son for us.

Those of us who have recognized Jesus as our Savior have many reasons to celebrate. We've been forgiven, released from eternal punishment, and can enjoy eternal fellowship with God. If some in the group haven't yet made the decision to ask Jesus to be their Savior, give them the opportunity to accept this gift that God offers today and to enjoy eternal life with Him. The Bible reminds us that whoever believes in the Son of God has eternal life, which is God's desire for all (John 3:16-18).

Review/Application:

Christ - only means of salvation

1. According to John 1:29, what did John the Baptist say about Jesus being the Christ? **That he was the Lamb of God who takes away the sin of the world.**

2. Why is Jesus compared to a lamb? **Because the Jews had a sacrificial system in which a lamb without blemish was sacrificed for the forgiveness of sins.**

3. What is the function of a mediator? How is Jesus a mediator between man and God (1 Timothy 2:5)? **Sin created an abyss between God and human beings, so a "bridge" was needed. Jesus is that bridge through which we have access to God.**

4. Give some examples of the actions that characterize the life of the person who's experienced salvation through Jesus, the Christ:

   a. **Help those in need**

   b. **Sharing the message of salvation**

   c. **Encourage others and treat our neighbor with dignity and respect**

   d. **Tell the truth**

   e. **Act honestly**

Challenge:

God initiated the greatest rescue operation that has ever existed. This operation included sending his own Son to give his life in your place. If you have asked Jesus Christ to be your Savior by faith, the operation has been a success in your life. So, you have a very big reason to celebrate. If you haven't made that decision for Christ yet, don't wait any longer. Jesus has given his life so that you may be free from sin and have new life.

This week pray for someone who needs their life to be rescued, by Jesus, and then share the message of salvation with them.

Rescued

Objective: To understand the meaning of redemption and the importance of it in their life.

Memory Verse: "Israel, put your hope in the Lord, for with the Lord is unfailing love, and with him is full redemption. He himself will redeem Israel from all their sins." Psalm 130:7-8

Attention!
Ask some of the group to share about their decision to recognize Jesus Christ as their personal Savior.

Accept

Connect Navigate

Have you heard the word redemption or redeem? It is said that Jesus is our redeemer, that we have been redeemed, however, how clear do we have the concept of the word "redemption?"

Introductory Activity (12-17 years).
- Supplies: A quarter of a letter size piece of paper, pencil or pen.
- Instructions: After reading the introduction to this activity, distribute the papers and ask them to write in three words what "redemption" means to them. Give them a few minutes to think and write.

  After they finish, have each person read the three words. If someone needs help to put together three words only, they can ask for help. When all are done, ask them to put their name on the sheet and then post them on the board or wall and leave them there.

  At the end of the lesson, have everyone take their sheet and review their concept of redemption.

Introductory Activity (18-23 years).
- Supplies: A quarter of a letter size piece of paper, pencil, or pen.
- Instructions: After reading the short introduction to the group, ask them if they know what the word "redemption" means, and ask each person to write two synonyms for redemption or redeem on the piece of paper. (Some synonyms for redemption: Salvation, liberation, rescue, recovery, reconquest, emancipation. Some synonyms for redeem: Save, liberate, recover, rescue, exempt, forgive, regenerate).

  When finished, compare the answers and make one list with all the words used.

  As people who seek God, we must be clear about the concept of redemption and, above all, know its purpose.

Connect Navigate

Have you ever bought a poor-quality pair of shoes at an outrageous price but liked them so much that you still paid the asking price? Or have you ever helped someone pay off a debt by paying it yourself? Jesus Christ did something similar for us, which we call redemption.

1. What is redemption?

The word redemption is mentioned in Exodus 8:23. But in Exodus 6:6, we find the word redeem. By reading this passage, we can see God's purpose to free His people from slavery. We can easily substitute the word redeem for the words "save" or "release" without altering the meaning of the passage, because redeem is synonymous with saving and releasing.

Let's look at some definitions of the word redemption:

- The process of redeeming someone or something.
- Another word for salvation (Eby, et al, 2004. A Dictionary of the Bible & Christian Doctrine in Everyday English).

Eby's definition of redeem is also helpful: To redeem means to buy back. It means to return something or someone to a position that had been lost. To redeem is to set something or someone free to fulfill his or her purpose."

Eby also offers a helpful definition of redeemer: "A redeemer is someone who redeems others. He helps those who cannot redeem, or free, themselves. Christ is the Redeemer of the world."

These definitions make the biblical meaning clearer. God is the only one who can pay, buy, deliver, and put an end to our spiritual condemnation of eternal separation as slaves to the enemy of God.

2. Only in Christ we find redemption

In the Old Testament, God promised redemption to his people. Now in the New Testament, all redemption is attributed to Jesus Christ, who came to save humanity. In Romans 3:23, we read that all of us have sinned and fall short of the glory of God. We often use this verse to share with other people about Christ. Imagine being destitute of the glory of God, that there was no remedy for such condemnation, that we were sinners without salvation option. But what a relief when we read the next verse: "and all are justified freely by His grace through the redemption that came by Christ Jesus" (Romans 3:24)! There is a way to return to the glory of the Almighty God. Redemption in Christ is the only solution for the forgiveness of sin, and Jesus paid the price for our deliverance.

Let's look at the differences between the Old and New Testament meanings. Remember that the people of Israel offered sacrifices for their sins, but that this action didn't redeem them; that is, it didn't take them out of the slavery of sin, because after a while, they had to offer another sacrifice. In contrast, the sacrifice of Christ paid such a high price that it's sufficient and doesn't need to be performed again.

In Ephesians 1:3-7, Paul blesses God for choosing the Ephesians before the world existed to be holy (v.4). The apostle says that this is possible through Jesus Christ (v.7). We see here a clear example of that undeserved gift from God which makes us acceptable and completely restores our relationship with Him. Again, we find the word redemption, and it's made clear that we have it only by the abundant grace of God. Glory to God for His love! Blessed be His name for not letting us die in sin. Do we really appreciate that Jesus, being the Son of God, decided to take all our guilt and die, condemned as the worst criminal, to free us from eternal death? We definitely should because, thanks to Him, we can live free, without debt.

As we continue reading the letter to the Ephesians, we find that in chapter 4, Paul instructed the people about the Christian life, giving them specific directions of what they should do as redeemed people. Among the directions, we read: "And do not bring sorrow to God's Holy Spirit by the way you live. Remember, he has identified you as His own, guaranteeing that you will be saved on the day of redemption" (Ephesians 4:30 NLT).

We clearly see the magnitude of that sacrifice, even though we'll only fully understand it on the day when we're freed from sin forever. That is, we're redeemed not only in our present life on earth, but our life in eternity is affected.

As with the Ephesians, Paul also wrote to the Colossians on this subject: "For he has rescued us from the dominion of darkness and brought us into the kingdom of the Son he loves, in whom we have redemption, the forgiveness of sins" (Colossians 1:13-14).

3. Committing to value my redemption

It's time that we pay attention to the deep meaning of "redemption"—a word that we use so often in our church services. Let's live in a way that we're grateful to God for redeeming us at such a high price.

The psalmist spoke of his desire to be heard by God and was aware that it's only by God's grace and mercy that we have abundant redemption from sin: "If you, Lord, kept a record of sins, Lord, who could stand?" (Psalm 130:3). Let us always remember that redemption is only by God's favor, His infinite mercy and His selfless love. This valuable redemption changes our future and our spiritual condition, blessing us "with every spiritual blessing in Christ" (Ephesians 1:3).

If you haven't yet been redeemed, ask God for forgiveness for your sins, and through Jesus Christ, your present and your eternity will be changed. Don't hesitate any longer and take this gift that's freely available to you. Let's remember that if we haven't asked God for forgiveness, we're still in sin. Perhaps we're not thieves or murderers. However, we're sinners, because as Romans 3:23 says, "we have all sinned and fall short of the glory of God." The only solution to our current spiritual situation is accepting the sacrifice of Jesus.

Let's take time to reflect and thank our heavenly Father for redeeming us. Let's pray together and make a commitment to take our redemption seriously from now on.

Review/Application:

Give them time to solve the crossword by reading the clues.

Horizontal

2. Benefit, concession given free of charge. *(Grace)*
3. The result of freeing a person from a bad situation. *(Redemption)*
5. Set someone free. *(Release)*
7. Release from danger, damage or obstacle. *(Salvation)*
9. To buy back. *(Redeem)*

Vertical

1. Recognize importance or merit. *(Value)*
4. Time after death. *(Eternity)*
6. To protect, to bring out of danger. *(Save)*
8. Freeing someone from their burdens, obligations, or guilt. *(Acquit)*
10. Compassion towards the sufferings or mistakes of others. *(Mercy)*

Challenge:

Over the next week ask your family and friends if they have heard the word redemption, if they know what it means, and whether they are Christians or not. Tell them what you have learned and invite them to appreciate what God has done for us.

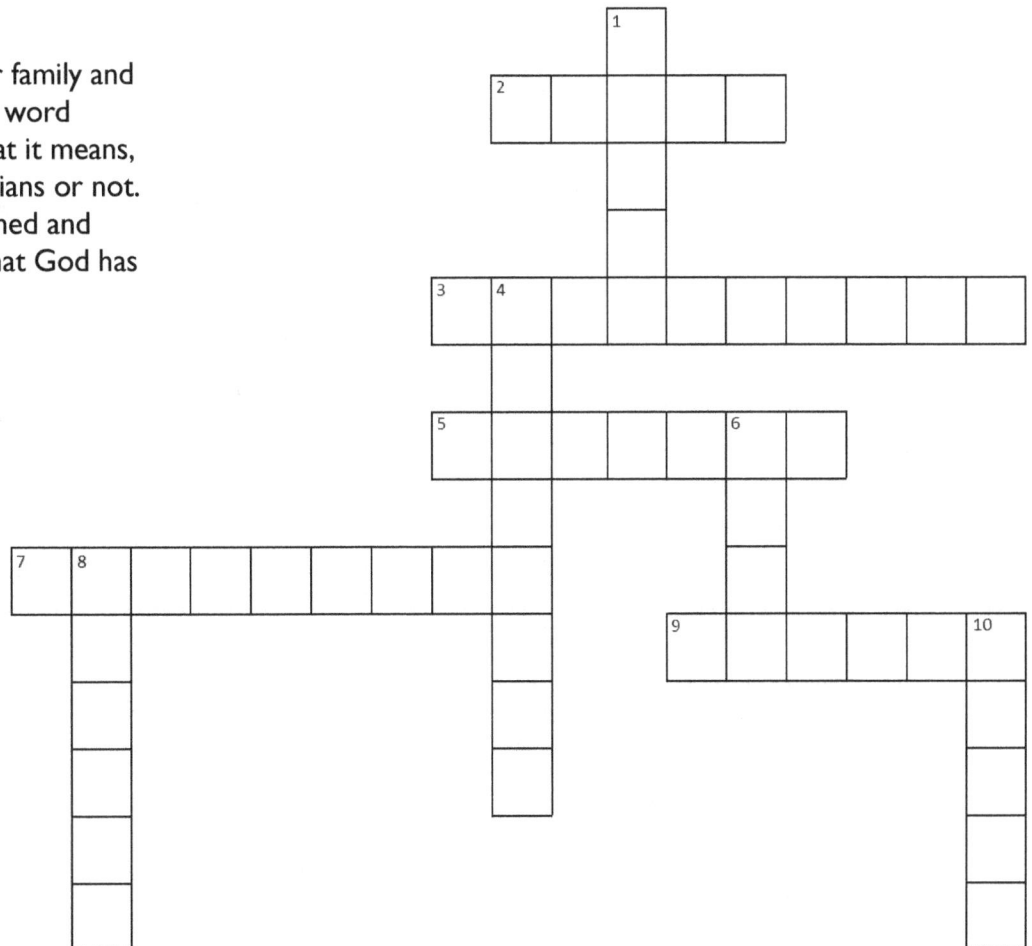

Is it just me?

Objective: To understand that justification is the result of faith placed in God.

Memory Verse: "Therefore, since we have been justified through faith, we have peace with God through our Lord Jesus Christ..." Romans 5:1

Attention!

x

Ask the group to discuss ways they shared the message of redemption with people since the last session.

Accept

Connect | Navigate

Introductory Activity (12-17 years).

- Supplies: Pencils and the story of Martin and Morgan.

- Instructions: Read the following story:

     Martin and Morgan were identical twins. Their physical appearance was the only thing in which they were alike. Martin obeyed his parents, had good manners, was studious and was kind to his neighbors. Morgan was always disobeying his parents, and he lied and fought with everyone.

     The differences grew with them. Martin finished his university degree and established a successful business. Morgan continued to make decisions that got him into a lot of trouble. He was in and out of jail until he was finally found guilty of murder and sentenced to the electric chair. The day before the execution, Martin came to visit Morgan. The guard left the two brothers alone in a room. Martin and Morgan switched their clothes just in time before the guard returned to take "Morgan" to his cell.

     The next day, Martin was taken to the electric chair instead of Morgan, and he died. Morgan was free but he had to make a decision: to continue living his life as before, or to imitate the life of Martin who died in his place. (Adapted from "Martin and Morgan," Jim Burns and Greg McKinnon, Illustrations, Stories and Quotes to Hang Your Message on. Gospel Light, 1997, pp. 11-12).

     Ask: What decision do you think Morgan made? Why? Do you know of another story where a person took the place of someone who was going to be punished? Would you be willing to give your life for someone else?

Introductory Activity (18-23 years).

- Supplies: Newspapers or magazines, scissors, pencils, and blank sheets of paper.

- Instructions: Divide into two groups. Each group will have all the required supplies. Ask the groups to scan the newspapers and cut out as many news stories, images, editorials, or advertisements as possible that exemplify the concept of justice, fairness, or the plea of innocence. Once they have these clippings, the groups will have to discuss and write responses to the following questions: "What did these clippings teach you about justice, fairness, or a plea of innocence? How do these situations resemble the biblical concept of justice?"

     Then ask each group to share their comments. Be sure to give each group an example they can find among the clippings.

     Human justice is hard to find around us. However, those small examples of justice resemble the intentions of our God wanting to reestablish a relationship with human beings, declaring us righteous through Jesus Christ.

According to the Argentinian newspaper Clarín: "In Japan about 96% of the homicides that are committed are solved. In France, 73%, and in the United States, 64%. In some Central American countries, it doesn't reach 10%. In Argentina… it can be estimated that the percentage of cleared cases is less than 50%" (http://www.clarin.com/diario/2005/05/22/policial/g-06001.html accessed on 10 November 2009).

The impunity in which we live in our world can cloud our understanding of what justice means, to be "just" and to be declared "innocent." Justification, regarding our relationship with God, has three fundamental elements: a. God's initiative; b. The human response; c. The results of the restored relationship.

Read Romans 5: 1-11, in different versions, if possible.

1. God's initiative

God, in his great love, wants to reestablish his relationship with humankind. That is, God initiates a process where human beings are able to be in full and direct relationship with Him.

Justification is affirmed as: "the gracious and judicial act of God by which He grants full pardon of all guilt and complete release from the penalty of sins committed, and acceptance as righteous, to all who believe in Jesus Christ and receive Him as Lord and Savior" (Manual, Church of the Nazarene 2017-2021, p. 30).

We understand that we've sinned and deserve death, but if we ask for forgiveness, God acquits us and makes us free from guilt (justification). Through divine justice we're declared innocent, we're accepted as righteous before God through faith in Jesus Christ and not by anything we've done.

Paul identified this divine initiative to declare us righteous and allow us to come into his presence with love (Romans 5:8). Ask: Is there someone in your life who has shown you true love? Who are they? How did they show their love for you?

2. How do we respond to this divine initiative?

Once we've recognized God's loving initiative through His Son Jesus Christ, we're confronted with the big question. What impact does justification have on my life?

The death of Christ was part of the Father's initiative for all of us to have a full relationship with Him. This relationship is characterized by the opportunity to respond in love and obedience. That is, once God's love has been shown and delivered, there must be a response from those of us who receive that love.

Many times, even as Christians, we continue to live as if Jesus' death has no impact on our daily lives. The news we hear every day of people suffering or dying desensitizes us to the pain and loss that it implies. Jesus voluntarily died for us to make us righteous, but what does it mean for us to be righteous? What does God ask of us?

Ask the group to find the answers in the following scriptures: Micah 6:8, 1 Peter 4:1-2, and 1 Peter 4:7-11.

A Dictionary of the Bible & Christian Doctrine in Everyday English explains: "Justification by grace through faith alone is the way people become Christians. The grace of God makes faith in Christ possible. Salvation is completely the work of God. Even faith is a gift [Romans 10:17]. But people must exercise faith to be justified. Good works add nothing to justification. But those who have been justified will do good works" (Eby, et al, 2004.)

As we know and experience the justice of God, the only thing left for us to do is to respond in love, obedience, and faithfulness to the purposes of the kingdom of God.

3. The results of restored relationship

Romans 5:1 identifies the great benefit of being in relationship with God through Jesus Christ. When Paul referred to this peace, his intention was to direct us to the fact that we have a new identity in Jesus Christ.

By faith in Jesus Christ, we draw near to God in such a way that we're no longer strangers or unknown to Him, but are called His children (1 John 3:1). Our Heavenly Father, by taking the initiative to come into the world, offers us the opportunity to be righteous. In this way, we've been declared fit to enjoy a total relationship with God, and so we begin a daily adventure of transformation and maturity as we commit ourselves to knowing the God of love in an intimate and dynamic way.

Review/Application:

Give them time to think and respond. Then ask them to share their answers with the group.

1. After what was covered in the lesson, how would you define justice in your own words?

2. What example would you use to explain divine justice?

3. What do you think is the result of a life that has been justified?

Challenge:

Since we are declared righteous before God, how can we live out God's righteousness in our neighborhoods, schools, families, and churches? During this week, think about and write a list of areas where you can serve your community to show reconciliation and restoration in God's name.

A new beginning

Objective: To understand what regeneration is and its importance in their life.

Memory Verse: "Put on your new nature, created to be like God—truly righteous and holy." Ephesians 4:24

Attention! Review and follow up on the lists of areas in which they proposed to serve in order to show reconciliation.

Accept

Connect | Navigate

I heard about a person who had videotaped the birth of their second daughter. That same afternoon, they went out to play with their elder daughter in the park and recorded her playing. At night, wanting to look at what they had recorded, they discovered that by recording the elder daughter in the park, they had erased the birth of their second daughter. Surely this parent wishes their newborn daughter would be born again! Is this possible? Can we be born again?

Introductory Activity (12-17 years).

- Supplies: 2 shirts or jackets, 2 hats, and 2 pairs of big gloves.

- Instructions: Divide into two groups. Choose two people to be referees (they'll not belong to any group). Ask the groups to line up, one group facing the other. In front of the first person in each group, place a T-shirt, a hat, and a pair of gloves. Tell them that each person will put on the clothes in order and then take them off as fast as they can, making room for the next person in line in their group. The first group to finish wins.

The referees will be the ones to decide if each participant put on and took off his or her clothes correctly.

Say: Everyone did a good job of getting clothes on and off quickly. Jesus can do the same with our lives. He removes everything old that sin has destroyed in our life and makes us new. When we receive Him in our hearts, we're born again.

Introductory Activity (18-23 years).

- Supplies: No material necessary.

- Instructions: Begin by talking with the young adults about what they understand about the term "regeneration." Share the example of a person who goes to prison to serve a sentence for a crime he has committed. Ask them:

What are prisons for? *(For people to "pay" their debts to society for their mistakes and to be rehabilitated.)*

Many prisoners leave jail saying that they have been rehabilitated; however, they continue doing the same things that led them to prison. Do they show signs of rehabilitation? *(No.)*

What kind of life do truly rehabilitated people lead? *(They should be new people, starting a new life. They stop doing what led them to be condemned and they live differently.)*

How is the life of a person who has been regenerated by the blood of Christ? Let the young adults give their opinion.

Begin by reading or have them read one verse each from the passage of John 3:1-16.

Nicodemus came to Jesus at night because he was afraid of being seen with Him. The important thing is that Jesus received him, and is always ready to receive us when we come to Him, even if it's at night and we're ashamed to be seen with Him. Nicodemus was a ruler and considered to be a godly Jewish man since he kept the law in detail. However, he didn't come to Jesus to speak about the law but about the interests of his own soul and his salvation.

Jesus spoke to him about the need for new birth, but Nicodemus didn't understand. Then Jesus explained and pointed him to the person who does that work: the Holy Spirit.

Regeneration isn't our work, but it's brought about by the power of the Spirit (John 3:5).

1. What is regeneration?

A Dictionary of the Bible & Christian Doctrine in Everyday English (Eby, et al, 2004) describes regeneration as follows:

1. Regeneration is the result of the saving work of God in the hearts of sinners. He causes them to be born again.

2. Regeneration is the spiritual work of God that completely changes sinners.

3. Regeneration refers to the same religious experience as justification, adoption, conversion, and initial sanctification.

(John 3:1-8, Ephesians 2:1-10, Titus 3:4-7 and 1 Peter 1:23)

The word regeneration literally means "to create again" or to be born again. This refers to the act by which the sinner is recreated to a condition that allows him to have communion with God. That is, to be reborn to a new and perfect relationship with God.

Eby also describes "regenerate.

1. (verb) To regenerate is to cause someone to be born again spiritually. Sinners are dead. They receive spiritual life from God when they are converted. It's as if their lives are started over again, created new. This is the means for God to regenerate a sinner.

2. (adjective) Regenerate describes a person who has been born again. A regenerate person is one who has become a born-again Christian (Titus 3:5).

In addition, Eby explains what it means to be born again.

1. (verb phrase) To be born again means to become a Christian. To be born again is really to be born from above. This means that God, not man, causes this birth or new life to happen. God gives believers a new start. He gives them a spiritual or new birth. God frees people from their old lives of sin.

2. (adjective phrase) Born again describes a person who is a Christian. Evangelical Christians believe that the new birth is necessary for salvation. Right ideas about Jesus Christ aren't enough. God must change the lives of people. They must be born again. (John 3:3-8)

Being born again provides us with a new nature, new principles, new life. To be born again is to start living again. Since in our first birth we're corrupt, formed in sin, it's necessary that we be made new creatures, completely different from what we were.

This new birth is from heaven, from above. It's a total change made in the heart of the sinner by the power of the Holy Spirit. This work is done in us and for our benefit, and it's something that we cannot do for ourselves. Redemption, justification, and regeneration are the product of salvation in Jesus Christ. Although we study them separately to clearly understand the meaning of each one, all of these happen the moment we're saved by Jesus.

The author of the letter to the Ephesians speaks of dying to a way of life that doesn't please God. We're urged to renew ourselves and be a new creation according to God's designs (Ephesians 4:22-24). This new person symbolizes the regenerating nature that enables us to live a just and holy life. But this only happens by the power of God.

2. How does regeneration work in our lives?

Without new birth, there's no salvation! So what must a person do to "be born again"? How does regeneration work in our lives?

Regeneration is a spiritual phenomenon that occurs inside a person. It's a heavenly work in which God takes the initiative (Titus 3:2-7).

We don't receive regeneration because of good works of justice. In other words, there's nothing we can do to earn salvation, or the right to be born again. God's mercy has enabled the cleansing of all our sins. It's through the work of Christ on the cross of Calvary and God's grace that we become partakers of a new life in Him.

It's His love that moved Him to extend His grace to those who believe. When we accept Jesus Christ as our personal Savior, we're no longer lost but experience a full, holy, and eternal life in Him (John 3:16). All of this takes place when we're reborn. We recognize our sinful state and our need for God, and prayerfully we ask Him to make us a new creature.

3. What are the benefits of regeneration in our lives?

With regeneration, a new way of life opens up for the believer. In John 3:16, Jesus uses the figure of the "new birth" to indicate three things or three benefits:

With new birth, there's a new relationship with God.

First of all, new birth initiates our relationship with God. In John 14:6, Jesus declares that He is the way, the truth, and the life; no one goes to the Father except through Him. This tells us that if we don't accept that way, truth, and life through new birth, we cannot have a relationship with God.

This is the main benefit of regeneration, the power to have perfect communion with God—a communion that isn't possible by our own means since the sin that dwells in us separates us from Him.

Being able to have direct access to God is the most wonderful miracle we can experience. Nicodemus didn't know this, so he approached the Master at night, afraid of being seen with Jesus. This indicates that Nicodemus had doubts that He was the Messiah, so he could not approach Jesus freely. He couldn't have a perfect relationship with Him. But new birth gives us that freedom, the freedom to have a relationship with God without fear.

With new birth, we see the kingdom of God.

New birth gives us a new perspective, a new vision. We see the "kingdom of God" as it is, as it says in John 3:3. New birth opens our eyes to the Word of God and helps us experience the work of the Holy Spirit in our lives.

In 2 Corinthians 3:15-18, Paul explains this phenomenon by comparing it to the material veil of Moses. Moses' veil represents the spiritual veil that prevents us from reading the Word of God with spiritual understanding. The veil prevents us from seeing the Glory of God that's in Christ.

The new birth removes the veil from our eyes and allows us to see in a new way, to see true spiritual reality.

Through new birth in Christ, we enter the kingdom of God.

Through the new birth, we're literally introduced to a heavenly realm. We become part of the kingdom of God on earth, and this prepares us for our eternal salvation (John 3:5).

This new birth opens the doors to the kingdom of God. It makes us heirs to "an inheritance that can never perish, spoil, or fade...kept in heaven" for us (1 Peter 1:4).

This wonderful regenerative work is available to each and every one of us. It's the work of the Holy Spirit in our lives. Jesus compares the Spirit with the wind (John 3:8). Although we may not understand where the wind comes from, we hear it, and we know that it's there. Likewise, we can experience the influence of the Holy Spirit in our lives.

Review/Application:

Ask them to write in their own words how they would explain to a friend what regeneration is, how it works in us, and how it benefits our lives. In other words, ask them to summarize what they learned today.

Challenge:

This week remember that God has given you the opportunity to be born again. The challenge for each of us is to reflect that new birth in our lives. What would you do differently this week that gives evidence that you've been born again in Jesus?

We're adopted!

Objective: To understand what adoption is and its importance for their spiritual life.

Memory Verse: "So you are no longer a slave, but God's child; and since you are His child, God has made you also an heir." Galatians 4:7

Attention! x

Ask the group some questions in relation to new birth and its reality in their lives.

Accept !

Connect | Navigate

Many of your youth may have heard the word "adoption" and are familiar with its definition. However, not many of them probably know an adopted person personally. In this lesson, we'll discuss the concept of adoption between human beings, and we'll also study the process of spiritual adoption through which we can become "children of God" (John 1:12).

Introductory Activity (12 - 17 years).

- Supplies: Write 2 Samuel 9:1-13 on the board or a large piece of paper. If possible, provide your group with a little information about the close friendship that David and Jonathan (Mephibosheth's father, found in 1 Samuel 20) shared.
- Instructions: Have your group read the Bible verses about David and Mephibosheth as a team. After a few minutes, ask them to prepare a simple skit or role-play to act out this story of adoption.

  As we saw in this story, King David loved Jonathan's son as one of his own children. In the lesson that we'll study today, we'll see how God has the desire to do the same with us.

Introductory Activity (18-23 years).

- Supplies: Whiteboard and whiteboard markers or large poster paper and markers.
- Instructions: Divide the board/ paper in two with a straight line down the middle. On one side write the title "Positive aspects" and on the other "Negative aspects." As a group, write down the aspects of the adoption process (positive and negative). Encourage your group to think from the perspectives of the adopted person, birth family, and adoptive family.

  Make sure that your group recognizes various positive aspects of the adoption process (family, love, shelter, food, etc.) and that the discussion doesn't turn into the negative connotations that adoption is sometimes given. Help them think about the difference between being adopted and being raised on the street and how each situation can impact a child.

  Christ does the same with us. He adopts us to change our earthly life and our eternal destiny.

Connect | Navigate

Humans are created with the ability to emotionally attach themselves to those who care for them from birth. Unfortunately, there are times when a person cannot be cared for or raised by their biological parents. For this same reason, since the beginning of time, people have taken care of children who weren't their biological children and looked after their well-being as they would have (or did) with their own.

1. The concept of adoption

A Dictionary of the Bible & Christian Doctrine in Everyday English (Eby, et al, 2004) notes:

1. To adopt is to make a child one's own son or daughter. This happens by law and not by birth. The adopted person has all the rights and duties of a child by birth.

2. God adopts people spiritually when they trust Christ for salvation. They become God's children. Christians are adopted into the family of God.

3. Adoption is an act that makes a person a member of a new family. This happens by law.

4. Adoption describes part of the new relation sinners have with God after He forgives them. Sinners who trust Christ for salvation are no longer separated from Him. They become children of God. Spiritual adoption is by grace, not by law.

(Romans 8:15, 23; 9:4; 2 Corinthians 6:14-7:1; Galatians 4:5 and Ephesians 1:5)

Imagine for a moment a girl who, due to life circumstances, cannot be cared for by her biological parents. How do think this girl would feel if she received an invitation to be part of another loving family? Let the group have a say.

By being adopted and loved, the person feels part of the family. It's wonderful to think about the possibility of feeling truly welcomed or included in a family that loves us, without having the obligation to do so, but as a voluntary decision.

The definition of adoption speaks of certain "legal procedures" that declare to others that the one who is adopted now belongs to the new family with equal rights and obligations. In the same way, adopting also means taking someone and making that person your own, assuming or accepting that person. The wonderful thing about studying the adoption process is that a person or persons clearly choose to adopt another person who will be in their care.

Adoption is a process that offers a disadvantaged person an alternative to a life that would otherwise be negative and full of pain.

If we take time to reflect on our own lives and how we lived without the presence of God, we'll realize our need for spiritual adoption.

2. The process of adoption

Spiritual adoption is the process by which God becomes our Father and we become His children. Like adoption between human beings, it's a process that includes responsibility of both parties involved.

In Galatians 4:4-5, we see how God Himself took the initiative to begin the process of our adoption. God has every desire to adopt us and make us part of His family. God desires to have us as His children and has prepared everything for such a relationship to be possible. From before the foundation of the world, God planned the coming of Jesus to earth, so that through His sacrifice on the cross, we would be adopted as His children (1 Peter 1: 19-20).

Our part is simply to accept and consciously receive the life that God offers us. Accepting Jesus as Lord and Savior can be done through prayer, which expresses repentance for sins and the desire to be a child of God (John 1:12).

Over time, as you pray, read the Word, and serve in church, you'll discover what it means to be a child of God. Part of the process of being adopted into the family of God is to accept and adopt the "customs" or identity of the parents—in this case, the identity of our Father God (1 Peter 1:17).

3. The result of adoption

Like a child adopted by a loving family is happy and comfortable with the parents, so are we when we're received by the members of the church; we feel part of a new family and enjoy the fellowship.

Let's think for a moment about the benefits that adopted children would enjoy: they would receive a new family name, which would make them a member of that new family, which would guarantee the same benefits and responsibilities that the other members of the family have.

In the Christian life, it's similar after spiritual adoption: God adopts us and we enjoy all the benefits of an adopted child. We become part of the family of God (Ephesians 2:19) that will accompany us in all circumstances. As children, we have direct access to our Father God to tell Him about our triumphs, dreams, hopes, difficulties, and more (Romans 8:15).

Ask your group if they have needs that they're facing in their life. Encourage them to think about them and share those needs with God in prayer. God can help and guide them as their loving Father. The most beautiful thing about the whole adoption process is that God wants to love us with all His heart, and we'll be His children forever.

As a group leader, be sure to guide anyone who wishes to pray to receive Jesus as Lord and Savior and become part of the family of God.

At the end, make it clear that in the very moment we ask for forgiveness and accept Jesus as our Savior, God redeems us, regenerates us, justifies us, and adopts us as His children. These are the previous four concepts studied. And you must make it clear that everything happens simultaneously.

Consider ending the session by praying. Thank God that He adopts all of us who want to be His children, no matter who we are.

Review/Application:

Divide your class into groups and ask them to write down definitions of the following words. Then share with the whole group the different meanings that each team gave to each concept. These are possibly answers:

- Abba: **Dad, daddy.**

- Father: **One who gives life, protects, educates and raises.**

- Orphan: **One who is not raised by his biological parents.**

- Adopt: **Take in or include a person in one's family through legal procedures and raise them as one's own child.**

- Protect: **Provide care, guidance, comfort, and help from negative influences or experiences.**

Challenge:

As a class, think about the possibilities you have as a group of God's children to show God's love to orphaned children. Consider whether you might want to visit a local orphanage as a group and spend time with the children who live there, or send an offering to organizations that help children in other countries, such as AIDS orphans on the continent of Africa, etc.

The Neverending Story

Objective: To understand what eternal life is and to see its benefits in their own life.

Memory Verse: "And this is what he promised us — eternal life." I John 2:25

Connect | Navigate

Introductory Activity (12-17 years)

- Supplies: A blank sheet of paper for each person, colored pencils or crayons.

- Instructions: Give each person a piece of paper and ask them to draw things they would do if they were immortal.

  Use the pictures to talk about how life is so important to us and how death prevents us from experiencing certain things or achieving certain dreams. Explore the idea of what spiritual death causes and how it prevents us from experiencing the blessing of living a life with God and fulfilling His will.

Introductory Activity (18-23 years).

- Supplies: Half a sheet of paper for each person and a pencil to write with.

- Instructions: Give half a sheet of paper to each person and ask them to write down things they want to do or achieve before they die. Then ask each one to share what they wrote. Discuss what things they wrote about would be considered important and what things secondary.

  At the end of the activity, help them to reflect and think about the many times in life we pay attention to secondary and fleeting things and don't attend to things of more importance that affect our eternity.

Connect | Navigate

Death fills us with great pain because it causes separation between us and someone we love. With this separation, dreams and plans that we had with that person come to an end.

Sometimes with the death of someone, our habits change. For example, if our grandmother with whom we had lunch every Sunday dies, we would no longer attend Sunday lunches. Other times, the death of someone changes the lifestyle we have. For example, if a father who supports the family dies, everyone might have to go to work to make financial adjustments.

But for those who have a personal relationship with God, we know that this separation is momentary, because we have eternal life in God.

1. What is eternal life?

A Dictionary of the Bible & Christian Doctrine in Everyday English (Eby, et al, 2004) notes:

1. Eternal life is the quality of life that God gives. Those who trust Jesus Christ for salvation receive the gift of eternal life. People begin to enjoy eternal life when they become Christians.

2. Eternal life is life with God, who is eternal.

3. Eternal life also means life after death for Christians. They will live forever with the Lord in heaven. Eternal life in heaven is sometimes called everlasting life.

(Matthew 19:16, 29; Luke 10:25; 18:18, 30; John 3:17; 5:24, 39-40; 6:27-69; 10:27-29; Acts 13:46, 48; Romans 2:7; 5:21; 6:22-23; Galatians 2:20; Titus 3:4-7; 1 John 1:2; 2:25; 3:15 and 5:11-12)

Make two columns on the whiteboard, and in one write "Life without Christ" and in the other "Life with Christ." Ask the group to talk about things we do when our life is without Christ , and what we do when our life is with Christ. Use their contributions to discuss what spiritual life (life with Christ) is, compared to spiritual death (life without Christ).

We cannot explain what eternal life is without talking about what eternal death is. Eby (et al, 2004) also explains eternal punishment.

1. Eternal punishment is the separation from God of those who finally refuse His salvation.

2. Hell is a place of eternal punishment.

(Matthew 18:8; 25:41-46; Mark 3:29; Luke 3:17; John 5:28-29; 1 Thessalonians 1:8-9; 2 Peter 2:9-10; Revelation 20:14-15 and 21:8)

As we said earlier, physical death is a separation between us and those we love. The same applies to spiritual death, but in this case, it means the separation of people from God. Sin separates us from God, and this is spiritual death (Romans 6:23). As a consequence of Adam and Eve's first sin, humanity was separated from God and is in a state of spiritual death. But it isn't only because of original sin that we're far from God. Paul shows us that, "all have sinned and fall short of the glory of God" (Romans 3:23). Our own sins separate us from God. However, out of His great love, God provided a means by which we can have life. John 3:16 says that Jesus came to give eternal life. Through His life and sacrifice, our sins are forgiven and we're made clean so that we can live a holy life before God and in communion with Him. This is eternal life, freedom from death, which is the consequence of sin, and a life of communion with God.

When we sin, we hurt ourselves and those we love, we break friendships, and many times, we compromise our own health. The consequences of our sins affect other people as well. But when we have life in Christ, we can walk safely in the presence of God.

The Bible also tells us about the assurance the believer has that after earthly death or physical separation, they'll be in the presence of God for all eternity (John 14:2-3). In this way, we won't only live eternal life on earth (since the Holy Spirit is with us) but also, when our time to leave comes, we have the assurance that we'll spend an eternity in the presence of God.

2. Requirements for eternal life

Many people aren't assured of eternal life in Christ or of their salvation because they don't understand the concept of God's grace. They believe that it's by their own effort that they can achieve God's forgiveness, or that God will eventually forgive them. But in the end, they meet the sad reality of sin and its consequences in their lives.

John 10:28 says that Jesus is the one who gives life: "I give them eternal life, and they shall never perish; no one will snatch them out of my hand." In other words, eternal life can only be received as a gift. There's nothing in our sinful condition that we can do to qualify for the gift of life that Jesus offers us.

You could explain this concept during the session by bringing a gift-wrapped box and giving the box to someone. Discuss with the group what a gift is, how much the gift costs to the recipient, and the possibility of the recipient rejecting the gift. Also, explore how we would feel if someone returned a gift that we gave them.

Just because eternal life is a gift doesn't mean it was free. Eternal life was bought at a great price, the sacrifice of God's Son on the cross. Jesus declares: "...the one who believes has eternal life" (John 6:47). Believing in God and in Jesus' sacrifice for the forgiveness of our sins is the first step to accessing eternal life. Salvation is a gift, but then we must be faithful to keep that gift.

3. Practical benefits of eternal life

The life that Jesus gives us is something we can experience from now on if we decide to trust Him and accept His wonderful gift of salvation. By living a life of communion with God and obedience to His Word, we're freed from the burden and consequences that sin causes in our lives. We can also have the peace and security that when we die, we'll be with God for all eternity (Matthew 25:46).

Look at the board again (using the division from before: life without Christ and life with Christ) and talk with the group about it. Help them see that life with God isn't about a set of rules that we have to fulfill so that God doesn't punish us, but it's a free life, full of benefits. Finish this section by reading John 10:10: "The thief comes only to steal and kill and destroy; I have come that they may have life, and have it to the full." Accepting the gift that God offers us makes the story of our life a never-ending narrative.

In case some of your group members haven't yet received the gift of eternal life, challenge them to do so today. If they have already received eternal life in Jesus, ask them to write a thank you letter to God for this undeserved gift.

Review/Application:

Encourage dialogue through the following questions. And ask them to write down the answers.

1. Why is faith in God and in Jesus' sacrifice a requirement for receiving eternal life? **Because we cannot receive as a gift something that we do not believe exists or that we think is not for us.**

2. If faith is a requirement to receive eternal life, why do we say that eternal life is a free gift from God? What price was paid? **Because faith is simply believing in the gift, we don't have to do penance or sacrifice to get it. The price has already been paid by Jesus on the cross.**

3. What does John 14:2-3 say about where we will be after we die? **With Jesus in the place that prepares us for heaven.**

Challenge:

This week ask some of your acquaintances or friends if, in the event of their death, they know where they would go. You'll be surprised at the answers. It can be a way of sharing Christ with them.

Share the answers you got with the class next week.

It could get lost

Objective: To recognize the importance of taking care of their salvation.

Memory Verse: "Therefore, my dear friends, as you have always obeyed— not only in my presence, but now much more in my absence — continue to work out your salvation with fear and trembling..." Philippians 2:12

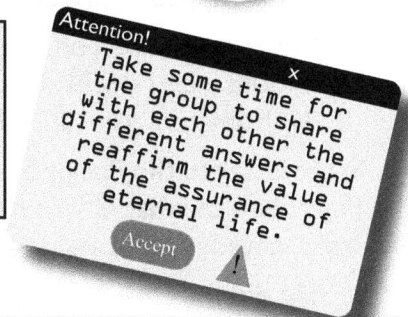

> **Attention!** x
> Take some time for the group to share with each other the different answers and reaffirm the value of the assurance of eternal life.
> Accept !

Connect | Navigate

Introductory Activity (12-17 years).

- Supplies: Two or three magnets, pieces of metal, and a stopwatch.
- Instructions: Form two or three groups, and on a table or on the floor mark a start and finish line. Each group must use a magnet to carry a piece of metal to the finish line, without the magnet and metal touching. Each participant gets one try and the group that does it in the least amount of time wins. If one of the pieces sticks to the magnet, the group is disqualified. If all the groups stick the pieces to the magnet, they all lose.

    In the same way that metal is attracted to the magnet, so is temptation in our life. It tries to attract us like a magnetic force. If we flee and withdraw in time, we'll beat it. Let's flee at the right time

Introduction dynamique (18 à 37ans).

- Supplies: Advertisement cutouts from newspapers of food, car sales, houses, religious items, betting, etc.
- Instructions: Draw a line in the middle of the board or on a piece of paper. On one side, write POSITIVE, on the other write NEGATIVE.

    Hand out the clippings and ask the young adults to place them under the word positive or negative according to their own criteria, and then talk about the reason for classifying them that way.

    Many times, it's easy to identify what's good or what's bad. But at other times, bad is disguised as good and can lead us to major sins.

Connect | Navigate

One of the current trends is the culture of the "fast," the "instant." What is surprising is that this trend is being applied to the Christian life. We want to grow into the image of Christ immediately. We want God to act instantly in our lives, without the work of maturing daily. Another tendency is to believe that God is love, and that no matter what we do, everything will turn out well in the end. While it's true that God is love, it's also true that the consequences of sin are real and that God is just.

It's sad to know the number of youth who, after having chosen to live a Christian life, have turned away from God. Some return as adults with lives beaten by sin, and others don't even return to the Lord and end up giving up salvation.

1. A great and valuable salvation

A Dictionary of the Bible & Christian Doctrine in Everyday English (Eby, et al, 2004) notes:

1. Salvation is the complete process by which God redeems His creation. The Bible tells the many ways God acted to bring salvation to His world.

2. Salvation is the love of God at work in the world. It's the way God takes away sins and reconciles people to Himself. Salvation is for all who call upon God for forgiveness.

3. God completed His work of salvation through His Son, Jesus Christ, who sets people free from sin. The Holy Spirit works through the Church to make Christ known to the world. Salvation makes possible the holy fellowship of the Church.

4. All Christians agree that there are two parts to salvation. These are justification and sanctification. Christians don't fully agree on the order or content of these parts. Protestants believe that justification returns believers to favor with God. Sanctification is the method God uses to make Christians holy. This begins in justification. Wesleyans speak of initial and entire sanctification. These are two stages within the total process of salvation.

5. Salvation will be completed at the second coming of Christ and the final resurrection. (Genesis 49:18; Exodus 12:31-15:21; 1 Samuel 2:1; Psalms 3:8; 74:12; 89:26; Isaiah 12:2-3; Luke 1:69, 77; 19:9; Acts 13:26, 47; Romans 1:16; 10:10; 13:11; 2 Corinthians 6:2; 7:10; Philippians 2:2-13 and Revelation 12:10)

In the letter to the Philippians, Paul explains the value of salvation. In Philippians 2:5-11, the apostle reminded the Philippians of what Christ did for them. Ask the group to read the passage and point to the stages of Jesus' life represented in the passage.

1. He didn't esteem being equal to God (v.6).

2. He stripped himself of His divinity (v.7). The Word became flesh and dwelt among us. He took the form of a servant, in the likeness of man Jesus was 100% God and 100% man (John 1:14).

3. As a man, He humbled Himself and sacrificed Himself for us (v.8). Death on a cross was the worst punishment for a criminal of that time.

4. 4. He was exalted by God (v.9). Jesus was resurrected and took back the glory that He had in the beginning, becoming the author of salvation for all mankind.

What Christ did on the cross makes our salvation possible today. Thanks to His sacrifice, we can draw closer to the Father and are free from condemnation.

"Therefore, ..." so Paul continues his letter in verse 12. He meant, take the above into account, consider what Christ did for you. We receive our salvation freely, but Jesus paid a very high price for it. The punishment He received was out of love for us, and He did it voluntarily.

In considering this, what does salvation mean to me? Something superficial? Of course not!

Paul commands the Philippians to work out their salvation with fear and trembling. What does fear and trembling mean? Take a few moments to discuss the meaning of this phrase with your group. It doesn't indicate fear or terror; on the contrary, it indicates reverence, respect, and consideration.

Paul encouraged the brothers and sisters in the church in Philippi to place a high value on the new life they had in Christ, taking care not to stray from the path. Talk to your group about how salvation can be lost.

We can lose our salvation when we sin and fail to abide in Christ. We must repent and confess our sins to the Lord in order to continue to abide in Him (1 John 1:9). We read in Revelation 3:5 that we must be overcomers so our names won't be erased from the book of life. This helps us understand Paul's concern in pressing this issue with the Philippians. Salvation isn't just a matter of accepting Christ as Savior, but of maintaining a personal relationship with Him (John 14:21).

2. A salvation to take care of

Read Hebrews 2:1-4 with your group. Discuss with them the advice the writer gives in verse 1. Divide into three groups and ask them to comment on this verse, keeping in mind the following: "Careful attention," "to what we've heard," "so that we do not drift away."

From this verse, we get two tips for taking care of our salvation.

A. We must strive and be intentional in wanting to maintain our salvation. We care for salvation by maintaining our relationship with God every day. Talk to your group about dating relationships. To keep that relationship alive, many people spend hours on the Internet or on the phone in order to be connected to the person they love. In the same way, we must take care of our relationship with Christ, the author of our salvation.

B. We must pay attention to the Word of God and fulfill it. Every day, the Word of God will bring new light to our life, but if we don't put it into practice, it's useless (James 1:22-25).

If we don't do the above, the author of Hebrews says we'll drift away, or "slide." Talk to your group about a person slipping on a wet floor. The person doesn't fall immediately; he begins to slip little by little. In the same way, in our Christian life, temptation seduces us with the purpose of making us fall. By following the above tips, we'll gain the strength to face temptation. Comment on Joseph's action in Genesis 39:7-12.

3. A salvation to live out each day

As we've seen in the previous points, maintaining our salvation means maintaining a personal relationship with Christ, a relationship that's permanent and not intermittent.

Have your group read Hebrews 4:14-16 and guide them through the questions.

A. What is verse 14 saying about Jesus? *This passage tells us that Jesus as the chief priest ascended to heaven and he is alive now!* What does it mean to you that Jesus is alive? *The fact that Jesus is alive is the reason for our faith, our Christian life and hope in eternal life. We must also trust that as our High Priest, He intercedes for us, loves us, listens to us, helps us, and cares for us.*

B. What are the reasons to trust that Jesus can help us in temptation (v.15)? *Because Jesus was tempted.* Ask about the three known temptations of Jesus in Luke 4:1-12—turning stones into bread, jumping off the high place of the temple, worshipping Satan. Emphasize Luke 4:13. *Those weren't the only temptations Jesus faced. Jesus went through more temptations. That's why Scripture tells us that Jesus has compassion on us, because He can understand us! He was tempted in every way like humans (Hebrews 4:15). It doesn't mean that He went through the same things as us, but He was tempted in every way according to human nature. In Gethsemane, He was tempted to disobey His Father (Luke 22:42). Jesus overcame temptation! Jesus is our example.*

C. What stands out to you in verse 16? *There the verse tells us that we can approach Him with the assurance that He will help us. Someone who has gone through the same situation is better able to understand us. For example, someone who is afraid of dogs, can understand another person with the same fear.*

We must approach Jesus in faith, believing that He can help us. That way, we can get help at the right time, before giving in to temptation. It's true that we can always ask God for forgiveness, but we can also ask Him for help before falling and thus continue to grow in His image and likeness.

As you conclude, ask your group to reflect on how they have been living the Christian life. Have a moment of prayer with them and encourage them to consecrate their lives to God and strive to care for their salvation. Remind them that Jesus is alive, that He understands them, and that He is willing to help them.

Review/Application:

Ask your students to explain the sentences and share their answers with the rest of the group.

"...a great high priest who has passed through the heavens" (Hebrews 4:14). *Jesus is risen, He is ascended, He lives and He intercedes for us.*

"...lest we be carried away from them" (Hebrews 2:1). *Temptation draws us little by little.*

"...a high priest who cannot sympathize with our weaknesses; on the contrary, he was tempted like us in all things, without committing sin" (Hebrews 4:15) *Jesus was tempted, but he overcame and he can help us overcome temptations too.*

Challenge:

How have you been taking care of your salvation? Are there any decisions you have to make this week in order to improve? Prepare a personal project in which you can increase your time with God this week. Find a friend or your teacher to be your partner and report back to them at the end of the week.

Holiness = Relationship

Objective: To understand what holiness is and its importance in their life.

Memory Verse: "May God himself, the God of peace, sanctify you through and through. May your whole spirit, soul and body be kept blameless at the coming of our Lord Jesus Christ." I Thessalonians 5:23

Attention! x
Discuss with the group about the importance of taking care of their salvation.

Accept

Connect | Navigate

Introductory Activity (12-17 years)

- Supplies: A bandanna per person.

- Instructions: Divide into two groups and form two rows. Choose two people as guides to go first in the lines with their eyes uncovered. The rest of the participants will cover their eyes with their bandannas. Each person will place his or her hand on the right shoulder of the person in front. Ask the guides to lead each group around and return in about 2 or 3 minutes.

At the end, lead a brief discussion with the following questions: How did it feel to walk without being able to see? What would have happened or what happened to those who let go of their partner? Is the guide's work valuable? Focus the discussion on how holiness in our life is based on our relationship with Christ and the guidance of the Holy Spirit.

Introductory Activity (18-23 years)

- Supplies: A white or blackboard and chalk or whiteboard markers.

- Directions: Ask your class to write on the board things or activities that damage a relationship. After they have finished writing, ask them to read their responses.

Lead the discussion to the point where they understand that just as we care for our relationships with family and friends, we must care for our relationship with God.

The objective is to emphasize that the principle of holiness means to maintain a relationship with God and to obey Him in all that He asks of us.

Connect | **Navigate**

Ask the group what their concept of holiness is.

1. The meaning of holiness

A Dictionary of the Bible & Christian Doctrine in Everyday English (Eby, et al, 2004) notes:

a. (noun) Holiness is the quality of God that makes Him completely different from His creation. He is the Creator. Everything else is His creation. No created being is His equal. The correct relation of a created being to God is one of worship. He alone is worthy of worship. He alone is holy.

b. Jesus Christ is the perfect revelation of God's holiness. He shows what God is like. His life also shows how God wants people to live.

c. God's holiness doesn't simply mean moral perfection. He's holy not just because He's morally perfect. He's holy because He alone is God. God's will is right because He wills it. Thus, He's the Judge of what's morally right. Morality is human behavior that agrees with God's will.

d. God desires to make Himself known as the holy God. He shows His holiness in His redeeming acts. He shows Himself to be a God of justice and mercy. This shows His righteousness. He also wants His people to show His righteousness in all they do. They, too, should act justly and love mercy (Micah6:8).

e. Christian holiness is the sanctification of believers through Jesus Christ. This comes when Christians give themselves fully to God. They receive this cleansing by faith. This makes them holy before God. God alone is the source of all holiness.

f. (proper adjective) Holiness sometimes describes denominations that teach the doctrine of entire sanctification.

g. (proper noun phrase) The Holiness Movement is a term that refers to churches that stress entire sanctification. These churches understand entire sanctification as a second work of grace. They generally have viewed "entire sanctification" and the "baptism with the Holy Spirit" as the same...A number of denominations came into existence as a result of the Holiness Movement. They include, among others, the Church of the Nazarene...

(Deuteronomy 7:6-11; I Samuel 2:2; I Chronicles 16:8-34; Isaiah 5:16; 6:1-9; 40:25; 45:20-25; Luke 1:68-79; Romans 1:1-6, 19-32; 6:15-22; 12:1-2; 2 Corinthians 6:14-7:1; Ephesians 4:22-24; I Thessalonians 3:11-4:7; 5:23-24 and Hebrews 12:10-14)

The following words show us a similar work:

- Holiness (Luke 1:74-75; Romans 6:22; Ephesians 4:24; I Thessalonians 2:10; 3:13; 4:17; I Peter 1:15-16).

- Purity of heart (Ezekiel 36:25,27,29; Matthew 5:8; I Timothy 1:5; I John 1:7-9).

- Baptism of the Holy Spirit (Joel 2:28-29; Matthew 3:11; John 1:33; 14:16,26; Acts 1:8; 8:15,17).

- Perfect love (Deuteronomy 10:12-13; Luke 10:27; Ephesians 3:17-19).

- Entire sanctification (John 17:17; I Corinthians 1:30; 6:11; Hebrews 13:12; I Thessalonians 4:3; 5:23).

- Christian perfection (Genesis 6:9; 17:1; Deuteronomy 18:13; I Kings 15:14; I Chronicles 28:9; Job 1:1; Matthew 5:48; 19:21; John 17:23; Ephesians 4:12-13).

Through these terms, the Bible leads us to understand that holiness must be sought, obtained, and lived out daily. God wants us to live holy lives, consecrated to Him. The only way to gain this experience is through the blood of Jesus Christ and the constant presence of the Holy Spirit in our lives.

A holy person is a person consecrated to God, and therefore, separated from sin. To reach this condition or stay in this state, we must consecrate our lives completely to Him. Some think that it's a state of absolute perfection (without errors). However, it's a perfection in relational love with Christ by the Holy Spirit in our lives.

2. I can be holy

A Dictionary of the Bible & Christian Doctrine in Everyday English (Eby, et al, 2004) notes:

a. Holy describes the perfection and purity of God that's His alone. Holy also describes that which is set apart for God's use. People, days, places, and things become holy when they're set apart for God's service. These are called holy because the presence of God sanctifies them.

b. The Holy Spirit is the Spirit of God. Jesus Christ is "the Holy One" and "the Holy One of God" (Mark 1:24; Acts 3:14). He is called this because He is the incarnation of God. The Holy Spirit came on Him when He was baptized. He is holy also because He gave Himself to do His Father's will perfectly. He obeyed His Father and gave His life on the cross for people's sins. He makes it possible for all people to be holy through His full salvation.

(Leviticus 19:1; 20:7, 26; Numbers 5:17; 6:5-8; Deuteronomy 7:6; 14:2; Colossians 1:22 and Peter 1:15-16)

From the beginning, God called his people to be holy (Leviticus 19:1), and the with for His church (I Peter 1:15). Is it possible that God asked the people for something that was impossible for them? Not at all! God asked and continues to ask us to be holy because He knows that through His help, we can be.

In John 17:15, when praying for His disciples, Jesus said: "My prayer is not that you take them out of the world but that you protect them from the evil one." This means that no matter where we live, there will always be the possibility of doing wrong. We, as children of God, must not let ourselves be molded by the society; but it doesn't mean that we have to live in a bubble so that nothing contaminates us and thus remain pure for God. Rather, we should pray that in the midst of any situation, God will keep us from evil and help us to remain holy before Him.

3. Living holiness

God's call to live a life of holiness doesn't mean that we should isolate ourselves and live as hermits. John Wesley said that he knew no holiness but social holiness. What was he referring to?

A Dictionary of the Bible & Christian Doctrine in Everyday English (Eby, et al, 2004) notes:

a. John Wesley preached that all people could know the grace of God. He preached to the poor and to those oppressed by society. Wesley fought to change evil social conditions. But his main message was that people could be completely changed by the grace of God.

b. He believed that by the help of God, Christians could live holy lives. He believed this was possible through entire sanctification. This is a second work of grace.

Wesley was referring to the fact that holiness is possible in the midst of everyday life and in relation to others. This means that wherever we are, we can be holy.

At all times, people of all ages had and have to struggle with conflicting issues and so-called social pressure. Joseph (Genesis 39:1-12) and Daniel (Daniel 1) are examples of holiness in daily life. You can divide your class into two groups and ask them to study both passages. Ask them to present their findings to the group.

Then ask, how do you make a difference in the places that you go every day? Take the discussion to the practical life of holiness. You can use one of the following cases or a real-life experience. If everyone in your school makes copies of a book instead of buying it, would you do the same, even though the book has copyrights? Or, on the contrary, do you find a way to buy or borrow it? If your friends invite you to go out with them one day when you're usually active in church, do you choose to go with them or do you take a stand about your time dedicated to the Lord's work? How much do you defend your convictions? If everyone has copied music CDs or everyone buys movies that aren't original, do you also do it? Or, what is worse, do you make excuses because they're very expensive and otherwise you couldn't afford them? And on the Internet? What pages do you visit? What do you spend your time looking at? Do you download illegal music and computer programs from the Internet? Have you ever wondered if illegal things please God and how different you are from others?

Maintaining this holy lifestyle is a decision that only we can make. God is willing to help us.

Review/Application:

Ask them to read the passage from 1 Thessalonians 5:12-25 and write, in their own words, a practical summary for their life.

For example: I should recognize those who work for the Lord with appreciation. I should not despise those who are idle and depressed, rather I should support and encourage them. I must always seek the good, always be joyful, never stop praying and be grateful.

Challenge:

As we have seen, holiness is love of God, that is, a close relationship with Him, but it's also love of neighbor as an expression of that relationship. So getting to work, plan to express that love to others by organizing a day of service in a care center (a hospital, a nursing home, an orphanage) and express that love by bringing gifts, doing some activity, etc., but above all, bringing love.

Teacher and Disciple

Objective: To understand that being a disciple requires constant learning from the teacher.

Memory Verse: "But as for you, continue in what you have learned and have become convinced of, because you know those from whom you learned it..." 2 Timothy 3:14

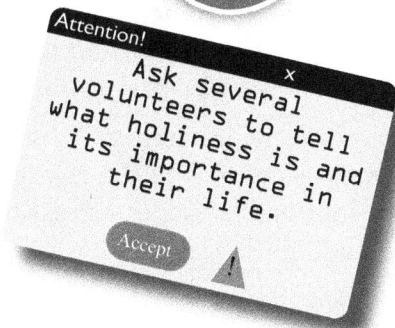

> **Attention!** x
> Ask several volunteers to tell what holiness is and its importance in their life.
> Accept

Connect | Navigate

Introductory Activity (12-17 years)

- Supplies: Colored poster paper, markers, and masking tape.

- Instructions: Write on each poster safety warnings, such as "stop," "caution," "do not take." These should be posted throughout the room (before the group arrives). To begin, ask: What are these signs for? What happens if we don't pay attention to them?

    Failure to heed warnings can have very painful consequences.

Introductory Activity (18-23 years)

- Supplies: Bandannas (two or three depending on how many pairs there are) and obstacles, (chairs, tables, poles, tires, etc.)

- Directions: Make two or three pairs. One of the members of each pair will cover their eyes with a bandanna. The other member will guide them along a path that you have set out, preventing them from tripping over previously placed obstacles. At the same time, the rest of the class will make noise to prevent the blindfolded person from listening to their partner's instructions.

    It's important to obey the words of the one who guides us. Despite the fact that there are other voices and distractions that say otherwise, if we don't do so, we'll stumble or be led astray.

Connect | Navigate

Our Lord Jesus, before leaving to the presence of His Father, left a commission (Matthew 28:19-20). Jesus wanted his disciples to teach others everything that He had taught them so that everyone would know Him. Each of us is the result of the fulfillment of that commission, and responsible for continuing it.

1. The teachers: Moses and Paul

Moses is one of the most outstanding Biblical characters in the Old Testament. Through him, the people of Israel were liberated from the hands of Pharaoh. His story is found in the books of Exodus through Deuteronomy. God used him to a great extent, which is why he earned a place in the 11th chapter of the letter to the Hebrews (Hebrews 11:23-29). In Moses, we see an ordinary person who placed himself in the hands of God, and by his obedience, God made him an extraordinary person. This teaches us that God's great works are often done by "ordinary" people who are willing to obey Him.

Moses was the greatest Jewish leader used by God to free His people from Egyptian slavery. He was a prophet, legislator, writer, but above all, a teacher. A man who modeled with his own life God's lessons to teach others.

In the New Testament we find Paul, who was a religious man, a fanatical follower of the religious laws of his people, even to the point of persecuting the Lord's church. As an intellectual, Paul was brave, determined, and firm in his convictions. However, after his encounter with the Lord, he placed himself in the hands of God, ready to do the good, pleasing, and perfect will of God.

Paul, the last apostle as he called himself (1 Corinthians 15:8), was God's instrument to continue His work, particularly outside the Jewish community. In addition to being an evangelist, Paul was a missionary, a pastor, a counselor, a preacher, a great New Testament writer, and a teacher.

Desiring deeply to be like Christ, Paul was so committed to the God he modeled in his life that he had no qualms about asking his disciples to imitate him as well (1 Corinthians 4:16, 11:1; Philippians 3:17; 2 Thessalonians 3:7,9).

True teachers are those who, like Moses and Paul, model God's teachings in their lives and inspire those around them.

2. The Disciples: Joshua and Timothy

From the beginning of Israel's pilgrimage through the desert, and before they went into the promised land, Joshua was an apprentice (disciple) of Moses. Based on God's instructions, before Moses died, he chose Joshua to be his successor. Joshua was a great teacher like Moses, who trained him in an extraordinary way for such an important position.

In Joshua 1:8, Joshua was given a very important recommendation on which his success as a person and leader of the people of Israel would depend. Throughout his life, Joshua left an example of obedience. Even in his final speech, he challenged the people to live in obedience to God while confirming his own unconditional commitment.

Like Joshua in the Old Testament, in the New Testament we find Timothy, who was a disciple of Paul. Timothy is believed to have been converted by Paul on his first missionary trip to Lystra (2 Timothy 3:11). Then on Paul's second trip to Lystra, they found each other again and Timothy distinguished himself by being a good witness in the congregation. Paul took him as a traveling companion (Acts 16:1-3).

This young man was Paul's faithful disciple. Even though in his house only his mother and grandmother were Christians, he remained faithful to God and an obedient collaborator with Paul. Thus, he became a great instrument of God in the spreading of the Kingdom (1 Corinthians 4:17, 16:10; Philippians 2:19-23; 1 Thessalonians 2:6, 3:1-5; 1 Timothy 1:3- 4).

3. A disciple obeys and never stops learning

Generally, we give people titles based on their tasks. How would you define a Christian, church member, teacher, and disciple? Allow people to come up with their own definitions.

Christian: The one who believes that Jesus is the son of God who died for the redemption of their sins and has accepted Him as his or her personal Savior.

Church member: Someone associated with a congregation, who agrees with its doctrines and serves in it.

Teacher: A person who has the ability to help others learn. Teachers are characterized by the commitments of their life and knowledge to the formation of Christ-like disciples.

Disciple: It's another name for a true Christian, who follows and learns from Jesus Christ, and enjoys serving Him with a totally surrendered of life. A disciple exercises a radical obedience to the teacher, is responsible for the assigned tasks, and is committed to common goals.

Our great teacher Jesus Christ has shared His teachings with us: what His Father made known to Him, He has made known to His disciples. Jesus teaches us through reading His Word, communing with Him in prayer, reading books by Christian authors, and having Christian friendships and fellowship that inspire us to a holy life. Jesus is our ideal teacher from whom we all learn.

Like Joshua and Timothy, we must have a teacher with whom we share experiences, learn from, and seek advice when we need it. A disciple must never be alone but must have a close mentor who can advise, correct, and encourage him or her throughout life's journey.

Review/Application:

These are characteristics of discipleship. Ask your students to write next to each word an example of how they would apply these disciplines in their daily lives.

- SERVICE: *I need to get involved in ministry.*

- PERSONAL DISCIPLINE: *I have to organize my time so that I can pray and read the Bible during the week.*

- OBEDIENCE:

- DELIVERY:

- INITIATIVE:

- RESPONSIBLE:

Challenge:

This week think of a person you would like to choose as your discipler. Pray and then approach him or her and tell them that you want to share and learn from them. On the other hand, you can be aware of someone you can help.

How much does it cost?

Attention!
Start the session by talking about discipleship and let the group share if they're discipling anyone and who is discipling them.
Accept

Objective: To understand the cost of being a disciple.

Memory Verse: "In the same way, those of you who do not give up everything you have cannot be my disciples." Luke 14:33

Connect | Navigate

Introductory Activity (12-17 years).

- Supplies: Sheets of paper, pencils or pens, a container.

- Instructions: Before the session, have a container with two folded papers inside—one with the word "teacher" and another with the word "disciple." Start the session by asking two people to come forward and each take a piece of paper from the container. The one who gets the word teacher will give an order to the disciple (e.g. a movement, dance, gesture, etc.). Then call two other people, but now the one in the role of teacher will have to do the action and the disciple will mimic them.

  Discuss the differences between the types of teachers. This activity will help the group think about the concepts of teacher/ disciple maker and disciple, and they'll get a glimpse of what it means to be a disciple.

Introductory Activity (18-23 years).

- Supplies: Whiteboard/blackboard, whiteboard markers or chalk

- Instructions: Divide the group into two teams. One team will discuss the concept of teacher and the other team about the concept of disciple. Give each team approximately three minutes. Then a representative of each team will write the definitions of teacher and disciple that they worked on.

  From this dynamic, the teacher will know how much the group understands about the subject.

Connect | **Navigate**

It seems that the tendency of some Christians is to settle for keeping their salvation and only sharing with other Christians, as if the church were a social club. Where is our commitment as disciples? To what extent have we assumed the role of disciples? How are we imitating Christ?

1. What is being a disciple?

A Dictionary of the Bible & Christian Doctrine in Everyday English (Eby, et al, 2004) notes:

a. (noun) A disciple is a person who follows the teaching and example of another person. Those who follow Jesus Christ are His disciples. They're sometimes called followers of Christ. They're also called Christians.

b. Jesus had 12 disciples who were later called apostles.

Hal Perkins (Walk with Me, 2008: 15) asked "What is a disciple of Jesus?" His response was: "A disciple of Jesus knows and follows Him. He or she walks with Jesus for a lifetime."

In Matthew 11:28, Jesus invited people to "Come" to Him. In Matthew 16:24 Jesus said, "Follow Me." I John 2:5-6 reminds us: "This is how we'll know we're in Him: whoever claims to live in Him must walk as Jesus did."

David Busic in Way, Truth, Life (2021, 13) describes discipleship as a "journey with Jesus". He notes:

a. Jesus invites us to a journey. "Come follow Me." It's a simple invitation to go on an adventure with a beloved friend. The Christian life is more than right belief. It's more than intellectual assent. It's an invitation to a journey with Jesus.

b. Another word for the journey with Jesus is discipleship. Discipleship, following the way of Jesus with Jesus, has many twists and turns and unexpected bends in the road. Sometimes the path feels easy and other times like a demanding incline. But the end goal…of discipleship is always the same: to be like Christ.

c. If that seems impossible, you are actually in a very good place to start. In fact, it would be impossible if it weren't for a very important certainty: we make the journey with Jesus. That's why it's a journey of grace.

Immediately when we think about the definition of disciple, we may relate them to: student, apprentice, pupil, etc. and we're not really far from the true meaning. The concept of disciple was established in New Testament times when it was common to be a disciple of a leader or teacher.

The responsibility of disciples was to follow and obey the teachings of their teacher, who taught these truths by embodying them in their own life. The disciples felt a deep respect for their teacher or tutor and obeyed Him in everything. But what does Jesus Christ expect of His disciples? He gave himself completely to the ministry of the kingdom of God, to the gospel of salvation, and expects no less from His followers. To be His disciples, Jesus asks us to bear much fruit (John 15:8).

This fruit is in two senses: first, our own life must be holy and pleasing to God. Second, consequently, we'll be the means for the glory of God to be manifested and to impact other people.

Another characteristic of a disciple of Christ is found in John 13:35. Love is a primary distinction of all of us who are His disciples. It's the love of God that moves us to go to others, the one that worries us and makes us feel the need of the world that doesn't know the Lord and the many people who are dying without hope.

2. God is calling you: Be His disciple

The mission that Jesus Christ entrusted to His church was clear, we have to be disciples and make disciples. Even though we may clearly know our call to share with others about God, we may ignore it and continue to place such responsibility only on others, such as: pastors, evangelists, missionaries, and other leaders. In this way, we fail to fulfill the great commission.

God is calling us, placing such responsibility in our hands because He chose us (John 15:16). Jesus Christ makes us partakers of His life and mission (John 3:16). The question is: how are we going to respond to God's call? It may even be that this call is taking us by surprise. Perhaps some of us are in a comfortable position, spiritually asleep, resting, or simply thinking about the problems of our daily life and in that state, God surprises us and calls us to get up. It's time to make a decision; God doesn't withdraw His calling or change His purpose for our lives (Romans 11:29).

We might want to excuse ourselves for lack of experience, fears, or limitations, but we must bear in mind that:

a. Evading our duty doesn't change God's purpose.

b. Just because everything seems fine with doing nothing doesn't mean it is.

c. Running away from God and His call is costly for us.

Let's make up our minds and be true disciples of Christ. There's nothing more satisfying than to be used by God in His work.

3. Discipleship: A high price to pay?

Jesus said that those who want to be His disciples must deny themselves and take up their cross and follow Him (Matthew 16:24). Jesus Christ not only asks us to give up comfort, wealth, and family, but also ourselves! Not only does it imply saying: "I am God's"; but it also means doing so by submitting our thoughts, actions, dreams, and desires to His will. According to psychology and philosophy, the only thing that belongs to each human being (and that's where one's wealth resides) is one's soul. That includes one's mind and will. This is precisely what Christ asks of us.

The concept "take up your cross" is loaded with meaning. It's a symbol of sacrifice, and the greatest example of this was Jesus himself. For Jesus, taking up the cross meant humiliation (2 Corinthians 5:21) and obedience (Philippians 2:8).

Luke 14:25-33 describes the cost of following Christ, and we'll discover this as we draw closer to God and seek to do His will. On many occasions, it will be necessary to detach oneself from what is loved (family, work, friends, etc.) if this is opposed to the demands of the gospel (v.26). Once again, the Bible emphasizes that above all things, we must first seek the will of God.

In Luke 14:28-31, we find two examples from the life of Christ's disciples that help us understand the importance of calculating the cost of discipleship.

Following Christ means that we no longer depend on ourselves but on Him. When we trust Him and give up our own desires, it's right in that moment when we begin to be true disciples of Christ. For example, to strip away everything except God's will is to pray and ask God to help us know His will when choosing a career to pursue. It also means praying before choosing the person you'll share your life with.

The commitment to be Jesus' disciple is radical. Disciples must not look back; they must adopt a lifestyle like Jesus and participate in the same destiny. If we truly want to be disciples of Christ, we must be aware that there's a price to pay, and we must be willing to do whatever the Master asks of us.

Review/Application:

Ask your students to answer the following questions (Answers are only guidelines; each student should express it in their own words).

1. What is our calling as Christians? **To be disciples of Christ.**

2. What is it to be a disciple of Jesus Christ? **It's to be imitators of Christ, to follow him and give ourselves to him, to work to extend the kingdom. It's letting God act in us and through us.**

3. What must we do to be Christ's disciples? **We must deny ourselves and sacrifice whatever it takes to follow God. At all times, we must let go of anything that keeps God from being first in our lives, including our will and our life.**

4. How should we prepare ourselves as his disciples? **Commune with God, obey and calculate the costs.**

5. Why should we be followers of Christ? **Because if we are Christians, we must be his disciples, his supporters and his imitators.**

Challenge:

We know that being Jesus Christ's disciple is no easy task; it's a battle that's fought every day. But seeking strength and following the example of Christ takes us forward and we can continue. So daily, we must write down what's keeping us from following him and what's keeping us from discipling others. Then, we must put it in prayer and give ourselves to the task of avoiding actions that divert us from Jesus' call.

A Diverse Call

Objective: To understand that regardless of the characteristics, we can all be disciples of Jesus.

Memory Verse: "Don't let anyone look down on you because you are young, but set an example for the believers in speech, in conduct, in love, in faith and in purity." I Timothy 4:12

Attention!
Ask the group to share ways they have experienced the cost of being a disciple.

Accept

Connect | Navigate

In Biblical times, it was common for people to walk many miles to follow a specific teacher. So many people followed Jesus through the regions where He moved. The account of Luke 6:2-16 shows us a different kind of day in the life of Jesus. Jesus spent many hours in prayer, seeking the guidance of His Father to decide who would be His closest disciples. These men were ordinary people, with extremely different characteristics, who became followers of Jesus. This is what Jesus continues to do today!

Introductory Activity (12-17 years)

- Supplies: Blank sheets of paper and pencils

- Instructions: Distribute the paper and ask your group members to write their names in the center in large letters, and around their name, their most outstanding characteristics (in any area: physical, emotional, spiritual or others). Once this is finished, they'll select someone in the group and write the name and characteristics of that person on the back of the paper. They'll mark with a circle the characteristics that are repeated in both and will share the most important ones (the same or different characteristics). They should conclude that we're all generally different.

    At the beginning of His ministry, Jesus chose His 12 disciples who were all different, and yet they made a good team.

Introductory Activity (18-23 years)

- Supplies: Different colored party hats (or you can make them in the shape of paper boats), white sheets of paper and pens for each person.

- Instructions: Write common, non-offensive adjectives on the hats, for example: "punctual," "nice," "spiritual," "intellectual," "cheerful," "strong." Mix up the hats and distribute one to each person, no matter what is written on it. Then ask them to read the adjective on their hat and find a person that could be described using that adjective, and put the hat on them. Each person must have a hat. When each one has a hat, ask the group to look at the hats and what they say. Comment on the fact that we're all different but we can still share so much together.

    Sometimes it's difficult to choose people when we're going to do an activity or create a group. Jesus faced that same situation when choosing his disciples. Nevertheless, the Master was able to sustain a group even with all their obvious differences.

Connect | Navigate

From the beginning, Jesus knew that He would have to make difficult decisions. One of them was to choose His disciples. How many times have we been in a similar situation having to decide between people?

1. There's beauty in variety.

Today there's much talk in favor of diversity. As Christians, we believe that we don't need to be the same to have peace. In fact, our faith in Jesus Christ is above differences. We're all different, we all think differently, we all react in a particular way, and we don't all give the same importance to the same things.

This happens for two reasons:

a. God created us to live in community (Genesis 1:27; 2:18). By nature, we're social, relational beings—people who are constantly interacting with the environment that surrounds us and able to receive new information and make decisions.

b. Our formation in society has been different for each of us (habits, family customs, the schools where we study and even the climate, geography, and history of the place where we grew up). We're endowed with different natural and acquired characteristics. Obviously, this applies to the church as well (1 Corinthians 12:4-6). It's something complex but wonderful when we recognize that it's part of God's will.

Notice how Jesus chose His 12 apostles:

• Jesus prayed. He did nothing without praying first (Luke 6:12), for He would decide who would continue the work He started!

• Jesus called His disciples (Luke 6:13). He already had a group of followers who accompanied Him in the first months of His ministry. It means that He had already started to know them and interact with them personally. Out of all of them, He chose some as His closest disciples, and 12 of these are referred to as apostles.

Two things surprise us: that He selected these people and that even knowing their flaws, He trusted them!

2. Just as we're different, our calls are different.

A *Dictionary of the Bible & Christian Doctrine in Everyday English* (Eby, et al, 2004) notes:

a. An apostle was a special kind of minister. The risen Christ called certain people to be apostles. Their mission was to preach so that people would become disciples of Jesus Christ.

b. Therefore, apostles were a type of missionary. They included Paul, the disciples of Jesus, and a few others.

(Matthew 28:16-20; Acts 1:1-2:42; Romans 1:1-6; 16:7; 1 Corinthians 9:1-27; Galatians 1:1, 11-2:10 and Ephesians 4:11-16)

Jesus recognized that each one of them was different. He lived with most of them during three years of ministry. Surely that wasn't easy. On one occasion, they were frustrated because they barely had enough to eat and a crowd accompanied them, and on another, they argued about who would have higher leadership positions in the "new movement." But Jesus was patient with them and lovingly taught them what He wanted for them. Jesus knew them, and yet, with those flaws that weren't going to change overnight, He decided to share with them the eternal inheritance of the good news.

3. Me? A disciple?

Yes! Jesus' call to the disciples challenges us to:

• Love and be patient with all people, even with those who don't share our habits, or whom no one cares about; even those we've already "labeled" (as irresponsible, late, etc.). The challenge is that, as followers of Jesus, we remove labels from everyone and see each of them as someone with whom we can and should share salvation.

• Become aware that, if we've already responded to Jesus' first call to our lives, it's our duty to listen to Christ, who wants us to stop being "followers" and to become true "disciples," that is, people sent by Him with a special commission.

It doesn't matter that we don't know how to speak or be in front of an audience; perhaps until this day we haven't discovered our gifts, or we don't know what abilities we have. Let's get rid of the labels that we have put on ourselves! Let's stop saying we're useless! If God called us, He has a specific area of service for us. Let no one look down on you for being young! Paul wrote to Timothy (1 Timothy 4:12). Hear God's call and accept it!

Review/Application:

Ask your students to make a list with 2 columns. In the first column, put the names of those who have been in the class. Next column - what differentiates them. In the third column - what unites them ("child of God", "disciple of Christ," "disciple of Jesus", etc.). Conclude the activity with prayer, interceding for everyone to accept God's call.

It must be remembered that this calling is not an exclusive title, such as pastor, missionary or evangelist, but something that even includes professions, trades and basic vocational aspects.

The last prayer is as a group: while I pray for my companions, they pray for me..

Challenge:

Many people today have low self-esteem. Help the group to understand that regardless of their characteristics, we can all be disciples of Jesus.

God has not put a label on you. During the week, from this day on, try to discover in prayer who you are (virtues, qualities, capacities or defects) and who you can become if you respond affirmatively to His call.

Help me to be different

Objective: To understand the importance of the faithfulness and consecration of God's disciples.

Memory Verse: "But nothing that a person owns and devotes to the Lord—whether a human being or an animal or family land—may be sold or redeemed; everything so devoted is most holy to the Lord." Leviticus 27:28

Attention!

Start the session by asking about the qualities and gifts that they discovered through prayer.

Accept

Connect | Navigate

Introductory Activity (12-17 years).

- Supplies: Toothbrush, hairbrush, a deodorant bar or some other personal item.
- Instructions: Present the selected materials to the group and ask: If any of those items belonged to them, under what conditions would they share them with another person? Why don't they share these objects? There are items that are for "exclusive use" of the owner, for personal use. That exclusivity makes us jealous. Ask the group what other things they consider exclusive that they would not share.

These objects become a part of us; they can even identify us in some way. In the same way, God values His people, and He paid a price that escapes human reason in hopes that we would be exclusive to Him and that people can see Him in us.

Introductory Activity (18-23 years).

- Instructions: Ask someone to share an experience where they have acquired something by working hard, something they desired deeply and that had a special meaning for them. But for whatever reason, it was broken when someone else used it with or without their permission. Encourage them to express their feelings at that time.

We value what costs us hard work—more if it's something we have wished for, and even more if it's for our personal use. These objects become a part of us; they can even identify us in some way. God values His people, and He paid a price that escapes human reason. We're His property and a reflection of Him. The world should see God in us.

Connect | Navigate

One mother had a set of elegant cutlery that she kept in its original case, a well-made briefcase, indicating that there was something precious inside. She used this cutlery only on special occasions and she spent time cleaning and polishing it. When the guests recognized her excellence and dedication, she felt that the purpose for which she reserved them was fulfilled. She said that the silverware was a reflection of her. Under no circumstances did she use that cutlery on a different occasion. Although her family begged her or when a friend asked to borrow them or offered to buy them, she never gave in. She was very careful with that which she already had "dedicated" to something special.

Do you know someone who's very protective of something that belongs to him/ her? Perhaps you yourself are protective about something personal. That mother's attitude towards her cutlery reminds us of God's attitude towards His people.

A Dictionary of the Bible & Christian Doctrine in Everyday English (Eby, et al, 2004) notes:

a. To consecrate means to give oneself or something to be used only by God. God makes holy what is consecrated to Him. (Exodus 28:3;30:30; Numbers 6:7, 9, 12; Joshua 6:19; Micah 4:13 and Hebrews 10:20)

b. Consecration is the act of giving or presenting something to God. People or things may be consecrated to God.

c. Consecration means giving oneself to God to live a holy life. God sanctifies people who trust Him and consecrate themselves to Him. (Exodus 28:3, 41; Matthew 12:4; Luke 2:23; Romans 6:15-19 and 12:1-2)

1. Consecration to God in the Old Testament

Ask: Do you know of someone who stands out because they're different? How are they different? How are you different?

A. Consecrated to worship

In Leviticus, God speaks precisely to His people about what it means to be God's people. In the first chapters, He points out how the high priest was to sanctify himself and sanctify the objects that he used in the tabernacle and later in the temple. He did it by sprinkling the blood of an animal without blemish, usually a sheep, a steer, or a dove, specially chosen for it, on the people and utensils. Everything that was used to worship God was "cleansed," "set aside," and "dedicated" just for that purpose. They couldn't be used for anything other than sacrificial worship to Yahweh. They belonged to God, and they were elements sanctified to Jehovah.

B. A jealous God

One of God's names is "jealous" (Exodus 20:5, 34:14; Deuteronomy 5:9). Certainly God is a jealous God. He cares for what belongs to Him and He doesn't share, lend, or sell it (Leviticus 27:28). When God chose the people, He "sanctified" them, that is, He "set them apart" and gave them a special "purpose" (Leviticus 20:26). This is what it means to be consecrated to God. Through Leviticus, God taught His people what it meant to belong to Him. Something that was not holy couldn't be in relationship with the holy God.

2. Consecration to God in the New Testament

Ask: Do you think it's easy to be different? Being different implies sacrifices. What do you think is the price of being different?

A. A consecration that makes a difference

The New Testament teaches us that we're now a people of priests. Our consecration to God draws us closer to Him and equips us spiritually to be like Him (Ephesians 1:3-4; 1 Peter 1:13-16).

We belong to God, for He has redeemed (bought) us at a price, through the shed blood of Christ, who cleanses us and makes us a holy people. Every time the word "holy" is used in the New Testament, we must understand: "Set apart for God with a purpose in Him and for Him." This isn't easy and God knew that alone we couldn't be holy. To fulfill this purpose God decided to pour out His Holy Spirit on His new people, "the Church." Now, unlike the Old Testament, where only some were consecrated and fit to stand before Him, we can all come into His presence through Jesus Christ.

B. A complete consecration

The birth of the Church was accompanied by a supernatural event called Pentecost. At Pentecost, God sent the Holy Spirit to seal His children (Ephesians 1:13). From then on, those of us who repent of our sins not only belong to God, but He dwells in us (1 Corinthians 6:19-20). Those consecrated are now inhabited by God Himself. Every believer is a reflection of God. The New Testament writings reveal concrete forms of consecration to God, and their writers lived and died for Him (Romans 14:8). They were different because God was with and in them.

3. Let's consecrate ourselves today

Many who have accepted Jesus as their savior continue to live in their own way, without understanding that our whole being, soul, mind, and body have been set apart for Him. God has cleansed us and awaits a total consecration in order that we fulfill the purpose for which we were created (Ephesians 2:8-10).

We live in difficult times. The world tries to stop the gospel from progressing. We receive pressure from many groups, and even close family and friends may demand that we leave our faith or ask us not to be so extreme. Our minds are continually bombarded with messages that deny or question God's Word. We're invited to dedicate our body to sensuality. We're told that we're in charge of our own bodies, so we can abort or consume drugs. Our minds are filled with vain desires and needs and we're the object of ridicule and aggression. But God is with and in us, and in Him all things are possible (Luke 1:37). Being a child of God means walking as He walked. But how do we take care of our mind? How can we keep our body pure? How can we sustain our redeemed lives? Here are some suggestions for living a different life in Christ:

a. Talk to God on a daily basis. God is close to those who truly call on Him (Psalm 145:18). Tell Him about your situation, in your own words. Make Him your close friend and your first resource.

b. Read the Bible. God's Word is powerful (2 Timothy 3: 6-17) and helps you think about what pleases Him and gives you tools to do His will.

c. Surround yourself with other people who are "different in Christ," There should be no lonely Christians. Share with other Christians, encourage them and let yourself be encouraged (Psalm 133:1). Schedule fun activities—being a Christian isn't boring!

d. Get together with a church community. Make friends with your pastors. Get involved in the activities of your church because that will make you stronger in your faith. Participate in conversations about the issues of being a "different in Christ" person, such as maintaining sexual purity, handling the pressure to use drugs, obedience to parents, not participating in activities that separate you from God.

e. Find a "prayer partner" of the same gender, or small prayer group, those who are of kindred spirit. Find disciples who don't hesitate to call your attention if you do what doesn't please God. Commit to accompany each other in love and encouragement (James 5:16). Pray and talk periodically about your life in Christ.

f. Be sure your "Yes" means "Yes" and your "No" means "No" (Matthew 5:37). Aim to be a radical and passionate Christian. Believe it or not, that makes you different, and God will be pleased.

g. Witness about Christ to others (John 1:7-8, 15 and Hebrews 12:1-2).

h. Pay the price with joy! Consistently obey God. Being at peace with God is something incomparable! (Matthew 5:11-12).

Review/Application:

Give your students some time to match the following words with their definitions.

1. Consecrate (**K**)	A. The right or power to dispose of a thing.
2. Clean (**G**)	B. The objective.
3. Separate (**I**)	C. Reserve or save something.
4. Set aside (**C**)	D. Care for, have extreme interest in something.
5. Different (**E**)	E. Diverse
6. Purpose (**B**)	F. Price assigned to a thing or service.
7. Choose (**H**)	G. To remove dirt from a thing.
8. Buy (**J**)	H. To select one or more things or people from among others.
9. Cost (**F**)	
10. Zeal (**D**)	I. Establish distance or increase it between something or someone. Have something for a specific use.
11. Ownership (**A**)	J. Acquire something for a price.
	K. Dedicate something or someone to a certain purpose.

Challenge:

What do you think would happen in your life, family, circle of friends, fellow students, co-workers, if you were radically Christian? Write these thoughts and ask the Lord for help, and this week begin to make a difference.

Cheer up! Being different is brave.

Our goal

Objective: To understand that the purpose of discipleship is to be like Christ.

Memory Verse: "Instead, speaking the truth in love, we will grow to become in every respect the mature body of him who is the head, that is, Christ." Ephesians 4:15

Attention!

Let the group express themselves, and keep reinforcing the importance of being different in Christ, emphasizing the faithfulness and consecration of God's disciples.

Accept

Connect | Navigate

Introductory Activity (12-17 years).

- Supplies: Whiteboard or blackboard, chalk or whiteboard markers, blank sheets of paper, and pens or pencils.

- Instructions: Write "Characteristics of a Disciple of Jesus" on the board. As the students arrive, provide each one with a blank sheet of paper and a pencil or pen to write down the characteristics of a disciple of Jesus. Allow a few minutes for them to write on their sheets, and then ask a few volunteers to share their responses with the group. Let them express what they think. Make no judgment and no one should make fun of the others' answers. Guide the group to create a broad definition with all the thoughts expressed, without rejecting any of them, while encouraging free expression.

With this activity, the group will express their opinions on how they perceive a disciple of Jesus. By listing the characteristics of a disciple, they'll be expressing some personal beliefs that they may not have analyzed before.

Once everyone has voiced their opinions, you'll have an idea of what your group considers important to be a disciple of Jesus, and you'll later work with those opinions to lead the group to understand that Jesus' disciples should be like Him.

Introductory Activity (18-23 years).

- Supplies: Whiteboard or blackboard, chalk or whiteboard markers.

- Instructions: On the board, make three columns. At the top of the first column write "_____ Movement" (a movement/religion known to your group), in the second write "_____ Philosophy" (a philosophy known to your group) and in the third "Christianity." Ask them to describe in their words what the followers of each of these three are like and to identify a founding character or representative of each. Have them write their contributions on the board.

Discuss as a group what they wrote and ask if the followers of each of the three have remained faithful to the example of their founders.

The objective of this activity is that by comparing the characteristics of the followers of these three, the group establishes the bases to understand that the disciples should be like their teachers. But when this doesn't happen, the movement is derailed.

Connect | Navigate

Every disciple must be discipled. This doesn't seem to be an impressive statement; however, many people in the church claim to call themselves Jesus' disciples but don't want to go through the elementary process of daily training that will make them true disciples. Why? Some don't understand the purpose of discipleship and don't see it useful. Others do understand it, but aren't willing to pay the price for the daily discipline of preparation, reading the Word, prayer, fasting, service, etc.

A Dictionary of the Bible & Christian Doctrine in Everyday English (Eby, et al, 2004) notes:

a. (noun) Discipline is the control of life by values and rules. A person my accept discipline for himself, or discipline may be forced on him.

b. Christian discipline describes the life of a person under the control of Jesus Christ. Christian disciplines have usually included prayer, fasting, Bible study, and other habits of devotion.

c. The Bible sometimes refers to discipline as chastening.

d. (verb) To discipline means to improve oneself or another person through rules and values.

(Job 36:10; Hebrews 12:3-11 and Revelation 3:19)

Read Ephesians 4:1-2, 11-16. Try bringing different versions/ translations of the Bible to this session.

1. Let's walk worthy.

In Ephesians 4:1-2, the apostle Paul wrote and shared the circumstances that he experienced with the Ephesians so that they would take seriously his way of living now that they were Christians. Since the people of Ephesus observed his behavior and thus formed an idea of what Christians were like, Paul didn't want the Ephesians to take lightly the call they had received from God to be part of his flock. He implied that the commitment made to God upon conversion should be shown by their conduct.

As is the case today, Christians were observed by their community, and for this reason it was important that their way of acting was consistent with the faith they professed. When we accept Jesus as our Savior and Lord, we must conduct ourselves in accordance with Kingdom values (Ephesians 4:2-6). So, it's important to establish a solid relationship with God so that these values take root in our hearts.

a. Humility (v.2) isn't born from one day to the next, it's a behavior exercised over time. Eby, et al, explain:

1. Humility (noun) is an attitude of modesty. It sometimes means the quality of being gentle, meek, and full of mercy.

2. Humility is being not too proud of successes. I means freedom from conceit.

3. Humility is an important Christian virtue. It's a condition for receiving the grace of God. It's the attitude of people who depend on God. It's knowing that one isn't worthy of the grace and presence of God.

4. Humility includes respect for the worth of other people.

5. To humble means to produce the quality of humility. A person can humble himself or herself. Or one person may humble another. (Deuteronomy 8:2-3; Psalms 10:12; 34:2; Proverbs 15:33; 16:19; 18:12; 22:4; Daniel 5:22; Acts 20:19; 2 Corinthians 12:21; Philippians 2:8; Colossians 2:18, 23; James 4:6 and 1 Peter 5:5)

b. Meekness (v.2) is born from a noble heart, a heart where God has come to establish priorities. (Psalm 37:11; Zephaniah 3:12; Matthew 5:5 and 2 Corinthians 10:1)

c. Patience isn't bought; it's exercised in walking daily, hand in hand with God. Eby, et al, explain:

1. Patience means the ability to wait when it would be easier to act.

2. The New Testament names patience among the fruit of the Spirit. It says Christians should have patience even when they suffer. This shows their faith in God and hope for the future. (Romans 5:1-5 and Galatians 5:22-24)

d. Love isn't a level of improvement that's reached through hours of meditation. It's God who grants it. The word Paul uses at the end of Ephesians 4:2 doesn't refer to brotherly love, nor to romantic love for a couple, but to the love spoken of in 1 Corinthians 13. It's God's special "agape" love. It's expressed in God's special concern for people. Christians receive this special love from God. The Holy Spirit helps us love God and other people with this special love. (John 3:16; 1 John 2:15; 4:8 and 3 John 1)

Paul asked the Ephesians to live like Jesus: humble, meek (Matthew 11:29), patient, and love as He loves.

2. He perfects us for the work

Paul emphasized in his letter the gifts necessary for the edification of the church with the purpose of being perfected for the work (Ephesians 4:11). The Ephesians list is similar to the one mentioned in I Corinthians 12:10 and 12:28, but we should by no means think that they're the only existing gifts. (See also Romans 12:6-8 and Hebrews 2:4)

In verse 11, Paul talks about those 12 apostles that Christ personally prepared to found the church. The evangelists Paul mentions were preachers who traveled from place to place preaching the good news of Jesus. Pastors and teachers form the same group. For many, the pastor must be a teacher, and on the other hand, a teacher must do pastoral work with his/her students. The grammatical reference of the word used by Paul is the Greek poimen which literally means shepherd of a flock. And the ministry is to protect and nurture.

Paul explained the reason why God gave these gifts: "Their responsibility is to equip God's people to do his work and build up the church, the body of Christ" (Ephesians 4:12 NLT). God prepares His children so that they in turn can commit to ministries, serving and instructing other believers.

3. The goal: Christ

We always have goals in our lives, like finish our education, starty a career, get married, etc. What is the goal Paul intends for us to reach, according to Ephesians 4:13-16? Verse 13 makes it clear what the Christian's goal should be and speaks of a level of maturity within the body of Christ.

Discipleship leads us little by little to reach that point of Christian maturity that God expects. In this way, we approach the goal: being like Jesus Christ. It isn't about reaching a maturity to be independent of Him, but to arrive at an ever more intimate relationship with Christ: being one with Him and reflecting Him. This has to be part of our daily life, always asking ourselves: Where do I see Jesus in this situation? What would Jesus do in our place? Would Jesus act like I'm acting?

Do we behave in a way worthy of Jesus Christ (Ephesians 4:1-2)?

Review/Application:

There are no correct or incorrect answers. Seek God's direction to motivate the student to want to seek deep and meaningful discipleship with a view to reaching the stature of the mature person that Paul speaks of.

Answer the following questions.

1. Is there a point in the lesson that you would like to study in more depth? Which? Why would you like to know more about it?

2. What gifts have you seen being practiced in the congregation?

3. Are there gifts among the group of young people that you think are not being used? Explain.

4. In your opinion, is our church a body that works in unity, where the "joints help each other"? Explain your answer.

5. Based on today's lesson, how can a young person reach the "measure of the stature of the fullness of Christ" (Ephesians 4:13)?

Challenge:

Do you think you're seeking in your life to be like your teacher or other mature disciple? Make a list of what you think you're doing well and another of the things you think you need to improve. Discuss it with your youth leader or Sunday school teacher and make a plan to strengthen the strong areas of your discipleship and strengthen the weak ones.

Me? A Discipler?

Objective: To understand that being a disciple of Christ implies making disciples and that we're called to disciple others.

Memory Verse: "Therefore go and make disciples of all nations, baptizing them in the name of the Father and of the Son and of the Holy Spirit" Matthew 28:19

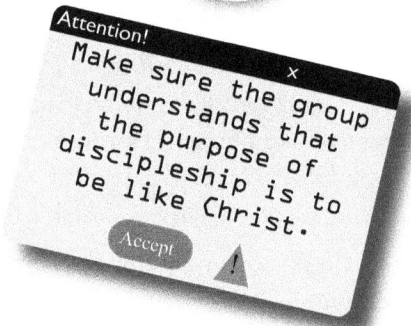

> **Attention!**
> Make sure the group understands that the purpose of discipleship is to be like Christ.
> Accept

Connect | Navigate

Introductory Activity (12-17 years).

- Supplies: Find phrases or Bible verses related to the topic of discipleship. Example phrases: I am a follower of Christ, Go and make disciples of all nations. Example verses: Matthew 10:25a, 42; 11:1; 12:1; Acts 16:1; 18:23.

- Instructions: The group will play broken telephone (similar to the old game Chinese whispers). Ask them to stand in a row or line. You can also have them compete in two teams. Each one will say the phrase or verse to the next in line or row, in their ear without others listening. The sentence should come to the end just as is was said in the beginning.

   God entrusts us with the message of the gospel and we must share it, just as He taught us.

Introductory Activity (18-23 years).

- Supplies: Cards, pens or pencils.

- Directions: Ask the group to think of someone who has influenced their life and then write on the card how that person influenced them. Ask them to write concrete things, visible changes motivated by this person (for example: Now I read the Bible because some time ago Peter motivated me to do it). Also ask them to write the name of a person they have influenced for better or for worse and how they did it. Ask a few to share.

- Mention that in life we all influence others in some way, but as disciples of Christ, our influence should always be for the better.

Connect | Navigate

A disciple is an apprentice who strives to learn a task or trade. Starting from this, we can say that we're disciples of Christ because we're learning from Him. We strive every day to be like Him so that those who observe us see Christ in us.

Let's reflect on the following: What do you believe about discipleship? Do you think discipleship ends with the completion of certain courses?

1. Is discipleship a commandment?

Generally in churches, very few people feel the need to be disciples, much less to disciple others. They have believed that the mission of: "... go and make disciples of all nations ..." (Matthew 28: 19a) is for a few who are called to professional ministry.

In Matthew 28:19-20, we see explicitly the command to go and make disciples. As we proceed in our Christian life, we must teach others all the things that we've learned from the Word of God and in our experience with the Lord. Possibly, many of us know it by heart, but do we put it into practice? Is this just for some few? No, Jesus entrusted it to all who were with Him. Ask the group: "Is anyone in our group discipling someone right now?"

Ask them to ponder the following example: Birds teach their young to fly. They do this naturally because they know that if their young don't learn, they won't survive; previously, the adult bird experienced the same lessons from its mother.

In the parable of the talents (Matthew 25:14-30), Jesus taught about the mandate to develop the gifts and talents that God has given us. The Lord has given gifts to us all (v.14). He will return and ask for an accounting of what we've done with them (vv.19-30). No matter what kind of talent we have or how many gifts God has given us, it's imperative to develop them.

To the question, is discipleship a commandment? The answer is a definite yes, since the command given by Jesus for the advancement of the Kingdom rests on discipleship.

2. Who should I disciple?

Discipleship is for all. Discipleship begins when we witness to even unbelievers, when we show and explain what Christ means to us. We help others seek a personal relationship with Jesus Christ. We help the newly converted to establish Christlike lifestyles. We help established Christians to meet their challenges. In this sense, it's important to recognize that discipleship is for everyone throughout their entire life.

Jesus' commandment to make disciples is for the whole church: children, teenagers, young adults, maturing adults, the elderly, men and women—no one is excluded.

Discipling unbelievers is frequently referred to as witnessing or evangelizing. An example is what parents do with their children by demonstrating and explaining Christian values in the home. In the local church, every Christian must be a disciple of Jesus Christ and be a disciple maker. However, when discipling, it's important to consider discipling someone of the same gender and to have a Christ-centered relationship with each other. This will allow for more Spirit-filled intimacy, which is beneficial for spiritual growth.

Personal witness is important in the New Testament. The first chapter of John's Gospel can be our pattern.

- Connection through a spiritual leader to point one to Jesus is helpful. John the Baptist pointed Andrew to Jesus (1:35-40).

- Family ties are important. Andrew found his brother, Peter, and told Peter about Jesus (1:41).

- Connection through place of origin is helpful. Next, Philip accepted Christ's invitation to follow Him. Philip was from the same place as Andrew and Peter (1:43-44).

- Connection through common religious background is helpful. Then Philip witnessed to Nathanael and invited him to come see Jesus (1:45-49).

A number of examples of evangelism are found in the Acts of the Apostles. Two examples of great witnesses are Peter and Paul.

- God led Peter to witness in Cornelius' home where Cornelius' family and friends had gathered. While Peter was speaking to them, "all who heard the message" received the "gift of the Holy Spirit" (10:44-45).

- Paul witnessed to a jailer. Then, the jailer and his whole family believed in God (16:31-34).

To disciple new believers, we need to help them become established in some of the basics of being followers of Jesus Christ.

- New believers need to understand that they now belong to God (Revelation 3:20).

- New believers need to understand how to walk with God (1 Corinthians 10:13).

- New believers need to understand how to learn from God, especially His plan for their lives (2 Tim. 3:16-17).

- New believers need to understand how to talk with God, praying always without becoming discouraged (John 16:24).

- New believers need to understand how to share their lives with God, living to please God (1 Corinthians 10:31-33).

- New believers need to understand how to speak about God. They tell others what Jesus has done for them. They testify about what they see and hear. They help draw others to Jesus. Their baptism shows others that they're Christians (Matthew 4:19).

- New believers need to understand their need to be filled with God's Holy Spirit. They need to be guided to receive the Holy Spirit by an act of faith, trusting God to entirely sanctify them (Ephesians 5:18).

- New believers need to join the family of God, the Church, where they'll mature and help others to grow in the Christian faith (Hebrews 10:25).

(See Charles Shaver, Basic Bible Studies for New and Growing Christians.)

3. Can I do it?

God has given us a responsibility and helps us carry it out. Remember that we're not doing this in our own strength. In Matthew 28:18, Jesus tells us that He Himself sends us, enables us, and goes with us.

We go in the power of Jesus. The one who gives the command is the risen Jesus Christ with all authority in heaven and on earth (v.18). Is there a greater power?

We go with training. Discipleship is an ongoing and lifelong endeavor. We're discipled to make disciples. Every day, we grow in Christlikeness and help others to grow as well. The things that Christ gives us are what we should give others (v.20).

We go with Jesus. We won't go alone on the path of discipleship, Jesus goes with us (v.20b). We should think that we can and must fulfill the command to go and make disciples.

Therefore, we must disciple others and we not leave it until tomorrow; it's time to start today. Seek to pray with others and make a commitment to be a discipling disciple.

Find someone who can disciple you. You need someone mature in faith to accompany you in the process through prayer and study of the Word of God, among others—someone you can trust to share what you are living, someone to pray with and share your walk with Christ. It isn't good to be alone and adrift; even Jesus himself submitted to the Father. Don't leave this until tomorrow; start looking for that person with whom you would like to share your doubts, burdens, desires, and wishes.

Also pray to God for someone to disciple. Remember that discipling a person is a natural process. You can begin to teach how to pray, read the Bible, intercede for others, share about Jesus, etc., which are simple but important things for your daily walk. And when something difficult arises, we should find someone who can advise us. It can be the pastor, a church leader, or a Sunday school teacher. If you don't know how to get started, find some discipleship material that can help you. A discipleship plan and resources can be found at: https://www.mesoamericaregion.org/en/package/additional-resources-for-the-journey-of-grace-discipleship/ and www.NdiResources.MesoamericaRegion.org

Review/Application:

Have each person answer the following questions. Here are possible answers but let the students answer them.

1. Write how you would define the word disciple? **A disciple is a student or apprentice.**

2. Who should disciples others? Why? **All Christians because Jesus tells us to disciple others.**

3. Do you think you need to be discipled? Why?

4. What do you do best and what could you do in your church?

5. What things should you take into account to be a discipler? We're not alone, we must be obedient, be communicated and our testimony.

Challenge: God is calling you today to start his work by looking for a discipler (someone to accompany you in your life of faith) and a disciple (someone you can accompany in their life of faith). In the week ahead, think about this and makes a decision.

My house

Objective: To understand what ecology is and the role of the Christian in it.

Memory Verse: "For the creation waits in eager expectation for the children of God to be revealed." Romans 8:19

> **Attention!**
> Make sure the group understands that being a disciple of Christ implies making disciples and that we're called to disciple others.
> *Accept*

Connect | Navigate

Usually Christians focus on the practices that help their spiritual life: witnessing, evangelizing, discipling, serving, etc. All this being very good, sometimes we forget that being saints implies being good stewards of God's creation during our time here on earth.

Introductory Activity (12-17 years).

- Supplies: A newspaper for each group

- Instructions: Organize the class into small groups, give one or several newspapers to each group (depending on the number of newspapers you have) and ask them to look for news related to ecological problems. Then ask them to take time to share how this problem affects humans and animals.

  Emphasize that most ecological problems result from people's ignorance and neglect of creation.

Introductory Activity (18-23 years).

- Supplies: Photos of animals, trees, or places typical of the place where they live, sheets of paper and pencils. If you don't have photos, you can put names of animals, trees, or parks that the group recognizes on the board.

- Instructions: Show the group the pictures or ask them to read the names (if you wrote them on the board), and then ask each one to write down the importance of these items.

  Emphasize that each element of the ecosystem in which we live has an importance for the survival of all.

Connect | Navigate

1. God's Creation

A Dictionary of the Bible & Christian Doctrine in Everyday English (Eby, et al, 2004) notes:

1. Creation is the act of making something. People may create things, but they really only shape material that already exists. Only God can create something out of nothing.

2. God made the world and all the people and things in the world. The New Testament says that God made the world through Christ. God told people to care for what God made. But God's creation has been harmed by man's sin.

3. Creation also describes the act by which God makes sinners into new people. The Church is sometimes called the new creation of God in Christ. God is making the whole world new through Christ. Thus, Christ is the Source of a new creation.

(Romans 6:4; 8:18-25; 2 Corinthians 5:16-6:1; Galatians 6:15-16; Ephesians 2:1-22; 4:17-24; 2 Peter 3:1-13 and Revelation 21:1-5)

The Bible begins with: "In the beginning God created the heavens and the earth" Genesis 1:1. This affirms that everything has its origin in God and that God created everything that exists. Both the Old and New Testaments show us the way in which all creation is sustained by God, which points to His great wisdom (Psalm 104:24). Passages like these should motivate us to contemplate creation with admiration for the multiple forms of life present in it. A careful look at creation helps us perceive how God is at work in all creatures, allowing them to exist and sustaining them, as expressed in Matthew 6:26-30.

We usually hear about natural resources, and environmentalists and ecologists talk about nature as a resource. God created nature as a resource, but also as a habitat for man and all His creation, both animals and plants. It was a suitable space to live (Genesis 1:28-30; 2:15-16).

The creation account in Genesis 1 shows us that God put everything in order and created everything that exists. He made human beings to live on earth and take care of all of His creation. They were to live on earth and enjoy it and not destroy it. Humanity has misunderstood the command to administer the earth and eat its fruit. We've made the earth a mere resource and forgotten that it's our habitat, and if it's destroyed, we'll be left unprotected. That's why God, by creating human beings as the only creation in His image and likeness, left them in charge of the rest of creation, the habitat that He had prepared for them. Humanity had to be a participant in the process of sustaining and caring for His work.

2. Ecology

Ecology is a science that arises from the need to find solutions to nature's problems that are generated by the misuse of resources. The word "ecology" comes from the Greek oikos, which means "house," and logos, which means "word." So we have a "word about our house." Thus, ecology is the study of the house or the world in which we live. As a science, it studies the relationships of living beings with each other and with their environment. According to the Merriam Webster Dictionary, ecology is "a branch of science concerned with the interrelationship of organisms and their environments."

A Dictionary of the Bible & Christian Doctrine in Everyday English (Eby, et al, 2004) notes:

a. Law means guidance or direction.

b. The Hebrew word for law is "Torah". Torah means "the way of the Lord". God showed Himself and His will for His people through the Law. The Law told the people how to be faithful to their covenant with God. The Law told Israel how to worship God and how to live with one another.

c. Torah is the name given to the first five books of the Old Testament.

d. God gave His law to Moses, and Moses gave it to Israel. Thus, the books of the law, the Torah, are called the Law of Moses.

The Law of Moses contains a series of principles to protect the environment. Thanks to the commandments and prohibitions established in the Law, the people of Israel were able to live in harmony with nature in their pilgrimage through the desert. The people of God subsisted in such a difficult environment only by faith in God, abiding by all his norms, which included ecological norms, established in the five books of the Law of Moses. To show that the Old Testament is an effective guide for sustainable development, we can cite in particular the rules of food and hygiene.

a. In Leviticus 11: 1-8, it was established that any animal with a split hoof that chews the cud could be eaten, but not those that only chew the cud or only those that have split hooves. In this case, the camel and the pig would be unclean for them, but why? The division between clean and unclean animals makes sense from a biological point of view. Although pigs are good forage eaters, they also have nutritional needs similar to those of man, and perhaps rivaled the Jews for food. The pig is an animal that easily contracts diseases. It cannot travel long distances, doesn't tolerate high temperatures in dry weather, and isn't a grazing animal. All these factors made pork a difficult food item to serve for the Jewish people who were a nomadic people. God wanted to avoid diseases in the midst of Hs people. The raising of sheep and goats was healthier and more profitable too.

Camels, despite being ruminants, were indispensable as beasts of burden; so they were among the protected species.

b. Another example was the prohibition of eating aquatic animals that feed on parasites and insects. The prohibition in Leviticus 11:9-10 referred to amphibians that feed on insects, especially frogs. Let's look at a current example: In the 1970s, in Bangladesh, frogs were caught in large numbers for export. Soon after, there was an outbreak of Malaria in the country. As the frog population declined, Bangladesh lost its cheap and effective defense against Malaria.

c. In Deuteronomy 20:19, we find a clear ordinance regarding cutting down trees.

3. The responsibility of human beings

Human beings and nature have been created as parts of the same process. Man was the head of God's creation, but by yielding to temptation, he sinned and thereby affected the purpose for which he was created. Today, many of the ecological problems that surround us are the result of disobedience to God.

Humans don't own creation; we're not free to do whatever we want with it. The biblical account says that as representatives of the creator God on earth, we're called to administer creation, with responsibility before God and before other creatures. According to Genesis 3:17, the land was cursed because of man's disobedience, and for that reason he would eat from it with pain. Sin affected our relationships: with God, with ourselves, and with nature. Although sin distorted the image of God in people, it didn't change our place in creation. Likewise, nature has not completely deteriorated. It's still governed by the same laws that God established from the beginning (Genesis 8:22, Psalm 19:1-3, Romans 8:19-23). We can affirm that we continue to be administrators or stewards of all creation. As such, we must understand that we're not the owners, since an administrator or steward manages the properties of another. Our role is to carefully guard the property of others that have been placed under our responsibility (1 Corinthians 4:2).

Our current relationship with nature is typical of those who have lost focus of their administrative responsibility. As we return to our original position of steward and custodian of the environment, the abuse against our habitat will diminish. Our faith prompts us to take care of creation and the promotion of ecological justice as a personal and Christian responsibility.

Review/Application: Ask your students to fill in the following ecological interaction chart, filling in the relationship between the detailed parts and the appropriate action on them. We give answer options below, but the students don't need to do it exactly the same.

Relationship between God and...	Relationship between people and...	Special care for its conservation.
Plants: God made plants to bear fruit.	Plants: They provide food and it is people who must harvest them. Plants generate oxygen.	Plants: Do not fell trees improperly.
Water: God Himself created it.	Water: It is essential for life.	Water: Must not be wasted or polluted.
The earth: God is the owner.	The earth: It is the habitat of all beings and provides resources.	The land: It must be administered equitably and not abused.
Animals: God is the creator.	Animals: Serve as food, company and service.	Animals: They must be protected and not abused or .

Challenge:

During the week, place wet cotton in a glass container. On the sides (between the cotton and the glass) place seeds (beans or kidney beans) and monitor the growth of the seeds, checking that the cotton always remains moist. Share the result of the work after a couple of weeks, and symbolically reward those who managed to take proper care of the germinated plant.

Caring for animals

Objective: To understand the responsibility we have towards animals as part of God's creation.

Memory Verse: "Pairs of clean and unclean animals, of birds and of all creatures that move along the ground, male and female, came to Noah and entered the ark, as God had commanded Noah." Genesis 7:8-9

Attention! x
Review what the group understands what ecology is and the role of the Christian in it.
Accept

Connect | Navigate

Introductory Activity (12-17 years).

- Supplies: Pictures of animals, blank sheets of paper, and pencils.

- Instructions: Show the group the selected pictures and ask them to write down what feelings they have when looking at the pictures. Ask how of the students many have pets and how they would feel if their pet got lost and was found injured, dirty, and poorly fed.

    If our heart is saddened when we think about the suffering of animals and is further accentuated when we imagine them as our own, ask the group: How would God feel when He sees that many animals, which He created and belong to Him, are exposed to so much aggression?

Introductory Activity (18-23 years).

- Supplies: Poster sized card, paper of different colors, erasers, and scissors.

- Instructions: Divide the group into pairs, ask them to make a collage about nature. Encourage the group to be creative and do their best. At the end, take the collages and crumple them, soil them, walk on them, and throw them into the trash can. They may be surprised. Talk about the feelings this action caused in them.

    If we become angry or sad when we see that others don't appreciate or treat with disrespect what we've done with so much effort, how will God feel seeing that many animals that He created are exposed to so much aggression and abuse?

Connect | Navigate

1. Animals are God's creation

Genesis 1:20-25, 28-30 narrates the process of creation, and especially verses 20-25 detail the creation of fauna, closing this process with the statement: "And God saw that it was good." As believers, we must clearly understand that all creation belongs to God (Psalm 24:1). He isn't only the Creator but also cares for and sustains creation. The Word tells us how God takes care of animals as an important part of His creation (Psalm 84:3; 104:10-14; Matthew 6:26).

According to what is expressed in Psalm 96:1 and 148:7-10, all creation praises its creator and expresses the glory of God. Through nature we can show others the vastness of God as creator, but certainly all of His creation expresses His greatness as well. Animals, as part of His creation, are sensitive to God's voice. A shocking case is Balaam and his donkey (Numbers 22: 23-33). Also in the story of Elijah, we see that the ravens sent by God fed him (1 Kings 17:4-6).

2. Animals as helpers and pets

God gave human beings the power to be administrators of His creation within the limits that were set by the Law. His commandment also had restrictions, reminding humans that they would exercise power over something of which they weren't creators or owners of, but stewards (1 Chronicles 29:11-12; Psalm 50:10-11).

God assigned people the task of being stewards (Genesis 1:28; 2:15). A steward or administrator is a person who manages the assets of his master. In the New Testament, the Greek word for administrator means stewardship. It's a compound that means "house" - "law," referring to the administration of a house, under the law or principles of the owner. A principle for exercising stewardship is to recognize that nothing belongs to us, although everything was created for our well-being (Psalm 8:3-8) and for us to care for it with love. Human beings are endowed with noble and wonderful powers: (1) We're crowned with glory and honor (Psalm 8:5b). Our ability to think of ourselves is our crown of glory; we must not desecrate that crown by misusing it, nor lose the right to it by doing wrong. (2) God has put all things under the feet of people (Psalm 8:6b), but we must not abuse creatures. Rather, we must care for them with love, remembering we're also God's creation, and awaiting our final redemption (Ephesians 1:14).

The correct stewardship of animals will bring multiple benefits for humanity:

- Balance the ecosystem. Psalm 104 is the perfect account of the balance of the ecosystem and there we can appreciate how animals play a role in the conservation of the ecosystem.

- They benefit our health. Some animals provide help to people in crisis. Animals don't have the power to heal, but through their affection and unconditional love, they promote relaxation, stability, and help to face critical situations with greater serenity.

- They provide good company. Taking care of a pet mitigates the feeling of loneliness, fills the empty spaces in life, especially for elderly people who may be abandoned.

- They facilitate productive work. Working animals have played a considerable role in the cultural and economic development of humankind since ancient times. However, the spread of industrialization machines in many places has displaced animals.

- They generate food and shelter. The food that we obtain through animals, not only from their meat, but from their products (eggs, milk and their derivatives, etc.), are of great importance for proper human nutrition. They also provide resources for footwear and clothing.

God has given animals to be a benefit to people so that we in turn exercise our authority over them with the love and respect that they deserve as a creation and as an expression of the glory of God..

3. Our responsibility to animals

People have to exercise stewardship under divine principles, but when they didn't do so, sin distorted their ability to act. Because of sin, people decided to rule by their own will and this brought an imbalance in the entire ecosystem. Human beings felt ownership of their possessions, and in their ambition to have more, they have caused irreparable damage to the animal world. Today, people resist believing that their abilities come as a gift given by God, and they exalt themselves by damaging the world around them. The result has been temporary economic gain through environmental loss. The consequence of this ambition, referring to the animals produced is:

- Greater demand: To meet the current demands for meat in some countries, it's necessary to intensively confine the animals in so-called factory farms. These farms have a single objective - to obtain the maximum benefit without looking at the welfare of the animals, using any method, no matter how cruel it may be, as long as it's profitable. Some of these methods are: Putting animals in extremely small spaces with no place to move, since by the simple fact of moving they waste food in their activity. In some cases, they're fed excessively to get more out of them.

- Unsuitable premises: They keep animals living in windowless buildings. They only see the sunlight and feel the fresh air when they leave the warehouses to go to the slaughterhouse.

- Hunting: A large number of species have disappeared due to hunting, either for skins or other valuable elements such as ivory or their meats.

- Fun: Bullfighting and other festivals. When the bulls come out of a state of panic from the bullpen, they're dizzy in the bullring, and finally killed with a sharp spear. There are countries where their national holidays include slaughtering roosters and hens, stabbing calves and bulls, throwing goats over cliffs, etc.

- We could talk about other aggressions such as experimentation on animals, mistreatment of pets in general and disrespect for animal rights. All of these activities go against God's creation. We don't have the right to do what we want with the natural environment. "Dominion" isn't synonymous with destruction. Since creation has been placed in our charge, we must manage it responsibly and productively for our own good and that of future generations.

- One man lost two otter cubs when someone, walking along the beach with a rifle, found them playing near the water and shot them. One cub died instantly and the other later died from its injuries. The shooter apologized but tried to justify his actions saying: "God gave man control over the beasts of the field." How wrong he was. As Christians, we have to start thinking and acting like God's stewards.

Review/Application:

Discuss the following questions with the class and ask them to write down their responses. You can tell them about the suggested answers after they have written down their own answers.

1. Do animals have rights? *Although there are rights to animals, they have not yet been recognized as such. What the laws for the protection of animals or the proclamation of the rights of animals, if they have achieved is, to a certain extent, "cut the absolute rights that were previously granted to human beings" over animals. (Razón y Fe magazine, The rights of animals and the moral value of living beings, Miguel Sánchez González, Volume 223-No. 1190-March 1991).*

2. What is the statement that, as believers, should move us to a respect for animals? *That they are part of God's creation that we have been given to care for Genesis 1:28.*

Challenge:

Be sure the group understands the responsibility we have towards animals as part of God's creation.

Coordinate with the class to visit a nearby animal shelter. Perhaps they can offer themselves for a day of volunteer work. The purpose of the activity is to sensitize their hearts to the suffering and abandonment suffered by animals, and to know the good disposition of those who dedicate their time to caring for them.

Contamination

Objective: To comprehend the relationship that exists between contamination of the human heart and contamination of the planet.

Memory Verse: "The Lord God took the man and put him in the Garden of Eden to work it and take care of it." Genesis 2:15

Attention!
Start the session by encouraging the group to share testimonies about the responsibility we have towards animals.
Accept

Connect | Navigate

The word contaminate is synonymous with corrupting, spoiling, debasing, and infecting. In the Bible, the idea of contamination is applied first to the profound degeneration that sin can cause inside people. Many times, God warned His people not to be defiled (Ezekiel 20:1-7, 42-43); and likewise, Jesus taught the same thing (Matthew 15:10-20).

Since ancient times, the contamination of the heart has been linked to the contamination of the earth (Numbers 35:30-34). This remains true to this day. The contamination of the earth begins with the internal contamination of the human being. Pride, envy, ambition, and greed have generated economic, political and social systems that are polluting creation.

Introductory Activity (12-17 years).

- Supplies: A glass container, filled with clean water; some chemicals commonly used in our homes (powdered soaps, liquid cleaners, chlorine, etc.); garbage (plastic packaging, metals, toilet paper, etc.)

- Instructions: Show the container of clean water and then pour the chemicals or trash into it one by one. With each item, check the changes in the smell, color or consistency of the water. Then ask the following questions: Why does our society contaminate water? How easy or difficult is it to contaminate something? How easy or difficult is it to clean contaminated water? Could contaminating the environment be considered a sin? Why?

  According to the memory verse, what is the Christian responsibility to creation?

Introductory Activity (18-23 years).

- Instructions: Ask the young adults if they know of any human diseases related to contamination. Ask about other consequences that contamination causes in plants and animals. Make a list on the board. If possible, bring some visual or documented examples of diseases and consequences generated by water, air, and land pollution. Then ask:
- How is contamination related to wellness?
- How is contamination related to disease?
- Is it necessary to contaminate to live well?
- Why does today's society feel that it needs to contaminate the environment in order to live well? Is this idea true?
- How many things would you have to change in society and in your daily life to help stop contamination?
- What does the Bible say about illness?
- How can we as Christians give hope to a sick world?

Connect | Navigate

Since ancient times, civilization has polluted the earth as part of its idea of material progress. However, in the last 200 years, with the emergence of industrial development, there has been more pollution than at any other time in history.

Currently, a factor of contamination is the emission of so-called greenhouse gases (GHG). These gases are formed by the use of fossil fuels such as coal, oil, and natural gas, used to move many things such as industrial machines, generators, ships, trains, automobiles, and airplanes. Also, the appearance of plastics and other synthetic materials, as well as fertilizers and various chemical compounds, have contributed to polluting both water and land.

1. The consequences of contamination

One current concern of contamination of the earth is climate change or global warming. It's feared that thousands of species of plants and animals may be lost due to this phenomena. Added to this are the human consequences that may result from the rise in sea level and changes in temperatures in different areas of the planet, affecting the life, diet, and health of millions of people.

What exists behind this is the idea that humans are the owners of the land and that all the things that exist must be at their service. This idea is known as anthropocentrism. In short, human civilization has seen in nature an inexhaustible source of exploitation of resources for its benefit. Therefore, forests have been seen as suppliers of wood and wind as a supplier of energy for movement. But a forest is more than wood and wind is more than energy. Forests and wind are part of natural cycles that generate life for animals, plants, and people. By forgetting this, men and women have affected their own livelihood, along with the livelihood of other beings. Ask: What benefits has industrial development brought us? Why has development that brings benefits also harmed the earth? Is humankind the owner of the land and everything that exists on it?

2. A Biblical Perspective

From the beginning of creation, God entrusted men and women to maintain a relationship of "caring and working" with the planet. He commanded them to rule over the earth (to cultivate it) while also seeking its preservation (to keep it) as part of their commission from their Creator (Genesis 1:28-31). The correct lordship of humanity over the other beings on the planet produces well-being. As the biblical text points out, as sin entered the heart of man, the earth also suffered the consequences (Genesis 3:17-19). Therefore, the internal contamination of man is in direct line with the contamination of the earth. Both things are tied in a common destiny. The epistle to the Romans tells us that the earth has been "tied" by God to the destiny of its caretakers (Romans 8:19-23). The sin of humankind against the earth has serious consequences since it implies failing to recognize that creation belongs to God (Leviticus 25:23; Psalm 24:1-2; 102:25). The manifestation of the kingdom of God includes destruction for those who destroy the earth (Revelation 11:15-18).

A contaminated humanity generates a destroyed and suffering earth. But a redeemed humanity produces a living earth for the glory of God. Thus, the arrival of our King and Lord Jesus Christ is good news for the earth (Luke 2:10-14). Jesus is the one that God provided to redeem the earth as well. From ancient times it has been prophesied that the kingdom of God will bring prosperity to creation (Isaiah 11:1-9) as it will mean the end of those who destroy it. Thanks to the redemptive work of Jesus, we too, the children of God and witnesses of Christ, are part of that hope for all beings that inhabit the planet (Romans 8:21-23), provided that we give a real witness as God's people. Ask: What is the difference between an owner and a caretaker or manager? Why is the contamination of the heart linked to the contamination of the earth? What is, according to the Bible, the fate of the ones who destroy the earth?

3. The alternatives

Christians can work to care for the earth in two ways:

a. Fighting the effects of pollution and its causes.

- Reduce pollution, using recyclable materials, and biodegradable products; changing plastic consumption habits, extending the life of household appliances or, if necessary, replacing them with appliances with a more efficient use of energy.

- Refuse, reduce, reuse, and recycle are keywords to mitigate the effects of pollution.

b. Fighting the causes is more complex, but much more important than fighting the effects, since it means fundamentally changing the forms of production and consumption in the current economy.

- Demand companies and countries lower contaminating gas emissions.

- Develop laws that oblige polluters to clean and repair what is contaminated or damaged.
- Demand that technological advance complies with ethical principles of preservation and precaution.
- Fighting the causes of pollution also implies the use of alternative energies that don't put nature's cycles at risk.

Today, Christians have the important challenge of making God's mandate to care for the earth come true. Ask: What are some possible alternative energy sources? What concrete actions can you start taking today to avoid contamination? (Make a list on the board). Why is it more difficult to combat the causes of pollution than its effects? Why are Christians a hope for the earth?

Review/Application:

Ask your students to divide into groups and write the definition of the following words, and using organic and inorganic material found in the garbage, in the gardens or in the pots of the church, develop a poster to represent one of the following words:

Reuse, recycle, reduce, renew

At the end, each group should explain their poster and talk about the alternatives that exist to avoid pollution, and give Christian testimony of care for creation.

Challenge:

Review with the group the relationship that exists between contamination of the human heart and contamination of the planet.

Using the proposals that emerged from the lesson, work with your teacher and class to develop an annual work plan so that actions can be taken in the church to avoid contamination, and care for creation. The plan may include the voluntary collaboration of children and adults who are interested, as well as a series of sermons by your pastor in which the subject is discussed.

Taking care of water

Objective: To understand that water, something that everyone must have access to, has a material and spiritual dimension.

Memory Verse: "Let the one who is thirsty come; and let the one who wishes take the free gift of the water of life." Revelation 22:17b

Attention! Check how well the group comprehends the relationship that exists between contamination of the human heart and contamination of the planet.

Accept

Connect | Navigate

Introductory Activity (12-17 years).

- Instructions: Ask your group to close their eyes and begin to imagine the place where a clean river begins (it's essential that they keep their eyes closed during the whole dynamic). Provide some detailed mental pictures that can help your group's imagination. Give them enough time to visualize the details of the place: "Maybe there are trees and fish; maybe you can see the bottom of the crystal clear river and the sunlight."

  Then tell your groups to imagine that they are that river and think about the feelings that arise. Comment: "You are that river!" How do you feel? (Allow some to express their feelings.)

  Invite them to imagine that the river has started its course and they're feeling the water flow. They're that running water. What do they see? What are the places they pass through like?

  Have a time of silence and say: "At this moment you begin to feel that something strange enters your waters, it's oil!"

  Continue by saying: "It also begins to collect a lot of garbage, industrial substances, oils, insecticides; then the fish die, the colors fade and everything turns gray and stinking."

  Finally have them open their eyes. Ask: "How do you feel now? How does a clean river relate to the physical and spiritual well-being that God gives us? What does a dirty river mean?"

Introductory Activity (18-23 years).

- Supplies: News clippings from local newspapers about problems related to water in all its contexts (a polluted river, construction of a dam or hydraulic work that represents a social conflict or an advance, water scarcity, etc.).

- Instructions: Using the news, lead the group to reflect on a water problem that they know about: Maybe from their home, neighborhood, city or country, and ask: "What is the cause of the problems for which you're going through the current water situation? What problems in physical life and in spiritual life does water pollution or poor distribution reflect?"

  Write on the board a list of problems this creates in life. (Illness, thirst, malnutrition, etc.) Write the relationship that this has with our spiritual life, for example: When some people waste water and other people who need it don't have access to it, injustice, selfishness, lack of neighborly love, etc. are reflected.

  How can we give water back the meaning of life that God gave it? What is the meaning of water when it's scarce or cannot give life? How could we Christians help solve the water problems in our city or country? What could I contribute?

Connect | Navigate

All beings on the planet depend on water. For this reason, water is presented as a need that doesn't distinguish between rich and poor, men and women, race or nationality. Even the need links us with that of plants and animals.

By giving us water, God testifies of His goodness and caring for our needs. Water is life and this poses a very important relationship with God, the Creator of life.

1. The current situation

Multitudes of people around the world don't have adequate access to drinking water and sanitation systems, which implies various health risks. Numerous deaths are reported each year caused by diarrheal diseases. Likewise, various social conflicts are unleashed by injustices related to the distribution of water. Multitudes of people have been displaced from their places of origin, many times by force, due to the construction of dams. There are also inequitable payments in water rates while other areas enjoy subsidies for their water consumption. The sale of bottled water has become a big business, to the extent that, in some places, a liter of bottled water is more expensive than a liter of gasoline. It costs thousands more than a liter of the public network, which means that many people are excluded from the quality water that should be for everyone.

On the other hand, the best use and saving of water implies a comprehensive effort: The most important consumer of water is the agricultural sector, which uses 70% of the water worldwide. This is followed by the industrial sector with 20% and is the area that pollutes the water the most. The urban sector uses 10%. Although the effort of citizens is important to save water, it's the largest consumers who must save the most. To this is added that in very few places in the world do the ecosystems of rivers, lakes and aquifers exist that we need to live. Ask: "What does this water situation tell us about the spiritual life of human beings? Are there "rivers of living water" in this data?"

2. The perspective of water in the Bible

God has put testimonies of His goodness in creation in order for us to recognize His presence and His desire for well-being towards the creatures of the earth. The existence of water is one of those testimonies by which many men and women bless God (Psalm 104:10-13, 24-26). In fact, the creation of water is, by itself, a clear reason to give reverent praise to our King (Revelation 14:6-7). A demonstration of the kingdom of God is the abundance of water for His people (Psalm 73:10). The condition of water being free extends to a dimension that combines the need for physical and spiritual water (Revelation 21:5-7).

A person who is able to freely give physical water to another manifests, deep down, a spiritual act (Mark 9:38-41). On the other hand, spiritual water is also a gift, which, being far superior to material water, is given freely to all those who are thirsty and need to know that God is the one who satisfies them (Psalm 42:1-2; John 4: 6-15). Ask: "Why can we say that giving someone good quality water to drink is a spiritual act? Is this part of the act of 'feeding the hungry'? Why?"

3. Alternatives

Water should be for everyone. Governments, businesses, and citizens must prioritize the water used to sustain life over water to sustain business or the economy. According to the UN, people need about 50 to 100 liters of water a day to cover basic needs. (see https://www.un.org/waterforlifedecade/pdf/human_right_to_water_and_sanitation_media_brief.pdf) Thus, some governments, such as South Africa have proposed that 50 liters of water be free for all, to maintain the constitutional human right to life. In many towns and cities of the past, there were sources of public and free drinking water. Hence the saying: "A glass of water isn't denied to anyone."

There are four levels of priority in water consumption:

a. Meeting and guaranteeing the water needs for the life of all (including ecosystems).

b. Water for everyday citizen consumption, which should have fair rates according to the volume of consumption of each person.

c. Water for the economy—that is, for industry, business and sustainable development, whose rates would also have to be staggered and without unfair subsidies; paying all the costs generated by pollution.

d. Establish regulations and laws to sanction those who use water irresponsibly.

Christians have the responsibility to think and propose strategies to take care of water, as a testimony of God's goodness.

Review/Application:

Ask your students to first write on their paper ideas of how they can make people aware of the importance of conserving water.

Then give them the following materials: poster board, folded paper, markers, colored pencils, colored paper, and crayons.

Finally ask them to make posters with practical ideas for saving water and then stick them in different places where they have access. For example:

1. Check in your houses and church and make sure that no faucet leaks even a drop.
2. Assess rest rooms for potential leaks.
3. Place bottles with sand in the tanks of the toilets so that they don't fill with so much water that is wasted when draining.
4. Turning off the water while brushing teeth or soaping dishes.
5. Not using hoses to wash vehicles.
6. Throwing left over water on a plant.
7. Watering before sunrise or after the sun goes down.
8. Making the community aware of the importance of saving water.
9. Praying that as Christians we can help raise awareness of the need to change our habits in our use of water.

Challenge:

During the week, take note of the habits you have begun to change to save water and with how many people you have shared what you learned.

Whoever throws away the least, wins

Attention!

Ask the group: How many people have you shared with this week about what you learned about material and spiritual water?

Accept

Objective: To be responsible with the trash they produce and learn the value of recycling.

Memory Verse: "For we're God's handiwork, created in Christ Jesus to do good works" Ephesians 2:10a

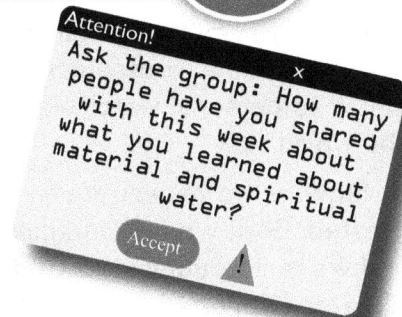

Connect | Navigate

Introductory Activity (12-17 years).

- Supplies: Different pieces of garbage: Potato peels, dead batteries (not sulphate), dry branches and leaves, etc.

- Instructions: Place each type of garbage in a container or bag without previously being seen by the group. With their eyes blindfolded, three volunteers will have to say which containers contain garbage by the scent.

  Learn that garbage or polluting wastes aren't only those that have a bad smell, but that there are different types of garbage. Sometimes those that don't give off odor are more harmful to the environment.

Introductory Activity (18-23 years).

- Supplies: Batteries, a picture of a notebook or computer, picture of a car, plastic bags, papers, some fruits and a cell phone.

- Instructions: Place each of the items in the previous list on a table and ask three people which of these items would be most useful to them. Most will surely agree on choosing the computer, cell phone, or car.

  Allow them to reflect on how, by fashion or custom, the elements that we consider most important or most useful are also the most polluting due to their components and the time they take to decompose.

Connect | Navigate

In general, it's said that garbage is everything that no longer serves a purpose.

Upon returning from shopping, bags and papers are thrown into the garbage because they're no longer useful. The "spoiled" fruit, the broken jar, the empty cans, etc. are also thrown into the garbage.

Resources don't disappear when they have been consumed to satisfy needs. The materials that make up the resources continue to exist, are returned to the environment, and accumulate as garbage.

1. The trash that we generate

Trash doesn't necessarily have to be odorous, disgusting, and undesirable; that depends on the origin and composition.

According to its composition, garbage can be classified into:

- Organic waste: Any waste of biological origin which was once alive or was part of a living being, for example: Leaves, branches, peels, and residues from making food at home, etc.

- Inorganic waste: Any waste of non-biological origin, of industrial origin or of some other non-natural process, for example: plastic, synthetic fabrics, etc.

It's a globally recognized fact that garbage is increasing day by day. The main causes of this increase are: the notable increase in the population in cities, the great variety of objects that are produced today, the way these objects are packaged, the excessive and compulsive attitude of buying and accumulating goods beyond what is necessary to live (consumerism).

Multiplying our personal waste by the number of people who inhabit the planet, the levels of pollution are very high and its consequences devastating in the short, medium and long term. And it's much more serious still, if to personal waste we add industrial, chemical, hospital, urban, and technological waste from around the world.

Now, as we've been studying, in the beginning, God established relationships together between everything created. Both women and men, as image bearers of God, are called to serve and love the rest of creation, and we're accountable to God as stewards. Our care of creation is an act of worship and obedience to our Creator (Genesis 1:26-30 and 2:15).

Invite three people to read the following verses: Genesis 1:26-30; 2:15. Each of these passages reminds us of what God commissioned Adam and Eve to do in the early days of creation, when everything was brand new. That sounds good, right? Let's imagine for a moment what this command from God would sound like today. Have some express what God would ask of us today, the same way He asked Adam and Eve. For example: "Carla, from now on you are the manager of everything I have just created; everything is at your disposal, under your care, so that you can enjoy everything; I hope you do a good job."

Without a doubt, a good dose of "pride" would go through our minds. However, one of these days, we could also imagine the Lord checking our garbage at home, work, or church; surely, the shame would be unimaginable! Let's think about how many batteries, cell phones, compact discs, DVDs, plastic bottles and bags, takeout containers, cans, etc., we irresponsibly throw away.

Although the words are different, what God said to Adam and Eve is recorded in the Bible and is a message for us today.

2. We're responsible

Consciously or unconsciously, every time we decide to buy or use an object (of any kind), and then transform it into garbage, we're exercising our right to choose; therefore, we also exercise our "responsibility." The word "responsibility" comes from the Latin "respondé" (respond), which means the ability to respond to our actions, performed in freedom and with the awareness that all our actions (including omissions and silences) have consequences for us, others, and our environment—the ecosystem that we're a part of.

Since we're in the world, we live among other creatures, and everything we do (or stop doing) will affect us and everything around us to some degree. We cannot run away from responsibilities. As consumers and producers, we're responsible for the way we work, the way we consume, the way we produce, the way we connect, and the way we relate to the environment, to nature, and to other living things. There's no innocent consumption. Every consumer is responsible. Ask: "How many cell phones have we thrown away? How many batteries or cell phones have become garbage? When we change cell phones, was each purchase decisive for the course of our life or were we only satisfying a desire? How many cans or plastic bottles have we thrown away in the last month? Could they have been less, looking for returnable packaging options or reusing the bottles?"

3. Good ideas, good works, good testimony

Above all, we must understand that we can improve our witness as Christians in the area of waste management. Our attitude towards caring for the environment is a central part of the gospel message. Why? Because the Bible says that in Jesus, God wants to reconcile all things (Colossians 1:19-20), and this includes our relationship with the environment that was broken with the appearance of sin in the Garden of Eden.

Much later, the apostle Paul wrote in his letter to the Romans: "We know that the whole creation has been groaning as in the pains of childbirth right up to the present time" (Romans 8:19, 22).

The gospel isn't only spiritual reconciliation but also social, physical, and ecological reunion. Therefore, everything that we can do and correct in the management of our waste, both personally and collectively, are parts of good works (Ephesians 2:10).

Some practical ideas that will help improve our habits and thus expand the influence of our testimonies as Christians are:

- Choose glass or plastic (returnable) containers to reuse.

- Do not use non-returnable containers or aluminum cans.

- Reduce the use of plastic bags when shopping, taking other appropriate non-disposable bags from home or, when possible, use your hands to carry small items.

- Buying rechargeable batteries, not only will this make a huge contribution, but even this implies a greater investment the first time, you'll see that your expenses on this product will be greatly reduced.

- Avoid compulsively changing your cell phone with each new model.

- Verify that the air freshener or personal deodorants you use don't affect the ozone layer.

- Classify and remove your waste in a timely manner so that it can be collected properly.

- Reuse sheets of paper with spaces or blank pages to write notes or for printing purposes.

- Don't print something that isn't extremely necessary. Think before you do it.

- Organize your files on the computer to avoid paper files.

Review/Application:

Ask your class: Is this statement correct?: "There is no innocent consumption. All consumers are responsible.

Answer: *If the statement is correct, depending on how we exercise our rights and obligations as consumers, we can be responsible for making a positive contribution and caring for the environment or responsible for a negative contribution and destruction.*

But we will always be responsible because we can think and choose how to act.

Challenge:

During the week, prepare a brochure with your class with these information and others that they consider striking, with practical suggestions that everyone can do, and distribute them in the neighborhood and also to the other members of the congregation.

Lungs in danger

Objective: To understand that we have the responsibility to do good to nature and protect the planet.

Memory Verse: "A tithe of everything from the land, whether grain from the soil or fruit from the trees, belongs to the Lord; it's holy to the Lord." Leviticus 27:30

Attention! Ask for testimonials of experience regarding the challenge of the past week concerning trash and recycling.

Accept

Connect | Navigate

Introductory Activity (12-17 years).

- Supplies: One inflated balloon per person and markers to draw pictures on the balloons.

  On one of the balloons, draw outlines similar to a world map (globe) or write the words "Planet Earth." On the other four balloons, draw ugly faces; they'll be the "threats," with the following words: pollution, irresponsibility, toxic waste, deforestation.

  The rest of the group will have balloons that will be the "protectors" of the planet. Their balloons will say: rivers, trees, seas, medicinal plants, bushes, lakes, herbs, etc. (You can repeat the protectors if you have more people in the group).

- Instructions: Ask one person to hold the "Planet Earth" balloon; four people who have the "threats" balloons and the rest the balloons with the "protectors."

  The "protectors" will circle around the globe "Planet Earth." Then the "threats" will try to break the circle that protects planet earth, bursting the "protective" balloons, each burst balloon must come out of the circle. On the other hand, the "protectors" will make an effort not to let the "threats" pass them and will burst their balloons. The idea is that the threats don't manage to burst the globe of "Planet Earth." If they happen to break the "Planet Earth" balloon, the activity ends, even though there are still "threats' and "protectors" balloons remaining. Another way to conclude is if all the "threat" balloons are popped. In this way, the planet is saved.

  God has control, an order, and a cycle of reproduction for all of His creation. We haven't taken care of what God gave us; on the contrary, we unconsciously or consciously contribute to its ruin.

Introductory Activity (18-23 years).

- Supplies: A sheet containing the following questions with the answer options and a pencil.

- Directions: Divide into two or three groups. Give each group a paper with the questions and the answer options. Then allow a few minutes for them to mark the correct answer with an X. When they find them, allow them to share their answers with the group. If they don't know any of the answers, give the biblical quote for them to read and find the answer.

1. What tree was the symbol of a righteous man?
   a. Oak ( )
   b. Acacia ( )
   c. Palm tree (X) Psalm 92:12
   d. Apple tree ( )

2. From what tree was the wood taken to make the ark?
   a. Acacia (X) Exodus 25:10
   b. Gofer ( )
   c. Cedar ( )
   d. Walnut ( )

3. The fruit of which tree was used to cure King Hezekiah of his illness?
   a. Pears ()
   b. Figs (X) 2 Kings 20:7
   c. Plums ()
   d. Raisins ( )

4. What tree did Zacchaeus climb to see Jesus?
   a. Oak ( )
   b. Sycamore (X) Luke 19:4
   c. Walnut ( )
   d. Canelo ()

   The Bible gives us examples of trees that were useful in history for different purposes.

1. Trees are part of God's creation

Read Genesis 1:11-12. These verses tell us the scene of a vital part of creation. God in His great wisdom made the perfect creation for Him and for definite purposes as written in Genesis 1:29.

It's important to know that in addition to serving as food, trees are the lungs of the earth. They transform carbon dioxide into oxygen. For example, a medium-sized Holm oak produces oxygen for 10 people daily. Ask: "What other benefits do we get from them?" Let them give their opinions. Some suggestions are: They stop the rain from washing away the humus layer of the earth. Some have healing properties. Some bear fruits that feed both animals and humans. With their wood, houses, furniture, and paper are made. They retain dust and particles floating in the air in their leaves, preventing us from inhaling them. They serve as shelter for insects, birds, and animals.

Ask: "Can we see and value God's purposes in creating herbs and trees? What is our responsibility to them?" Allow the group to respond. We must make good use of them.

2. The appropriate use of creation

Ask: What two actions does God highlight to man in Genesis 2:15?

When God put Adam in the garden of Eden, He gave him the command to till and care for it. This shows us that God didn't create people to be lazy, but rather He gave them an occupation. A farmer's occupation is as old as mankind; it provides for working directly with God's creation. Working the land means cultivating, plowing, planting, sowing, and in some cases, pruning (the vineyards). On the other hand, Adam also had to tend to creation. This means that he had to put diligence, attention, and care in what he did because it was his responsibility.

The people of Israel were a people who dedicated themselves to working the land. It's interesting to see how Jesus used objects and imagery from nature to teach spiritual truths. For example, trees (Matthew 7:15-20, 12:33, 21:19, 24:32); seeds (Mark 4:26, 30-32); sowers (Matthew 6:26, 25:24, 13:1-9; Luke 19:21-22).

3. Administration of creation: deforestation and reforestation

Ask: "But, what has happened over time? What have we done with the beautiful nature that our Creator gave us to manage?" Let's analyze terms related to the subject and of great value in the conservation of trees.

What is reforestation? Reforestation means the planting of forests on lands where they had historically existed but which suffered a change in their use. Today, we've lost many of the precious forests that existed. The fact that we see some scattered trees or some parks doesn't mean that forests haven't suffered damage. It's important to plant fast-growing native trees where the trees have been removed. At the same time, it's also essential to plant some slow-growing trees so that in 50 years, future generations can enjoy them.

What is deforestation? It's the process by which the earth loses its forests at the hands of humans. Any reduction of the forest is a problem for its ecosystem. Deforestation occurs when forests are turned into farms for food, cash crops, or ranches to raise livestock. Cutting down trees for commercial use or for fuel is also deforestation.

The construction of roads in the jungles has increased the fragility of this ecosystem. The forest is very fragile to cultivate. When disrupting factors such as roads are introduced, the fragility increases dangerously. When roads are constructed, the permeation of humans into the forest is extended. The construction of villages multiplies this and a chain of deterioration begins. At the same time, roads let huge vehicles enter that can transport large numbers of trees, bringing logging to industrial proportions. The noise and the production of pollutants, as well as the generation of deliberate or accidental fires, put the flora and fauna of that area at risk. Deforestation also creates rapid soil erosion, and what was a closed forest, part of the creation of our God, a lung for the planet, can become an immense desert.

Face to face are the interests of small communities of defenders of the environment and the interests of powerful transnational companies. The latter have the resources and techniques to exploit the forest in such a way that the way to achieve a new ecological balance in is minimized.

Many of the problems of floods, mountain landslides and climate disorders arise as a consequence of this disorder and lack of control in deforestation.

4. Our contribution as God's stewards

A Dictionary of the Bible & Christian Doctrine in Everyday English (Eby, et al, 2004) notes:

1. A steward is one who is trusted to care for what belongs to another.

2. A steward may be one who takes care of another person.

3. A steward may be the one who manages the property of another person.

4. Stewardship is the act of fulfilling the duties of a steward. The Christian life should be one of stewardship. All that a Christian is and has belongs to God. He trusts Christians to care for what belongs to Him. Thus, stewardship is a way of caring for what God has entrusted to Christians. Such care seeks to bring honor to God.

(Genesis 43:19; 44:4; Luke 16:2-4; 12:42; 16:1, 3, 8; I Corinthians 4:1-2; Titus 1:7 and I Peter 4:10)

We've been called to be stewards of creation. Therefore, it's important to start today. No matter how insignificant we think our contribution is, there's something we can do. Caring for trees and planting more trees can be good contributions.

Deforestation cannot be controlled overnight. What we must do is seek a change in mentality that begins with us. Some possible actions are: Obtain (through government forestry institutions or NGOs) trees and plant them in deforested places. Form an education and awareness program in our churches about this issue. If for any reason a tree must be removed, it's important to find a place to plant two more trees. Participate in campaigns to reforest your city. If you have a garden, plant trees and take care of them. Let's motivate people to invest their energy and resources in protecting, conserving, and preserving creation.

Review/Application:

Find the following words:

1. Creation
2. Cedars
3. Trees
4. Grass
5. Walnut
6. Green
7. Seed
8. Life

Y	V	G	R	E	E	N	E	A	O	S	K	A
B	H	K	D	P	A	R	G	T	S	E	P	T
J	C	R	H	E	C	B	E	I	E	M	B	R
G	E	A	W	L	F	B	X	A	E	E	U	E
C	R	E	A	T	I	O	N	Z	D	N	E	E
E	N	J	L	A	P	N	T	D	L	C	H	S
D	V	B	N	S	V	I	E	B	M	E	F	O
A	I	L	U	C	O	G	R	A	S	S	G	Y
R	K	A	T	R	T	A	U	W	R	E	M	V
S	T	E	U	A	Y	N	I	C	L	I	F	E

Challenge:

Make sure the class understands that we have the responsibility to take care of nature and protect the planet. With the class, take some time to get trees that can be planted in a park, road or place near the church. For this to take effect, each must plant at least three trees.

Use vs. Abuse

Objective: To take responsibility of their use of the earth.

Memory Verse: "a time to be born and a time to die, a time to plant and a time to uproot" Ecclesiastes 3:2

Attention! Take a few minutes at the beginning of the session to celebrate their achievements in their reforestation activities.

Accept

Connect | Navigate

Introductory Activity (12-17 years)

- Supplies: Newspapers, scissors, glue, and a large sheet of paper.

- Directions: Divide into small groups and hand out the supplies.

  Each group will make a mural with clippings of articles and images about natural disasters, and write in no more than three sentences who is responsible for the disasters.

  At the end, each group will present their mural and reflection. Encourage them to think about the responsibility God gave us to manage and use land properly.

Introductory Activity (18-23 years)

- Supplies: Video or news clippings dealing with the indiscriminate deforestation of trees, the extinction of some species such as the panda that are hunted for their fur, or some other related news.

- Instructions: Divide the group into pairs to answer the following questions:

  1. What leads humans to do these things?

  2. Name three reasons why you shouldn't carry out these types of actions. You can look up biblical quotes to defend your opinion.

Connect | Navigate

In 1992, the United Nations Framework Convention on Climate Change (available at https://unfccc.int/resource/ccsites/zimbab/conven/text/preamble.htm) was signed. It acknowledged that: "change in the Earth's climate and its adverse effects are a common concern of humankind". It also affirmed that: "'Adverse effects of climate change'" means changes in the physical environment or biota resulting from climate change which have significant deleterious effects on the composition, resilience or productivity of natural and managed ecosystems or on the operation of socio-economic systems or on human health and welfare."

1. Land use in the Old Testament

In Genesis 1:1-14, there's an orderly sequence of creation of days, seasons, and years. Then, we find God's plan for creation and reproduction and the products that would serve for food (Genesis 1:11, 22, 28, 29, 30). And then in Ecclesiastes 1:6-7, we find the air cycle and water cycle in detail.

When God spoke to Adam and Eve in Genesis 1:28 and referred to subduing and ruling creation, studying and understanding it were included. God also gave them responsibilities (working in it and caring for it) that they had to fulfill (Genesis 2:15). God established a time for everything—for example, the water cycle, the seasons of the year, the harvest time (Ecclesiastes 3). The earth is a perfect ecosystem that we humans share with millions of animal and plant species, but many times, we modify and destroy natural habitats, endangering their lives.

Read Deuteronomy 20:19-20, and answer as a group: What does God indicate about cutting down trees? What material can we use to build the furniture in our home?

God thought down to the last detail for our needs and expressed how we can make use of the earth and its resources. God put people in the garden to work it, take care of it and administer it. He gave people lordship over all creation, not to do with it what they saw fit nor to destroy it. God commanded them to work the land, to have dominion over creation, and to administer it, because God is interested in His creation and its resources.

2. The abuse of the earth today

From the first time that man decided to disobey God, we began to miss the responsibilities of managing and making good use of the land. All of creation was affected by sin.

Give cards with the following verses: Genesis 3:17-19, Romans 5:12, and Romans 8:20-22 so they can read and give their opinions about them.

The seriousness of all this is that people insist on disobeying the laws established by God. For example, the Amazon contains about 17% of the fresh water worldwide in liquid form, and human beings are determined to advance with an agricultural frontier (cattle raising and soybeans). The lack of water in the world is increasingly serious. We don't take care of it; instead, we damage its sources, wasting what God purposed for our benefit. We only think about our personal interests without taking into account how our self-interests harm humanity at large. (If you remember, tell an example or anecdote of yourself or someone where you show that you have abused or wasted the resources that God gave us).

In Leviticus 25:3-4, God gave the command of the Sabbath year for the earth. There He says that six years the land would be sown and six years the vineyard would be pruned and then they would collect its fruits, but the seventh year the land would have rest; it would not be used so that it would not be exhausted. Today, to make more profits and make the land produce more, it isn't given the proper rest, and hectares of land are destroyed because the necessary nutrients are taken from them. This misuse of the land and its resources brings consequences and alters the order and times that God marked.

Ask: "As Christians, what do we do in the face of God's instructions?" Give them time to answer.

3. Our responsibility

In Ephesians 2:10 it says that we were created in Christ Jesus for good works. Colossians 3:23 says: "And whatever you do, do it from the heart, as for the Lord and not for men ...." These passages urge us to do all things in the best possible way, both in our relation to people and the land with its resources.

Good works imply respect and proper use of the earth's natural resources. When we pollute water or the environment with garbage by throwing away batteries, nylon, or we kill animals as a hobby: Are they really good works? What does our responsibility to use the land correctly imply? Ask: "What do men's actions have to do with 'negligence'?" Let them have an opinion. According to the Merriam-Webster Dictionary (available at https://www.merriam-webster.com/dictionary/negligence, negligence is "failure to exercise the care that a reasonably prudent person would exercise in like circumstances." How are you treating the land and natural resources? Do you make a responsible or negligent use of the land?

In His Word, God urges us to humble ourselves, pray, seek His face, and repent of our evil ways. This also has to do with our actions, the damage we cause to others and to the earth. He promises to listen to us, forgive our sins, and heal our land (2 Chronicles 7:14). If humanity turned to its Creator and respected the established times to use each natural resource, how different everything would be!

Practical ideas

As children of God, we're no longer partakers of sin. We must do our part and always do our best not to become accomplices in the damage that's done to God's creation. At the same time, we must also faithfully witness with our voices. As we engage in activities to help save our planet, we must also tell others about God's saving grace in our lives.

Introduce the group to some possible projects for the community or neighborhood surrounding the church and encourage them to carry them out in the next two to three weeks, such as:

- Encourage the rescue of public wastelands and their subsequent conservation in orchards, green areas, etc.

- Design a brochure that raises awareness about the use of drinking water or explains how to classify organic and inorganic waste.

- Carry out a trash cleanup in the neighborhood.

- Think of phrases to make posters and hang them up in the businesses in your church's neighborhood, which encourage the correct use of God's creation.

- Collect paper, cardboard, plastic bottles, aluminum cans, and take them to a recycling center.

Review/Application:

Assignment: Write God's provision in each case

1. Genesis 1:29 - What was the supply and for whom? **(Seed-bearing plants and fruit-bearing trees. For the man.)**

2. Genesis 9:2-3 What did God establish after the flood? **(Every animal, plant and vegetable will be for human supply.)**

3. Psalm 104:9-13 What was God's provision for many needs? **(Water.)**

Reflect on what your responsibility is before what is established and provided by God for us: Use everything in its fair measure, without waste or abuse so that others can use it too.

Challenge:

Discuss with the group ways they can take responsibility of their use of the earth.

Read the following inscriptions, then choose one to prepare a poster to paste somewhere prominent.

- "Let's plant trees to have more oxygen."

- "Let's not use so many aerosols so as not to damage the ozone layer."

- "Let's recycle paper so we don't cut down so many trees."

- "Let's close the water faucet so as not to waste drinking water."

Or other tips to use on your poster.

To whom is each phrase addressed and what action does it demand from us? Ask God to help you make good use of the land.

This is hot!

Objective: To understand that global warming is a consequence of disobeying God and to recognize God's restoring mercy.

Memory Verse: "But the day of the Lord will come like a thief. The heavens will disappear with a roar; the elements will be destroyed by fire, and the earth and everything done in it will be laid bare." 2 Peter 3:10

Attention!
Discuss ways the group is taking responsibility of their use of the earth.

Accept

Connect | Navigate

Introductory Activity (12-17 years).

- Supplies: Statistics or photos and stories of catastrophes that have occurred in your city or country.

- Instructions: Find out if anyone has been in a similar situation. Explore feelings and thoughts around the topic. Then do a short role-play involving a "natural disaster victim" and "a rescue volunteer." In this role play, ask the group to develop a possible dialogue between the two after the disaster. Extract from the dialogue the feelings that arise in this regard, and you'll be able to see the knowledge and feelings that your group members have about these types of events.

Introductory Activity (18-23 years).

- Supplies: Statistics or photos and stories of catastrophes that have occurred in your city or country.

- Instructions: Form a "National Aid Committee" in a disaster situation. Imaginatively introduce them into a specific disaster situation in order to explore concrete and practical strategies that the group knows and could carry out. Find out if anyone has been in a similar situation.

Connect | Navigate

The Bible shows us that we haven't been good stewards of what God has given us. We find that from ancient times until today, mankind has disobeyed God and suffered the consequences. Have your students look up the following passages about disobedience and its consequences: Genesis 3:6 (Adam and Eve ate from the tree), Genesis 3:23 (the expulsion from Eden), Genesis 6:5 (man inclined to evil), Genesis 7:21-22 (the flood came and ended with people who didn't want to live according to God's will). Jonah 1:3 (he fled as not to do God's will); Jonah 1:14-15 (he was thrown into the sea). The current state of the planet is a true reflection of disobedience.

1. Global Warming

Scientists marvel at the perfection of designs found in nature. Everything has been created to work in perfect coordination, each element is interdependent, nothing is left over, and nothing is missing. Planet earth is a wonderful example of the interaction of creation. The planet was designed to be in balance, and human beings are part of that chain of interacting elements. God made us stewards of creation, and the axis of balance is the relationship with the Creator.

Ask: If God gave us a report card on our performance as stewards of the planet, what grade would we get?

Why so much concern about global warming? Most environmental scientists agree that our future depends on the control of the climate change that's being observed. This is the situation: The greenhouse effect is a natural mechanism of the planet to self-regulate the temperature that preserves life. In our atmosphere, there are a series of gases that trap part of the sun's heat that's reflected by the planet, thus maintaining an average temperature greater than 15 degrees Celsius - ideal for life. This helps the evaporation of water, which in turn, produces clouds that return the water to the earth in the form of rain or snow. This avoids the dehydration of the planet and its erosion by drought. This cycle favors the growth of plants and trees that absorb excess carbon dioxide and restore balance. If this mechanism were to fail, the temperature would drop or rise rapidly and life would be extinguished by extreme cold or heat.

In the last century, the consumption of fossil fuels and deforestation has increased greenhouse gases in such a way that the balance of this cycle has been broken. The average temperature of the planet is increasing. Without the natural greenhouse mechanism stabilizing it, this is called "global warming". To explain this concept, you can carry out the following activity: bring a winter coat to this session. Ask a volunteer to move vigorously for a few minutes and then ask him if he feels hot and wait a couple of minutes until his normal temperature has been restored. Ask another volunteer to do the same, but with their coat on. When he's done moving around, don't let him take his coat off for a minute. The second volunteer will take longer to regain his normal temperature (If you are in a location with hot weather, have fresh drinking water at hand). The human body has natural mechanisms of self-regulation of body heat, when these mechanisms are blocked, self-regulation is hampered.

2. What should we do?

Opinions vary on the contributions we can make. Different nations discuss and agree what should be done, but what can I as an individual do? Here are some tips to keep in mind. Cut out each suggestion below into cards, starting the sentence with: I can. My family can. My school can. My church can. My city can. My country can. Randomly distribute one or more cards to each person. Then ask them to read them and give their opinions.

- Use the four "Rs": Refuse, Reduce, Reuse, Recycle.

- Save water, and especially hot water. How? Take shorter showers; close the tap while brushing your teeth and using shampoo; install toilets that use less water.

- Save energy. How? Turn off lights that aren't in use; use energy-saving light bulbs.

- Dry your clothes in the sun and wind, don't use the dryer if possible.

- Use energy efficient appliances. Save money and pollute less.

- Don't just turn off, but unplug appliances when you're not using them or leaving the house.

- Reduce carbon dioxide in the environment. How? Plant more trees, use your car less, take public transportation, drive hybrid vehicles, ride a bike, walk more.

- Drive better. Drive at constant speeds, use the right gears, regularly maintain your car, use the air conditioning only when strictly necessary.

- Adapt your house thermostat. In winter, reduce the heating in your house when you aren't home, reduce the temperature to the minimum tolerable by you or your family, bundle yourselves up instead.

- Get involved. Actively participate in groups that plan and develop eco-friendly activities.

- Make yourself heard. Address your governments, companies and organizations that interfere in environmental policies and effects, through: Writing letters, emails, making phone calls and personal visits.

- Organize discussion groups, environmental action brigades.

- Do it personally. Remember, each of us is part of the environment. It affects us all.

- Proclaim, exhort, at all times and in all places.

- Pray constantly. The prayer of the righteous can do a lot. Include the theme of the environment in your prayer requests.

- Evangelize. Many people are hopeless and lost. Meteorological and geological phenomena are a topic that facilitates evangelism.

3. God is always in control

This bleak outlook has already been described in the Bible. Matthew 24:6-8 mentions wars, plagues, famines, and earthquakes as a painful beginning.

We must recognize that human beings in their selfish and ambitious endeavors have failed in their responsibility towards the earth, and have brought the planet into a situation of ecological disaster. The truth that we must accept is that human beings left the care of the environment at the mercy of their fallen nature. We need the restorer, reconciler, savior, and healer provided by God the Father in the figure of His Son Jesus (2 Corinthians 5: 18-20). The return of our Lord Jesus, His second coming, is set in the midst of extreme meteorological manifestations. The apostle Peter warns of the climatic disorder that will precede this second coming and the healing work on the planet that He will bring (2 Peter 3:13). A new heaven and new earth are the result of divine intervention, and we, His children, will be with Him for eternity. Are we prepared? (Revelation 21:1-3).

Review/Application:

Have the students respond with their own words.

We are responsible before God.

1. Do you think that mankind is responsible for the current environmental situation? Why?

2. Genesis 1:28 establishes something pertinent to the days we live in. What is it?

3. In 2 Peter 3:10-13 and Revelation 16:8-9, they mention notable weather phenomena. How many can you identify?

4. Do you think that as a church we can do something about this situation? How?

Challenge:

This week review your habits and begin to change. To change others, we must begin to change ourselves first. Then share with your family and together review the habits you can change at home. Share your results in our next class.

My neighbor

Objective: To understand who their neighbor is and the importance of gender, racial, and cultural equity.

Memory Verse: "...Love the Lord your God with all your heart and with all your soul and with all your strength and with all your mind'; and, 'Love your neighbor as yourself." Luke 10:27

Attention!
Discuss the group's understanding of global warming as a consequence of disobeying God. Also help them recognize God's restoring mercy.

Accept

Connect | Navigate

As we study the Bible, we realize that our relationship with others is very important to God. God Himself is love, and His desire is that we experience that love in our own lives, that we love Him, and that we also love others as we love ourselves.

Introductory Activity (12-17 years)

- Supplies: Blackboard and chalk/Whiteboard and markers/poster paper and markers, a sheet of paper and pencil for each person.

- Instructions: Ask the group to make a list with the names of up to 15 people they know and to write next to each name the kind of relationship they have with that person, e.g. María, mother; Estela, classmate; Mr. Martínez, math teacher, etc. As a group, explore the list of people each one knows and how they interact with each of them in light of the memory verse.

  Tell them that there are different types of relationships and the Bible commands us to love everyone the same.

Introductory Activity (18-23 years)

- Supplies: Blackboard and chalk/whiteboard and markers/poster paper and markers

- Directions: Separate into groups, and ask them to come up with a definition of "love." Then ask them to share their responses and you can write them on the board. Review the answers given to guide you in case any answer isn't entirely correct or appropriate.

  Share as a group how this definition would apply in the context of the memory verse.

Connect | Navigate

We all have a lot of different relationships - some people we see every day and others occasionally. However, God places great importance on the way we treat the people around us, whether they're very close or not. Today and in the following lessons, we'll study several passages that will help us understand what God expects of us in our relationships.

1. Who is my neighbor?

The word "neighbor" generally means "one living or located near another", but the Merriam Webster Dictionary also uses the definition of "fellow man" (https://www.merriam-webster.com/dictionary/neighbor?src=search-dict-hed).

A Dictionary of the Bible & Christian Doctrine in Everyday English (Eby, et al, 2004) says:

a. A neighbor is someone who lives close to another person.

b. A neighbor in the Old Testament was a member of the same tribe or nation. Jews didn't consider Gentiles who lived near them their neighbors.

c. Jesus didn't use the word "neighbor" in this limited way. He said a neighbor includes everyone. People should love everyone as they love themselves.

(Exodus 20:16-17; Leviticus 19:15; Proverbs 3:29; Luke 10:25-37; Romans 13:8-10; 15:1-6; Galatians 5:14 and James 4:11-12)

In response to the question, "Who is my neighbor?" asked by one of the teachers of the law, Jesus told the story of the Good Samaritan (Luke 10:25-42). In verse 27, we see that this teacher had just recited from memory one of the central passages of God's Law, (Leviticus 19:18 and Deuteronomy 6: 5). It's probable that that teacher of the law had studied the passage carefully before and knew something of its meaning, according to the concept of the time. However, he still asked Jesus "Who is my neighbor?" The answer that Jesus offered to the teacher of the law included a story and some characters that in the daily life of those times would not have spoken to each other: Israelites and a Samaritan.

A Dictionary of the Bible & Christian Doctrine in Everyday English (Eby, et al, 2004) says:

a. A Samaritan was a person who lived in the region of Samaria. Samaritans were hated by the Jews in the time of Jesus.

b. The Samaritans were descendants of Jews who had married Gentiles. These Gentiles were mostly from Assyria.

(Matthew 10:5; Luke 9:52; 10:33 and 17:16)

Those who lived in Samaria had developed religious practices different from those of the Jews. For this reason, the Israelites regarded the Samaritans as second-class citizens. The Samaritans and the Jews were enemies, so the parable is critical.

In this way, Jesus defined "neighbor" as a person who needs help. Jesus taught those who listened to him that the neighbor of a person includes not only blood relations, or someone who goes to the same school and they get along with, or the one who lives in the same neighborhood, or the one who dresses the same. According to the teaching of Jesus, our neighbor is every human being who needs help, no matter if the person is similar or different, in terms of gender, race or culture.

2. How should I treat my neighbor?

According to Luke 10:33-35, ask: How did the Samaritan help his neighbor? The Samaritan: (1) bandaged his wounds; (2) poured oil and wine (medicines of that time) on them; (3) put him on his donkey/animal; (4) took him to an inn; (5) took care of him; (6) paid the expenses that he accrued; (7) left money for any future expenses.

Jesus taught that everything within one's reach should be done for one's neighbor no matter who it is. Together with the group, answer these questions and put together your own story according to the context that you live in.

- What would this story look like if Jesus told it today in our context?
- Who would be the priest and the Levite?
- Who would be the Jew?
- Who would be the Samaritan?
- What would the Samaritan in our story do?

This story makes us think and ask ourselves: How do I show love to others? Careful! Not just the people I know, not just my church family, or just the people I love.

A Dictionary of the Bible & Christian Doctrine in Everyday English (Eby, et al, 2004) notes:

a. (verb) To love is to act in the best interest of another person. It's to act in a way that seeks to create fellowship with another. To love an object is to want to possess it.

b. (noun) Love is the action of one who seeks fellowship with another person. Love tries to create a bond of loyal friendship.

c. There are different kinds of human love. Friendship is a kind of love. The care members of a family have for each other is another form of love. The desire of a man and a woman for each other is another kind of love.

d. The love God gives is a special kind of love. He loves the world. He cares for His whole creation. But His special concern is for people. He loves them even when they don't accept His love. Sinful people reject the love of God. Instead, they love things that will destroy them. But God isn't satisfied to let them be lost in sin. He sent His Son to save them because of His eternal love. This is why Christians say God is love.

e. Christians know that God loves and accepts them through Christ. God gives them His Spirit as proof of His love. The Holy Spirit helps them love God and other people. Christian faith also shows love for God through good works.

(Leviticus 19:18; Deuteronomy 6:5; Proverbs 3:3; Matthew 5:44; Mark 12:30-33; John 3:16; 13:34; 15:12; Romans 5:1-11; 13:8-10; 1 Corinthians 13; 1 Peter 4:8; 2 Peter 1:7; 1 John 2:15; 4:8 and 3 John 1)

These passages in the Bible help us understand the kind of love that God wants us to express. Let's look at three:

a. 1 Corinthians 13:4-8: Here we find a unique description of the scope of love, and it helps us understand the kind of practical love that God expects to be given. It's important to reflect on each of the characteristics of love described in this passage, and think of practical examples that can help show that kind of love to others.

b. Romans 13: 8-10: The apostle Paul taught that the most important thing is to love people and in this way we'll fulfill all the law of God. Love for others includes doing all kinds of good and no kind of evil; that's why he said: "Love does no harm to a neighbor. Therefore, love is the fulfillment of the law" (v10).

c. Matthew 5:43-45: In this passage, as well as in the parable of the Good Samaritan, Jesus went beyond what is usually thought. He taught that even our enemy is the neighbor to whom we must do good. Anyone who needs our help is our neighbor. We must love such people and do for them whatever God enables us to do so they'll see and experience the love of God.

3. How can I love my neighbor?

Jesus concluded the story by saying "… go and do the same" (Luke 10:37). Jesus not only gave the interpretation of the law concerning the concept of neighbor, but also indicated how he should treat them. We must understand that Jesus doesn't expect us to carry out this task in our own strength but with the fruit of His Spirit, which is His love in our lives (Galatians 5:22-23).

The important detail is that God doesn't ask us to do something impossible; He doesn't ask us for anything that He Himself didn't do first. God sent Jesus, His Son, to live on this earth, and even more, He died in our place on the cross, so that we can experience His love and His forgiveness. Jesus first gave us an example of his sacrificial love, and then He commands us to follow in His footsteps (Matthew 5:43-44).

God longs to fill our hearts with His love and help us to love our neighbor in a way that pleases Him.

Take some time today to thank God for loving you in such a wonderful way. Thank Him for putting His love for you into practice by sending Jesus to die for your sins on the cross, forgiving you and giving you a new life. Ask God to put that same love in your heart for your neighbor.

Review/Application:

Next to each of the relationships described below, write specific ways you can put into practice the kind of love that Jesus teaches us in the parable of the Good Samaritan.

With teachers

With study or work colleagues

With neighbors

With people I don't like

For example with neighbors: **Start greeting a neighbor who doesn't greet me because he doesn't like Christians.**

Challenge:

This week begins to change your attitude towards someone you consider your neighbor with whom you do not have much relationship.

We are family!

Objective: To understand the relationship that they can have with their family and the responsibility they have toward their parents and siblings.

Memory Verse: "I will bless those who bless you, and whoever curses you I will curse; and all peoples on earth will be blessed through you." Genesis 12:3

Attention!
Start by talking about the difficulties faced in understanding who their neighbor is and the importance of gender, racial, and cultural equity.
Accept

Connect / Navigate

Introductory Activity (12-17 years).

- Supplies: Images of different people (men, women, boys, girls, the elderly, etc.), glue and sheets of paper or cardboard.

- Directions: Have the group sit in a circle and give each one a sheet of paper. Place the glue and pictures in the center.

   Ask them to form a family in one minute by gluing pictures on the sheet.

   Then ask why they included each person and what his or her role would be in the family.

Introductory Activity (18-23 years).

- Supplies: Paper and pencil for each person.

- Instructions: At this age, most young people have thought about whether or not they would like to start a family.

   Distribute the materials and ask them to write down three personal reasons why it's good to start a family. Then ask them to write down three things the Bible says about the family or its members.

   Then have everyone read what they wrote and together form the biblical and social concept of family.

Connect / Navigate

1. What the Bible says about family

It all started when God said: " It's not good for the man to be alone. I will make a helper suitable for him." (Genesis 2:18), and it was then that He created Eve.

We know the rest of the story. Adam and Eve were exiled from the Garden of Eden. They had children, who had conflicts. In Genesis 10:31-32, there's the list of their descendants, and we find the word family for the first time. We see that God himself promised to bless all the families of the earth, through His servant Abraham. "I will bless those who bless you, I will curse those who curse you; and all the families of the earth will be blessed in you". Through Abraham and his descendants, the Lord promised to form a great family that would grow into a great nation that He would call "His people" (Genesis 12:3).

2. The family today

Read Ephesians 6:1-4. Pause after reading the first verse and ask them what they think of that passage. Ask how many of them obey their parents, in everything. If no one answers, dialogue with them - they'll all give "good" reasons for not carrying out this request of Paul to the Ephesians. Even when the motives are apparently very good, this commandment of God is the only one that has a promise (v.3), that's to say that obedience to parents represents blessing and prosperity for the future life.

Explain that this is a commandment and commandments aren't negotiated, only obeyed. Point out that whatever they say, they have no valid excuse for not obeying.

A Dictionary of the Bible & Christian Doctrine in Everyday English (Eby, et al, 2004) notes several important aspects of commandments:

a. The Ten Commandments are the laws that God gave to Israel through Moses. The Ten Commandments are for everyone. They refer to all people of all places of all times. The Ten Commandments are found in Exodus 20:1-17 and Deuteronomy 5:6-21.

b. Both Testaments agree that all the commandments are summed up in one Great Commandment. This is to love God and one's neighbor as oneself.

c. God gave the Ten Commandments as a way of showing His faithfulness to Israel. Israel was to give testimony to the covenant by obeying the Ten Commandments.

d. Jesus Christ is the testimony or witness of the new covenant. He is the testimony through His life, death and resurrection. Those who receive Christ as Savior receive Him as the testimony of God. The Holy Spirit gives witness to Christians that Christ is the true testimony. Christians then become testimonies to Christ. They witness for Christ through what they say and do.

Even if our parents aren't believers, God commands us to obey them and we must. The only excuse would be if what they asked us to do would lead us to disobey a biblical principle.

If we obey, we'll set an example of our submission to God, and our parents will probably draw close to Him thanks to our good testimony.

Continue reading Ephesians 6:2-3. The Merriam Webster Dictionary (https://www.merriam-webster.com/dictionary/honor) understands honor as:

a. good name or public esteem;

b. a showing of usually merited respect.

Ask: Do I respect a person when ... I speak ill of them to others? Answer back to them disrespectfully? Deliberately lie to them? Yell at them and disobey?

As the answer to all these questions is "No", ask them to think for a moment that as children, we don't comply with this commandment daily.

Now let's talk about the prize that awaits us when we fulfill it: "... long life on earth." But we must obey with God's commandments for the promise to be fulfilled.

Lastly, read Ephesians 6:4, which will be a powerful tool for the group. Paul asked the church fathers at Ephesus not to provoke their children to anger, and the church fathers at Colosse not to exasperate them (Colossians 3:21). There are several reasons for this request. In Colosse, he told them not to exasperate them so they don't get discouraged. The word "exasperate," in addition to meaning to make someone angry, means to hurt. So we understand why Paul asked that parents not hurt their children, or irritate them so that they don't get discouraged or lose heart.

In Ephesians 6:4b, while parents are asked not to anger their children, they're also required to educate and discipline them. Here, it's worth asking the group if their parents are complying with their side of the bargain.

Some will fulfill the first part (v.4a), not because they're obedient to the Word but because the world has made them believe that they shouldn't deny anything to their children, or make them angry. On the contrary, they have to give them everything they want so that they aren't "traumatized." And what can we say about the second part? Ask the group this question and ask them to give examples of cases in which parents don't discipline their children, and to discuss the consequences of such lack of discipline.

Today's families show a worrying level of individualism, and parents and children live life without having any relationship. Many parents don't know where their children go, who their friends are and what they do in their free time. Many children don't assume responsibilities within the home and don't submit to their parents' authority. Even if the world wants to convince us otherwise, God's original design is still in effect.

God's plan is that families should be made up of a man and a woman, united in marriage, committed to raising children according to the ordinances of the Lord, disciplining them when necessary, and loving them in such a way that they never sadden their spirits. On the other hand, children must be subject to the spiritual and moral authority of their parents, committed as a functional part of the family, honoring their parents in obedience and love.

The real consequences that many families are experiencing today are the fruit of disobedience to God. Therefore, we see divorces, single parents, abandoned children, or simply children who are neglected and never disciplined, which is a form of abandonment.

We must insist and make it clear to young people that by following God's guidelines, much anguish in families today can be avoided.

3. A good relationship between siblings

This point may seem like science fiction. It's not easy, but it's not impossible either.

Most of us have been blessed with brothers or sisters. Although sometimes we don't see it as such, it's really a blessing to have someone to share parents, a room, toys, and even clothes with. It's a blessing that shapes us in all areas. Why should we see it this way? Because in this way, God perfects our patience, self-control, and love of our neighbors. God has given us people who love us, even if we don't see it at first glance; people who care about us, who, just as they protect their things from us, protect us against others.

Perhaps you prefer the company of friends to that of siblings. However, no friend, no matter how good, loves you as much, nor are they going to be at your side like a brother or sister in all circumstances.

Ask: Who hasn't had conflicts with siblings? Cain had them, and sadly he let the enemy work inside him, erasing the love for his brother. Esau had them, however, unlike Cain, he loved his brother to such a degree that he forgave him for having deceived him.

Let's love our siblings since they're also our neighbors, and most importantly, we share the same blood.

God has a plan and nothing that happens to us is chance or error. If you have siblings, He knows why, and when you are in the most difficult of situations, remember that God has a plan, and that He is shaping you according to His will. Let's not let the enemy triumph in our life, or sow seeds of resentment and hatred towards our siblings. Let's love them, however difficult it may seem.

God has given many of us a family, with a father and mother, brothers, sisters, uncles, cousins, nephews, etc. These are all designed according to God's perfect plan for us so that we arrive in this world protected, surrounded by love, affection, and security. God also left His Word to guide us, to show us how to act as children, parents, or siblings. Let's follow God's instructions!

Review/Application:

Match up the names in the left column with the names in the right column, and write the relationship between the two.

Jochebed (mother) - Aaron (son)

Noah (father) - Ham (son)

Abel (son) - Eve (mother)

Joseph (nephew) - Esau (uncle)

Simon (brother) - Andrew (brother)

Jesus (cousin) - John the Baptist (cousin)

Jonathan (son) - Saul (father)

Timothy (grandson) - Lois (grandmother)

Laban (father) - Leah (daughter)

Martha (sister) - Lazarus (brother)

Naomi (mother-in-law) - Ruth (daughter-in-law)

Abraham (husband) - Sarah (wife)

Challenge:

Ask several group members to explain the relationship that they can have with their family and the responsibility they have toward their parents and siblings.

Start thinking about the personal attitudes that don't benefit your family relationships; whether they're words, thoughts or gestures with which you don't honor your parents, and also words, thoughts or gestures that detract from and affect your relationships with your siblings.

Write this in the form of a list and try each day to modify one of those attitudes that you detailed. If you start small, it will be easier and you'll see how much good it does for your relationship with God and others.

These Kids...!

Objective: To understand the importance of caring for, understanding, and loving children.

Memory Verse: «"And he said: "Truly I tell you, unless you change and become like little children, you'll never enter the kingdom of heaven." Matthew 18:3

> **Attention!** x
> Lead a discussion with the group about how their family relationships have improved since last week's class.
> *Accept*

Connect | Navigate

Introductory Activity (12-17 years).

- Supplies: Pencils, paper cut into small squares, a stopwatch, and whiteboard. Write on the papers some activities that children commonly do, for example: Doing homework, playing games, going to school, watching television, studying, playing soccer, playing with dolls, etc.

- Instructions: Form two teams, and ask each one to choose a representative. Have a group representative take a piece of paper (without the rest of them seeing) and act out the activity indicated on the paper by acting out, without speaking, while their team guesses. The team will guess as many actions as they can in one minute. The team that guesses the most is the winner.

Remembering actions that children commonly perform helps us to be aware that they're part of our environment. Ask: "Do you notice when a child is by your side? What is calling your attention? Do you pay attention to them when they speak to you?"

Introductory Activity (18-23 years).

- Supplies: A couple of clothing items that resemble children's clothes (shorts, skirts, bows or hair ties, hats, etc.)

- Instructions: Divide the group into two teams, one for girls and one for boys. Ask each team to designate someone who will act like a little boy or girl throughout the whole group. They can do things such as: Asking to go to the bathroom, asking for water, constantly talking and moving. The responsibility of the team will be to care for and take care of their "child" as best they can. Five minutes before the end of the session, each team must make a judgment about the care that the opposing team gave their "child". They must evaluate three aspects: (1) The interest of all members in the child. (2) The patience of all team members towards the child. (3) The characterization and performance of the boy or girl child.

Connect | Navigate

Azalea is a young woman now, but she will never forget her childhood. She was sexually abused when she was just eight years old by one of her relatives. Azalea is a Christian now and she has forgiven that person who caused her harm. Only Jesus has been able to heal the wound that that situation caused her.

It's very sad to say but Azalea's situation is so common in the world today. It isn't only sexual abuse to which children are exposed today but other situations such as violence, bad habits, abandonment, neglect from their parents, labor exploitation and even slavery!

1. Jesus and children

The Bible passage of Mark 10:13-16 is also found in Matthew 19:13-15 and Luke 18:15-17. These gospel writers understood that this event was an important teaching for the followers of Jesus.

Mark 10:13 narrates that some people brought children to Jesus for Him to touch and bless them. Luke uses the term "little children" (NIV). Perhaps the disciples rebuked the parents, thinking that these children were too young to receive a blessing from Jesus.

A Dictionary of the Bible & Christian Doctrine in Everyday English (Eby, et al, 2004) notes: "To bless means to praise someone. It also means to wish happiness for someone…It may also mean to ask God to give His grace to them…Someone who is blessed has received the grace of God."

In Mark 10:14, we read that Jesus was outraged when the disciples didn't allow the children to be brought to Him to obtain His blessing and asked that the children be brought to Him. On the other hand, we see that: "It was natural that Jewish mothers should wish their children to be blessed by a great and distinguished Rabbi. Especially they brought their children to such a person on their first birthday" (William Barclay, Commentary on Mark 10:14). Perhaps this is why the children were brought to Jesus that day.

In Mark 10:15, Jesus set children as an example so that His followers would be like children so they can enter the kingdom of God. Ask: "What did Jesus mean?" This teaches us that heaven will be full of people who are like children. There won't be anyone there who has prestige and who sees himself as superior and who wants to walk around with a "Here I come" appearance. On the contrary, Jesus taught that to go to heaven you must have a child-like approach: faith, curiosity, and innocence .

2. The importance of children

In Matthew 18:1-5, we find that the disciples continued to think that the Kingdom that Jesus announced was of this world, and they continued to argue about their places in it. When Jesus heard their conversation, He called a child to Him, teaching them who would be the most important in His kingdom. Again a child takes the leading role in the teaching of Jesus. Let's see three lessons we learn from this teaching.

a. Don't exclude them!

Jesus took the opportunity to include children in the discussion: He put them at the center of the scene. Today there are many "modern" ways to exclude children, for example: sending them to play somewhere other than where you are, or constantly shutting them up and not letting them participate in any activity, not talking to them because you think they don't understand anything, ridiculing them, etc. Did this ever happen to you when you were little? Do you remember how you felt when this happened? Have you ever had any of these attitudes with a child? Allow the group to share their experiences.

The "little people" deserve the same respect as everyone. Young people today can make a difference for the new generations in this area.

b. Do good to them

It's very common to talk about respecting adults, being good to our parents, but what about children? Jesus sided with the children saying that if we receive a child, we receive Him. We must learn to always do good to children, to help them with their homework, answer their questions and teach them with patience and love how to do things. One of the most important commandments that Jesus left us is "Love your neighbor as yourself" (Matthew 22:39). Children are our neighbors so we must love them with the love we have for ourselves. Ask: "How has your relationship been with your younger siblings? Easy? Or difficult? Why? What aspects do you recognize as the most problematic in your relationship with the children around you?"

Christians must positively influence children through the love of Christ. It's public knowledge that children are currently being mistreated and abused even by their own siblings. Can you imagine what Jesus would say about this matter?

c. Follow their example

This passage shows the importance of serving and sharing with a child. If we saw Christ in a child, we would imitate His simplicity of heart, willingness to serve, selfless love, humility, dependence on the Father, His trust in Him. Ask: What qualities do your friends recognize in you? Are your qualities ones that characterize the kingdom of God?

3. Young people and children today

Have you noticed that Jesus treated children with the love that only God provides? God's love is a selfless love, it seeks the good of others and not its own. Think of a person you consider irresponsible with children, who doesn't love or care about them (they shouldn't give names). Ask them: "What attitudes does that person have that make you think this way? In the same way, think of a person who you consider responsible, who loves children and cares about them (they shouldn't give names). Ask them: "What behaviors make you believe that this person has these characteristics?"

Let us remember that although it's easier to see the attitudes of others towards children, we must be the first to positively influence the children around us, since they're also "our neighbor." The greatest good we can do for each other is to share the love that God puts in our hearts. Would you be willing to show your Christian love to the little ones? Would you be willing to ask God to fill your heart with a love for all children?

Review/Application:

Form two work teams and plan a project where all the young people of the church share a day of games and talking with the children. It has to be as friends and not in "teacher-student" roles in order to get to know them and get closer to them and learn about their interests. Develop the following project steps:

1. Project Manager:

2. Objective:

3. Date:

4. Place where the activity will take place:

5. Games:

6. Food:

7. Other resources:

Note: If you want, you can share the project with the other group.

Challenge:

See how well the group understands the importance of caring for, understanding, and loving children.

As a group, plan a prayer vigil for the children of our society and the world. Research the different reasons to pray for children, for example: For children who have been and are raped, for children who are abused, for orphaned children, for girls who are forced to marry in some places. You can involve the whole church and together develop a dynamic prayer program that raises awareness of the issue. You can get statistics on abused children in your city and the most common problems.

Young people and the elderly

Objective: To understand the relationship that they can have with the elderly and the responsibility they have toward them.

Memory Verse: "The glory of young men is their strength, gray hair the splendor of the old." Proverbs 20:2

> **Attention!**
> Discuss with the group the importance of caring for, understanding, and loving children. Have they made any changes yet?
> Accept

Connect | Navigate

Introductory Activity (12-17 years).

- Supplies: Drawings alluding to the elderly such as wheelchairs, a cane, medicines, etc.

- Instructions: Before starting the session, prepare the room with the pictures alluding to the elderly. Allow people to deduce what the topic of the session will be.

   Then, do a survey of those who have elderly people near or still living with them in the same house and encourage the young people to describe the characteristics of the elderly people they know. Write the characteristics of old age that they mention on the board. This way, you'll have ideas to contribute and enrich the group.

Introductory Activity (18-23 years).

- Instructions: Invite a senior adult from the church to share with the group a brief testimony about their life and what they have done to remain faithful in their Christian life. Include these questions in your discussion with him or her:

1. What was his or her profession?

2. What activities does the person get involved in now during their free time?

3. What was it like to retire and what was the most difficult part about retiring?

4. What social activities does the person get involved in on a daily basis?

5. How is his or her relationship with family members?

6. What information would be important for the youth to know about today's society?

Connect | Navigate

1. The elderly

The Merriam Webster Dictionary (https://www.merriam-webster.com/dictionary/elderly) defines the elderly as "a person who is rather old, or past middle age". Other concepts that we find for old age are: The last period of life, old age, longevity, living many years, golden age, old, senescence and older adult.

Sometimes the conception of old age is contextualized according to the cultures or the image of each one. In some places, when you retire, you are already considered elderly. There is also a tendency to think that a person is old when their hair is completely white, or when their skin has many wrinkles and they have different physical problems, diseases or they lose function.

Many of today's societies emphasize the image of eternal youth, discrediting the benefits and attractiveness of an elderly person.

2. Respect toward the elderly

Since ancient times, the elderly have enjoyed a certain respect and prestige in society. It was no different within the people of Israel (Exodus 3:16-18b). The elderly were sought out as counselors and to help resolve any moral or legal situation.

When we read the books of Exodus and Deuteronomy, we'll find several passages that speak about the elderly. An example of the importance of the elderly in solving legal questions can be found in the book of Ruth 4:2; 9-11. Ask: "Do you respect the elderly?"

Let's remember what happened to one of the kings of the people of Israel, Rehoboam. In 1 Kings 12:1-19, the story is told of a young king who followed the advice of his youthful friends and despised the advice of the elders, and this led to the division of the people he ruled. Ask: "Have you ever done something like that? What happened?" "Have you ever tried to become friends with an elderly person?" Generating a deep relationship with older people can bring a lot of wisdom to your life (Job 12:12).

In 1 Peter 5:5, the apostle Peter instructs young people to be subject to elders. As we continue reading, he tells us that we must be submissive to each other and clothed with humility, and with an attitude of understanding, communication, respect, and mutual care. If all generations work together, great things can be achieved for one's personal spiritual growth and for the growth of the people of God. According to what was stated by the apostle in the relationship that's generated between young and old, there's a type of subjection that enriches both. The word subjection refers to the respect and authority that older people have because of the experience and wisdom they have gained over the years.

Daniel 7:9 says: "I watched until thrones were set up, and an Ancient of Days sat, whose dress was white as snow, and the hair on his head like clean wool; His throne flames with fire, and his wheels blazing fire." In this passage, Daniel talks about his vision. The Ancient of Days he refers to is God himself. This is a tribute to our Heavenly Father's timeless existence. Likewise we show respect for the elderly around us.

3. Our responsibility toward the elderly

Young people must respect older adults and treat them with dignity, giving them their rightful place in the church and in society. We must listen to them and retain their teachings.

It's part of our responsibility to also watch over their physical and spiritual well-being, as we can recall in Paul's advice in 1 Timothy 5:8: "If anyone does not provide for his relatives, and especially for his immediate family, he has denied the faith and is worse than an unbeliever." Being young provides you with a lot of energy to achieve changes in the vision that you should have towards the elderly.

We must be patient with them, sometimes the elderly need special help—perhaps they have some health problems, and a young person can help them. It may be that an elderly man or woman feels sad, lonely, or angry for many reasons; then the young person can help the elderly person by showing the love of Christ.

Old age isn't a disease, it's a season of life that most human beings go through. During this stage of life, some come to lose their self-esteem; they feel that they no longer have the same value or performance, and sometimes they feel marginalized by their own families. Our job is to make them feel that they can still do and give a lot.

Let's remember that during this stage of life, some elderly people experience fear of the future and loneliness, especially if their spouse has passed away. Another of the most difficult aspects is economic insecurity, because what they receive in some cases, such as a pension, isn't enough to cover their basic needs.

Review/Application:

Describe or define elderly people using an adjective, for example: Good, isolated, tired, affectionate, etc.

Afterwards, ask each student to give their opinion or concept regarding older people. Classify them by words that qualify the observable positive or negative aspects.

Example:

Positive - *Kind, friendly*

Negative - *Pessimistic, Critical*

At the end, ask them to express how they can promote the positives and bring about change in terms of the negatives. How can we be active in the lives of our elders? They are also our neighbor!

Example: *I can visit them, bring them bread and have coffee with them and read some passages from the Bible that help them not to see life in a pessimistic way and strengthen their faith.*

Challenge:

Be sure the group understands the relationship that they can have with the elderly and the responsibility they have toward them.

Take time with the class and plan an activity with the elderly, whether it be a picnic, lunch or dinner, to spend quality time with them. A time where they share games that emphasize relationships. On that day, each young person can adopt a grandparent whom they will visit, greet on their birthday, call them and keep an eye on them, etc.

The Authorities

Attention!
Review with the group about the relationship that they can have with the elderly and the responsibility they have toward them.

Accept

Objective: To understand the relationship and responsibility they have with those in authority.

Memory Verse: "Let everyone be subject to the governing authorities, for there's no authority except that which God has established. The authorities that exist have been established by God." Romans 13:1

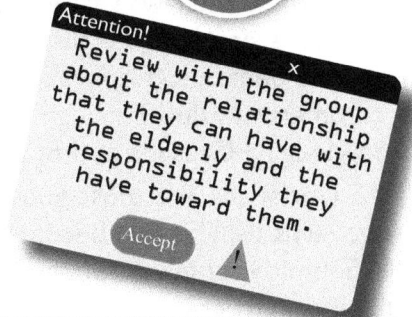

Connect | Navigate

What would happen if, in an orchestra, each musician chose what key to play in, what rhythm and what piece to interpret? The result would surely be a disaster. It's necessary to have someone in authority, in this case the conductor of the orchestra, to give direction to the musicians, achieving a beautiful symphony as a result.

The same happens in other areas, we need authority in every sphere of our lives to function in a correct and orderly way.

Introductory Activity (12 - 17 years)

- Supplies: A crown and an instruction sheet.

- Instructions: Name one of the group members as king/queen and give him/her a sheet with orders that he/she must demand that the others carry out (recite a memory verse, find a passage and read it, sing a song, etc.). Then "crown" him/her and explain to the group that whatever the king/queen requests, the "subjects" (the others) must comply with. Talk to two or three people in advance so that they rebel against the king's orders and refuse to do what is asked of them.

  When you consider it prudent, stop the activity and discuss with the group the attitudes that were generated, taking into account the perspectives of the king, obedient subjects, and rebels.

Introductory Activity (18-23 years)

- Supplies: Markers, colored pencils or crayons and sheets of paper.

- Directions: Make two groups and ask them to illustrate the following terms and write their definition.

  ◊ Group 1: Authority, honor, respect

    * Authority: the power to make decisions, the power to direct or control someone or something

    * Honor: good name or public esteem, reputation

    * Respect: a feeling of admiring someone or something that's good, valuable, important, etc.;

  ◊ Group 2: Government, submission, obedience

    * Government: the group of people who control and make decisions for a country, state, etc.; (

    * Submission: an act of submitting to the authority or control of another.

    * Obedience: an act or instance of doing something that someone tells you to do.

Ask them to present the pictures they have drawn and read the definition of each word.

Connect | Navigate

Throughout the Bible, we can see that God is our authority and works through authorities to guide His people. He expects us to respect and honor all authority, because all government is under His sovereignty. Read Romans 13:1 and start a discussion with your group about the secular authorities today and write their responses on the board (teachers, principals, mayors, government, police, bosses, etc.).

Knowing who our authorities are, we can ask ourselves: How should we behave towards them?

Let's look at the teachings that Jesus gives us in Matthew 22:15-22..

1. We need to recognize authority

In Matthew 22:19-20, Jesus said to them: "Show me the coin used for paying the tax." They brought him a denarius, and He asked them, "Whose image is this? And whose inscription?"

Jesus knew the laws that governed the empire, and for that reason, when they approached Him with such a question, He simply asked them to show them the coin they used for paying taxes. Jesus knew that they would give Him a denarius, this was a Roman silver coin that had the image and the inscription of Caesar, which gave it a commercial value. Through this action, Jesus was showing the people that He knew the law and that He was acknowledging Caesar's authority as ruler.

As Christians, we must know the laws that govern the place where we live and recognize the authority that governs us. This will become a powerful testimony for those around us. I Peter 2:13-15 expresses it very well: "Submit yourselves for the Lord's sake to every human authority: whether to the emperor, as the supreme authority, or to governors, who are sent by Him to punish those who do wrong and to commend those who do right. For it's God's will that by doing good you should silence the ignorant talk of foolish people." We can apply this passage perfectly not only to political authorities but also to supervisors or managers at work or to teachers or directors of educational institutions. Our attitude must be to know the rules that govern every institution (governmental, educational or labor) and accept and comply with them. If I don't agree on something, I must follow the corresponding channels to promote changes or make my position known, but rebellion or non-compliance aren't Christian attitudes.

2. We must have a good attitude toward authority

In the verse, "Give therefore to Caesar what is Caesar's" (v.21), we can complement Jesus' statement with Romans 13:7, which states, "Give to everyone what you owe them: If you owe taxes, pay taxes; if revenue, then revenue; if respect, then respect; if honor, then honor." This passage not only refers to the payment of taxes but to the respect and honor that must be given to the authorities. Although Jesus spoke out against some religious authorities, He didn't speak out against most of the political rulers, even though the time in which He lived the Roman Empire was an authoritarian, undemocratic, and abusive regime.

Based on the reading of Romans 13:1-7, divide into two groups and ask them to discuss and draw conclusions from the following phrases and then share them with everyone:

Group 1:

a. We must submit to higher authorities.

b. Authorities are appointed by God.

c. Whoever opposes authority resists what is established by God.

d. Those who resist authority will carry condemnation.

Group 2:

a. The magistrates are there to instill fear in the wicked.

b. The authorities are God's servant for your good.

c. One must subject themself to authority, not just to avoid punishment, but also for the sake of conscience.

d. The authorities are God's servants.

e. Pay to all authorities what you owe: If you owe taxes, pay taxes; if revenue, then revenue; if respect, then respect; if honor, then honor.

The Bible is very clear about responsibilities towards authorities. We must respect and honor them, pay taxes, pray for them, and be willing to cooperate. By doing these things, we honor God and bear witness to Him.

3. The biggest authority is always God

"...and to God what is God's" (v.21). As Christians we can affirm that we have two citizenships, one heavenly and one earthly. As earthly citizens, we must submit to the authorities, as explained in the previous point, but, what happens when the authorities require the implementation of laws contrary to divine laws? Let's analyze two examples:

- Sometimes laws are unjust. For example, what happened to women who attended deliveries in Egypt. The king ordered them that when a baby was born, if it was a girl they should let her live, but if it was a boy they should kill him (Exodus 1:15-16). The Bible mentions: "But the midwives feared God, and didn't do as the king of Egypt commanded, but kept the children alive" Exodus 1:17. The king's order was unjust, the women decided not to obey out of fear of Yahweh, the result is in Exodus 1:20-21, "So God was kind to the midwives and the people increased and became even more numerous. And because the midwives feared God, he gave them families of their own."

- It may be that obedience to human authorities conflicts with obedience to God. The High Priest was the highest religious authority of the Jews, and when he was full of jealousy, he put Peter in jail for preaching the gospel of Jesus Christ. But miraculously, God sent an angel and took him out of jail, because although Peter owed obedience to his earthly authority, he understood that above all he owed obedience to God. Acts 5:28-29 says, "We gave you strict orders not to teach in this name," he said. "Yet you have filled Jerusalem with your teaching and are determined to make us guilty of this man's blood." Peter and the other apostles replied: "We must obey God rather than human beings!"

Finally, it should be made clear that it's important to submit to any institution as long as it doesn't go against Christian principles. If in a job I am asked to lie or act improperly, I must make my principles clear. When I act like this, two things can happen, one may be that my life impacts my superiors and they respect me for my position. Another option is that I may have to suffer (possibly lose my job) for refusing to do something that goes against Christian principles. What will my attitude be from now on?

Review/Application:

Read the following passages and write them in your own words:

- Titus 3:1
- 1 Timothy 2:1-3

Challenge:

During this next week, read Romans 13:1-7 and 1 Timothy 2:1-3 and make a list of the attitudes that we have talked about in class that we should have towards authority and underline those that you have not yet developed, look for the closest authorities that you may have (teachers, directors, bosses), and share your desire to develop these new attitudes and ask that they help you do so.

Together but... not the same

Objective: To discover what is the correct type of relationship that Christians should have with those who aren't believers.

Memory Verse: "This is how we know who the children of God are and who the children of the devil are: Anyone who does not do what is right is not God's child, nor is anyone who does not love their brother and sister." 1 John 3:10

Attention! x

Talk to the group about how they have improved their relationship towards authorities in the past week. If appropriate, pray for the authorities in their lives.

Accept

Connect | Navigate

Introductory Activity (12-17 years).

- Supplies: Markers.

- Instructions: On small cards for each person, write certain behaviors: Scratch your nose, cry, laugh, limp, sneeze, stick out your tongue, (repeat two or three cards with each behavior depending on the number in the group). Write a card that says act normal.

  Ask a volunteer to go out of the room so that they don't hear the instructions. Hand out the cards and ask them to walk around the room in a circle, performing the assigned behavior. Bring in the volunteer who left the room. The goal of the volunteer will be to discover who it is that behaves differently from the rest of the group. After the volunteer detects who is different from the group for maintaining a normal behavior, allow the group to comment on the following phrases:

  - Together but ... not the same
  - The world must see a difference in us!

Give the group a moment to reflect on the memory verse.

Introductory Activity (18-23 years).

- Supplies: Poster board, markers, and masking tape.

- Instructions: Ask two volunteers who will be the "pickers" to leave the room while you give the group instructions. From the rest of the group, half will choose names of vegetables and the other half of fruits. The activity will consist of the "collectors" entering the room and asking the group questions to discover what fruit or what vegetable they are. The "fruits" and "vegetables" will be able to answer all the questions that the "gatherers" ask them, but they should never tell them the name of the vegetable or fruit they represent. As they discover them, they must move them to the place in the room indicated by the teacher (use the markers and poster board to make signs that say "fruit" and "vegetables." To find out what they are, the gatherers can ask questions like: What is its color? What is its taste or texture? In what season is it eaten? Does it have seeds? But they can never ask the name. At the end, both the pickers and the fruits and vegetables should share how they felt. Finally, comment that it's important for people to distinguish that we're Christians by our attitudes without us even having to tell them.

Connect | Navigate

Sometimes we hear phrases that say that if we hang out with certain people, something will stick to us, be it their way of dressing, speaking, behaving, etc. Some sayings in this regard say: "Birds of a feather, flock together" or "As thick as thieves." Let them comment on these sayings.

1. In the world ... but not of the world

Our parents taught us that we should choose our friends wisely. This is good advice since our friends are the people from whom we'll receive advice and with whom we'll have closer relationships. While we can choose our friends, we cannot always choose our coworkers or classmates.

It's impossible to separate ourselves from the world because we live in it! Jesus knew this very well. As His crucifixion drew near, He prayed, making a beautiful request to the Father on behalf of His disciples and said: "My prayer is not that you take them out of the world but that you protect them from the evil one." John 17:15. So how do we understand this? Should we stay away from non-Christian people so they don't "contaminate" us? No way. We must share life with them, but we must not let them influence us badly and end up doing what they want.

On the other hand, we must influence them and bring them closer to the truth that's in Christ; we must shine in the midst of darkness (Matthew 5:16).

Let's look at the passage from Mark 2:13-17. Jesus was teaching on the seashore and people were following Him and listening to His teachings. As Jesus passed by, He saw Levi, who is also known as Matthew, and called him to follow Him. Who was Matthew? We can start by saying that he wasn't a person loved by the people; on the contrary, he was a hated man. Tax collectors at that time were considered thieves. People never knew how much they should pay because tax collectors overcharged for their own profit and tried to get as much out of people as they could. Recall Zacchaeus (Luke 19:8) who, upon meeting Jesus, agreed to pay back those from whom he had stolen.

Matthew must have been a lonely man, since people didn't like him, and even less the religious leaders. How wonderful it must have been that Jesus spoke to him and called out to him! Once Matthew approached Jesus and met Him, he invited Him to his house and invited his friends and, as one might imagine, his friends were tax collectors and sinners (Mark 2:15). Seeing Jesus with these people, the Pharisees asked the disciples "Why does He eat with tax collectors and sinners?" (v.16b). Jesus' response was clear: "I have not come to call the righteous, but sinners" (v.17b). Jesus shone in the midst of those needy people. He went to Matthew's house and shared the table with these people who needed healing for their souls.

2. What should our relationship with the world be like?

It's important to note that there's a fine line that separates us from maintaining a holy and just relationship with God, or a shallow relationship with Christian overtones. Of course, we must interact with everyone around us, Christian or not, and it's part of our responsibility to be a light for them by being by their side (Matthew 5:16).

The problem is if by being with them, we become like them, and we stop shining and making a difference in such a way that people don't notice any difference. Ask: *"What differences are we talking about? What things will make us shine in the places we go?"*

This means shining our light in our way of thinking, seeing, expressing ourselves, in our day-to-day life, at school, on the street, with our group of friends, family, in sports, etc.

In all circumstances, we must be there to show the love of Jesus Christ through our actions as the apostle John says: "Dear children, let us not love with words or speech but with actions and in truth" (1 John 3:18). By being different in our actions and by acting sincerely according to what God commands us, we'll show others a different lifestyle.

3. We need to know the thin line that separates us

Knowing how to distinguish and respect that line will help to show unbelievers the difference that an intimate life of obedience to God makes.

When we're good friends, family, neighbors, coworkers or classmates in a world that lacks these characteristics, we're bearing witness to Christ. Even if in some circumstances that we encounter we don't say a single word, with a reaction or attitude we'll show what we are. Of course, we're not perfect, but we're in search of that Christian perfection called holiness (John 17:19). Correcting our mistakes, asking for forgiveness, forgiving, being gentle, striving in all that we do, and seeking to be better will help us speak with authority when necessary among unbelievers.

But how much should we be with the world without becoming like it or losing sight of our goal of being like Christ? We must not forget that we live in this world but don't belong to it, as Jesus himself indicates in John 17:16. We live as foreigners in a strange land. Ask: *"Do you know any foreigners? Have you noticed something different in the way they are or act? Have you noticed something that differentiates them from all of us who were born here?"* Let them comment; if you have an example take the opportunity to share it.

Here lies the difference between "being from a place" and "being in a place." "Being from" is the essence of the person; it's composed of their principles, beliefs, education, and training. It doesn't change due to circumstances since it's part of them. "Being in" is circumstantial; it speaks of a position, which can change permanently. Our goal is "to be holy" while "being in the world."

In our life as saints living in the world, obedience plays a leading role: "The one who keeps God's commands lives in him, and He in them. And this is how we know that He lives in us: We know it by the Spirit He gave us" (1 John 3:24)

The Bible is our truth, where we can find not only the commandments but also principles and values to lead a Christlike life. They'll help us make decisions about our interaction with the world and unbelievers.

The world must see a difference in us! We must share the gospel with people of the world and love those who don't know Jesus, but not do what they do (sin). It's up to us to ask for the guidance of the Holy Spirit so as not to cross that line between sharing with sinners and sharing in sin.

Review/Application:

Ask your class to list behaviors that can lead us to be confused or look like the rest of the world.

Example:

- Clothing
- Language
- Attitudes

Allow the group to share their conclusions about the risk of isolating ourselves in our Christian world or losing our Christian distinctiveness in our quest to gain access to the unsaved.

Challenge:

Do others see that you are different because of your Christian values and convictions? Ask your friends or the people closest to you. What do they see in you that's different? Examine your life and make the necessary changes. Every day when you get up, repeat the memory verse. At night, write down how it went and share it next Sunday with your classmates.

Who's in charge?

Objective: To understand the relationship that they should have with their church leaders and the responsibility they have toward them.

Memory Verse: "And the Lord's servant must not be quarrelsome but must be kind to everyone, able to teach, not resentful. Opponents must be gently instructed..." 2 Timothy 2:24-25a

Attention!
Create a safe space so that the group can testify about how they have been growing in Christlikeness in their daily life.
Accept

Connect | Navigate

Introductory Activity (12-17 years).

- Supplies: Sheets of paper and pencils.

- Directions: Ask your group to think of someone in the congregation that they admire for their leadership and service in the church. Then ask them to write down some characteristics of this person's life and ministry. Once they have finished, each person (if there are many, you can ask some of them to do it) will share their description and the others will try to guess which person it is. If the congregation is very small, they can describe zone or district leaders who are known to the majority.

Introductory Activity (18-23 years)

- Supplies: Poster paper and markers

- Instructions: Divide the group into teams of three or four and ask them to write down some characteristics that they think church leaders in different ministries should have. Then ask each group to present their findings.

Connect | Navigate

In the local church, God calls men and women willing to serve Him. Many of them began serving from a young age in children's church, as helpers in Vacation Bible School, in camps, etc. Over time, these people discovered their spiritual gifts or talents, gained experience, and were accepted and respected by the congregation. They came to be considered as leaders of the church in different ministries: Teachers, chairmen of departments, stewards, directors of worship, etc. Today, there's a leadership crisis in many churches since few really want to commit to serving God in various ministries and responding to God's call. We need to analyze why and also appreciate the importance of the leaders that God has called to serve in His work. We must also reflect on how we can collaborate with them so that together the church fulfills its purpose of "making Christ-like disciples."

1. Leaders are positioned by God

Begin this section by asking your group if they know how leaders are chosen in their local church. Perhaps if there's a young person who's a leader in a ministry, they can give a testimony of how they knew that God was calling them.

Normally, when a leader is chosen by the congregation to serve in a ministry within the church, we say that it was God who called the person to serve. On many occasions, God uses people in our church community to guide us to see in what areas God wants to use us.

When leaders need to be chosen, often an election will be held. Prior to this, the pastor and a board of leaders in charge pray and ask God for His direction. They then think of people who might fill the different positions and discuss their testimony, spiritual life, service, and gifts to perform a particular ministry. Once these areas are evaluated, the church's process is followed for the final election. In this process, the Spirit of God intervenes, speaking and confirming in the heart of the new leaders that they have been called to serve Him, and the congregation is used by God to support that call.

In Romans 12:4-11, Paul says that it's the Spirit of God who distributes the gifts and gives ministries, in the way that He sees fit.

Therefore, we must not doubt that God is the one who chooses leaders to serve Him, and therefore we must accept God's leadership and support them.

2. Leaders are an example to others

Team activity: Ask the group to divide into two teams and analyze the Bible passages, 2 Timothy 2:14-26 and Galatians 6:1-10. Comment and write down some characteristics or qualities that Christian leaders should have according to these verses. Each team will write down their answers and one person from each team will share them with the group. At the end, the teacher will summarize in a list the characteristics and qualities of a Christian leader.

a. 2 Timothy 2:14-26: According to this passage, Paul was exhorting Timothy to be an example, to take care of his spiritual life and his relationship with others.

The passage gives some guidelines to leaders regarding their ministry:

- Avoid pointless discussions.
- Strive to be a God-approved leader and have a good reputation
- Avoid idle talk or false doctrines.
- Flee from youthful passions.
- Follow justice, faith, love, and peace.
- Don't get involved in foolish discussions.
- Be kind to everyone and gently correct people.

b. Galatians 6:1-10: In this passage, the apostle Paul gives some exhortations and warnings for the brothers and sisters of the church and especially for those who are in leadership positions.

- Restore the one who has sinned with love and humility.
- Help each other carry their burdens.
- Don't think too highly of themselves
- Be grateful to those who teach us from the Word of God.
- Sow spiritual blessings, to please the Spirit of God.
- Don't tire of doing good for everyone.
- Don't give up, God will give the results.

Being a Christian leader implies not only receiving a calling, but also the great responsibility of fully fulfilling the task assigned to you, with a good testimony and love for others. This means above all not taking pride in the leadership position, but rather receiving that privilege with humility and as an opportunity to serve others.

3. We must obey our leaders

We have already discovered that serving the Lord involves a call and a commitment, but now we'll analyze why it's important that we as Christians respect and obey our leaders.

We usually like to come to church and be spectators of what others do, and sometimes we're tempted to criticize and comment or gossip about what we like or dislike. This has caused serious problems in churches and has sometimes even created divisions.

In our role as followers of Christ, our focus must be on Jesus Christ, who was not only Lord and Teacher but also Servant. We must always remember that God uses human beings, with defects and virtues, to guide his people (pastors, teachers, department presidents, etc.).

God puts in his servants the vision, the ideas, the projects of what is going to be done to fulfill the great commission. Our responsibilities to leaders are: Pray for them, support them, encourage them and help them in the task.

Leaders won't accomplish the vision alone but must work together with God's people.

Young people must be willing to accept leadership and obey directions to carry out the task which God has called them to.

It's also important to show a willingness to work as a team and to be encouraged to achieve the goals that you have set together as a church.

In Romans 12:9-21, Paul writes some recommendations on how interpersonal human relationships should be maintained among the members of the church. We should take them into account every day so that our relationship with our leaders occurs in an environment of love and equality.

Review/Application:

Give your students time to read the following passages: 2 Thessalonians 3:1-2 and 14-15; Romans 16:1-2. Then ask them to answer the following questions based on what they've read.

1. What responsibilities do we have to our leaders in the church?
   - *Pray for them and their ministry.*
   - *Obey their directions.*
   - *Support them in their ministry.*

2. What should be our relationships with our leaders?
   - *Of appreciation and respect.*
   - *Of love and care.*
   - *Of cordiality and teamwork.*

Challenge:

Think this week about how you can put into practice what you learned in class. What should you do if you feel God's call to serve? What can you do to support those who are the leaders in the church? Think about this and pray, asking the Lord to guide you in the service he wants you to do.

What I have I give to you

Objective: To understand that people with disabilities are also our neighbor and need Christ.

Memory Verse: "You see, at just the right time, when we were still powerless, Christ died for the ungodly." Romans 5:6

Attention!

Talk to the group about how they have improved in their relationship with those in authority. If appropriate, pray for the authorities.

Accept

Connect | Navigate

Introductory Activity (12-17 years).

- Supplies: Small table, a chair, a jug with water, rope or thick yarn, a glass, and a handkerchief.

- Instructions: Choose or ask for three volunteers, and position them a good distance from the table. On the table place the glass and the jug of water. Then, tie one person's hands together, tie another person's feet together and cover the other's eyes.

  Ask them to do whatever they're told together. Then tell the person whose eyes are covered to say "I'm thirsty!"

  Ask: *How will they solve this?* Only the two other participants will be able to respond and act.

  When they finish, ask the participants to express their feelings and explain how they felt. Allow the rest of the group to ask questions.

Introductory Activity (18-23 years).

- Supplies: A chair, rope or thick yarn, ribbon or scarf, and a sign that says "Ignore me."

- Instructions: Without giving further explanation, ask one group member to volunteer to go to the meeting room before the rest of the group enters. Tie the volunteer's hands or arms to the chair with a heavy string. Then put tape or a handkerchief over the volunteer's mouth so that the volunteer cannot speak, and hang the sign saying "ignore me" around the volunteer's neck.

  Act normally by greeting and welcoming everyone. Start the dialogue by asking how the challenge went or encourage a small dialogue. Then give everyone a treat except the volunteer with the "Ignore me!" sign.

  After a few minutes ask the group and the volunteer how they felt. (Be sure to show appreciation to the volunteer when you have finished this activity.)

Connect | Navigate

Have you ever wondered why God allows people with disabilities to exist in the world, that is, with physical or mental difficulties such as deafness, blindness, down syndrome, cerebral palsy, autism, intellectual deficiency, etc.? What do you think? Is it: Punishment from God? Did their parents sin? Did God make a mistake?

The World Health Organization estimates that disability is on the rise globally due to population ageing and the rapid spread of chronic diseases, as well as improvements in the methodologies used to measure disability. (https://www.who.int/teams/noncommunicable-diseases/sensory-functions-disability-and-rehabilitation/world-report-on-disability)

For some, their living conditions are further complicated by extreme poverty, the high rate of unemployment, little access to public services (education, medical care, housing, transportation, legal services) and in general, by a marginalized and isolated social and cultural status. Depending on how their needs and capacities are channeled, they'll become a social burden or they'll be able to contribute significantly to society.

1. We must not exclude people

When the Lord Jesus Christ gave the Church the mandate of the Great Commission, surely for the apostles it was not new to include people with disabilities among them. Many of the Master's miracles involved healing (lame, blind, lepers, etc.). So it wouldn't be strange to find people with physical and mental disabilities within the early church. Discrimination at that time within the church was towards Gentiles (Acts 10:34). Although at the beginning of the church, people with physical problems weren't discriminated against, somewhere in history, they were left out of many Christian churches.

The attitudes of society towards people with disabilities are many and varied. Some people show a harmful attitude of a mixture of compassion and pity towards people with disabilities. Others, out of ignorance or indifference, openly reject or discriminate people with disabilities.

First of all, we must understand that people with disabilities have a soul, body, and spirit. They feel emotions and have needs just like other human beings. Many times, people's actions are affected by the lack of information on the subject, which isn't adequately addressed. We must understand that every person is equal and deserves respect. Therefore, a person with disabilities is still a human who may be different than you and me.

People with disabilities, from a biblical point of view, are created by God, are reflections of His love, and are our neighbors. Both approaches point to the acceptance and integration of these people in different areas of society.

God is love, and if His love is in us, we can love all people (1 John 4:8). If we love God, we can love people with disabilities. God looks at our hearts, not our appearance. When Samuel went to anoint the future king of Israel, he never imagined that a skinny teenager with a young face could represent the authority that the role would demand. However, God confronted him with divine thought about people (1 Samuel 16:7). David, under an oath of friendship with Jonathan, promised to do good to him and his offspring. Years later, a surviving descendant of Jonathan was a crippled young man who crawled on the floor and felt worthless. David made Yahweh's words his own and looked not at his appearance but at his essence and did good to Mephibosheth as he had promised to Jonathan (2 Samuel 4:4; 9:7–9).

2. Obeying the Great Commission!

In Acts 3:1-10, Peter and John encountered a person unable to walk. The apostles took the time to listen to the request of this man, even though the request was financial and they didn't have money. The apostles' response was to act not by their strength or abilities, but "in the name of Jesus" (the key to Christian action), to act on behalf of Christ and pray with power in His Spirit.

God wants to heal people both spiritually and physically. *But what happens if God doesn't heal them physically?* Allow the group to have a say.

Jesus was careful to make it clear that spiritual healing was important, rather than physical healing. And more importantly, when Jesus healed, it was for the glory of God (Mark 2:1-12).

There is no greater misery than the vanity and pride that makes us think that we don't need God. Many times, we'll be able to see our little fears or selfishness by not being interested in taking the gospel to people with disabilities. We must be careful of phrases such as "they don't understand." We must investigate their ways of learning. We must seek evangelism strategies for people with disabilities and know the need for God's love in them and in their families.

3. Integrating people with disabilities in church activities

The lives of people with disabilities are testimony that the power of God is perfected in weakness, and through those weaknesses, God makes them strong in the face of adversity (2 Corinthians 12:7-10). People with disabilities need special attention in some areas. But above all, it's important to win them to Christ, baptize, disciple, and give them as much as possible an opportunity to serve the Lord.

It's true that people with disabilities sometimes require a greater investment of time and resources, but for Jesus, this is an investment that will bear eternal fruit. Every person, regardless of their physical or social condition, has something valuable to give to others. People with disabilities have determination, a desire to live, and a spirit of improvement and solidarity, which others often lack. Let's take time to get to know them and learn from them; let's not deprive ourselves of this enriching experience. As a church, we must fully integrate everyone.

As a Christian community, we must set the example of the integration of people with disabilities. We don't require regulations or a church code to integrate our brothers and sisters. We need the love poured out by the Holy Spirit in our hearts as well as the gift of intelligence that God gives us. If the world doesn't agree on including people with disabilities, as Christians, let's show that we can achieve it and not because of a government order or law, but because the love of Christ moves us to serve and love our neighbors.

Christians can give guidelines to society on how to treat its citizens with disabilities, because we are, as the apostle Peter says, "a chosen people, a royal priesthood, a holy nation, God's special possession, that you may declare the praises of him who called you out of darkness into his wonderful light" (1 Peter 2:9).

Review/Application:

Ask your students to respond to the following questions based on the account in Acts 3:1–10.

1. What did the lame man think he needed and why? *Money for his needs.*

2. What did Peter think the lame man needed? *The possibility of a radical change in his life.*

3. How do you think the man felt when he received healing? Why? *Surprised and happy because he received much more than he expected.*

4. Can you share your testimony or that of someone who has received physical healing?

Challenge:

Plan with your group a visit to a rehabilitation center or orphanage for people with special abilities. Schedule it in advance, requesting the pertinent authorizations and bringing a gift to leave them. This can be done periodically by planning activities according to the needs observed.

Rules of the game

Objective: To understand that there's a social ethic and a Christian ethic, and that by being part of the kingdom of God, we commit ourselves to live according to Christian ethics.

Memory Verse: "So in everything, do to others what you would have them do to you, for this sums up the Law and the Prophets." Matthew 7:12

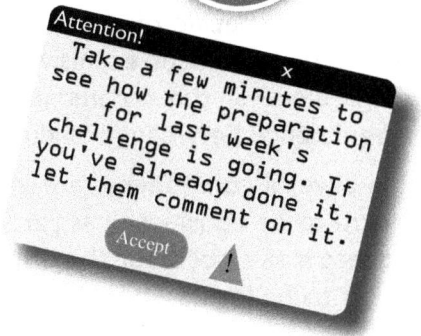

Attention! Take a few minutes to see how the preparation for last week's challenge is going. If you've already done it, let them comment on it. *Accept*

Connect · Navigate

Introductory Activity (12-17 years).

- Supplies: Balloons (two per person and some extras) and string to tie them.

- Instructions: Give two balloons to each participant. Ask them to tie the balloons to their ankles and when given the signal, in one minute, pop others' balloons without getting their own popped.

  Make sure there are still several teens with balloons at their feet, to make way for the next stage (if they all burst, put two balloons on each ankle again). Tell them that they should now follow some rules: (1) Must keep your hands behind you. (2) May not break the balloon of a person of the opposite sex. (3) Should always be in the certain area marked by the group leader, and leaving the area requires leaving the game. (4) Only have two minutes to try to break each other's balloons.

  At the end, ask the teens to share their comments about the activity: with rules and without rules. What differences did you find?

Introductory Activity (18-23 years).

- Supplies: Paper cards, pencils, whiteboard, and whiteboard markers.

- Instructions: Start the activity by giving a card to each participant. Mention that there has been a worldwide disaster and the only ones who survived were them. As a new society, they need to have rules that help them coexist. Ask each person to write, on the card that was given to them, a rule that will be included in the official regulations of their new society. Give them a few minutes and then collect the cards and write the rules on the board.

  At the end of the activity, ask the young adults to share their comments about the rules on the board. *Do you think the regulations show fairness? Do you think these rules will be enough to live in harmony? What do you think influenced each of the laws that each one contributed?* Once the majority have participated, begin the lesson.

Connect · Navigate

If you've ever played a sport, you'll know that every sport has to be played by the rules. As in sports and activities we're careful to follow the rules, even more so in life, it's important to have rules. There are questions that come to our mind, such as: Why do we need the rules? Who is in charge of setting these rules? What if I don't follow the rules?

1. Definition of social ethics

A Dictionary of the Bible & Christian Doctrine in Everyday English (Eby, et al, 2004) notes:

1. Ethics is the study of moral conduct.

2. It's a system of beliefs about how people should make moral decisions.

3. Morality is the practice of ethics. Ethics guides moral conduct.

Although there are several definitions, we can use a simple definition that's generally accepted by most schools of thought: ethics is the set of moral norms or values that regulate human behavior. These moral rules serve as the basis for determining the character of actions, whether they're good or bad. In other words, ethics are the rules of the game for our actions.

In the specific case of social ethics, we refer to the set of norms of moral conduct of a society. Social ethics doesn't focus exclusively on the individual, rather it concerns a person who interacts in a community. Regardless of the community we're talking about, social ethics aims to build an environment in which coexistence between individuals occurs consistently.

Several components are involved in this ethic, such as general acceptance. This means that for a moral norm to be considered as part of the community, it's necessary that the majority of the members of society accept it as a norm for them. It can be adopted in writing or understood by the community without the need for it to be legislated and put in writing.

Another important component is tradition, which is the set of actions or practices that a community adopts and repeats, from generation to generation. There is the following saying, "custom becomes law."

Social ethics is also marked by geographical, demographic, and historical boundaries. The set of moral standards that apply in one country, city, or community may be different from those that apply in another country, city, or community. For example, while in some countries, having multiple wives is approved within social norms, in other countries, this is rejected, classifying it as adultery.

The previous example makes us understand that social ethics has its limitations and cannot be perfect since it's a human attempt to achieve justice and seek goodness in the actions of individuals. This makes us wonder, what is it that makes the rules change, depending on the place or community? How can an action be considered good in some place or time, and bad, in another place or time? These questions make us conclude, or at least suspect, that there must be some ethics superior to social ethics.

2. The Supreme Law: The ethics of the Kingdom

Ethics is the set of moral norms that govern the conduct of human beings. So when mentioning specifically that ethics is Christian or biblical, the parameters of judgment aren't based on the traditions or the general consensus of the community that considers something just or good. Rather, the parameters focus on the person of Christ, as expressed in the Bible. Sometimes, social ethics and Christian ethics coincide, but not entirely.

Perhaps the clearest example of this full coexistence between social ethics and Christian ethics occurred in the formation of the people of Israel. When they received the Ten Commandments from God, the divine law was their social law. However over time, that moral law, expressed in the Ten Commandments, began losing its relevance in the daily life of the people of Israel. The problem wasn't the law itself, but the people, who began to design their own social ethics. However, in the Scriptures, we don't find another ethic revealed by God other than the one that's expressed in the Ten Commandments. Jesus perfectly summarized that in the great commandment, "love God, and love your neighbor." This great commandment was explained by Jesus through the Sermon on the Mount and was publicly modeled during His time of ministry.

One of the results of receiving salvation in Christ Jesus is that we're now citizens of God's Kingdom and as such, our commitment is to live according to the ethics of the Kingdom. Another result of receiving salvation is that we understand that we have social responsibilities and that we must seek the good of our neighbor (Matthew 7:12). But on many occasions, seeking the good of our neighbor isn't always a social ethic, since forgiveness and mercy may not be valued or plentiful in the laws and customs that govern some communities. That's why our primary Christian commitment is to live according to Christian ethics (Matthew 5:38-48).

Does the above mean that we must comply only with divine law and not with social rules? No, it means that as a consequence of living according to Christian ethics, we seek to comply with the rules of coexistence in our community, as long as they don't oppose Christian ethics.

The ethics of the kingdom of God are first our supreme law. First of all, it's because God created them, but also because of their scope. While the social law only has as its purpose to regulate the relationships between individuals, divine law (Christian ethics) is intended to restore the relationship with God, with oneself, with our neighbor and with creation.

Something that, although not new, is passionately promoted and defended by many today, is moral relativism. This is simply not having a single and consistent truth parameter to determine what's good and bad. This means having multiple criteria of judgment. Perhaps this is the greatest contradiction of some societies today: while social systems seek to regulate the coexistence of individuals, at the same time they promote that each individual dictates the rules of the game. The problem is that such societies are trying to live in harmony without including God in the design. We need to realize that if each of us follows God's will, then we'll be at peace as neighbors!

History has made it clear to us that no society has solved the problem of how to live in harmony without including God, and it's been proven that no social ethic that leaves God out can, in the long run, survive. The explanation of this reality is very simple: man-made rules will be outdated and imperfect. However, in the case of biblical ethics, we cannot say that they'll become obsolete, since it has its sustenance in God Himself as its creator, and He has no limitations of time or place. In fact, He's the creator of time, knowledge, wisdom, space and human beings themselves. Who is better than Him to determine what is good or bad, what is right or wrong, what is true or false?

Review/Application:

Kingdom Ethics

Every command God gave to the people of Israel had a purpose, which still applies today. Write down each of the 10 commandments (Exodus 20:3-17).

1. *You shall have no other gods before me.*

2. *You shall not make for yourself an idol in the form of anything.*

3. *You shall not misuse the name of the Lord your God.*

4. *Remember the Sabbath day by keeping it holy.*

5. *Honor your father and your mother.*

6. *You shall not murder.*

7. *You shall not commit adultery.*

8. *You shall not steal.*

9. *You shall not give false testimony against your neighbor.*

10. *You shall not covet.*

Challenge:

Memorize the golden rule "So in everything, do to others what you would have them do to you ..." (Matthew 7:12) and put it into practice this week, and share your experience next week in class.

We have an anointing

Objective: To understand the meaning of anointing in light of the Bible.

Memory Verse: "But you have an anointing from the Holy One, and all of you know the truth." 1 John 2:20

Attention!

Start the lesson by asking the group how they have been practicing the Golden Rule. Motivate them to go beyond just memorization.

Accept

Connect | Navigate

Introductory Activity (12-17 years).

- Supplies: Various objects such as a ball, candy, a stick, a colorful shirt or dress, a small container with oil, and any additional objects that are mentioned in the Bible or other objects.

- Instructions: Put the objects on a table. Ask each person to choose an object mentioned in the Bible, and to think about what the topic of the session will be. Then ask why each person chose that object. Whoever chooses the oil wins. Tell them that the topic of the lesson is anointing and that oil was used for anointing in Bible times.

Introductory Activity (18-23 years).

- Directions: Ask the group to think of something tangible that symbolizes "anointing" in the shortest amount of time possible. Take note of what they say. When someone says oil, stop.

   Explain that it's sometimes difficult to materialize something so spiritual, but the Jews used oil as a symbol of the Holy Spirit consecrating and setting apart.

Connect | Navigate

When we hear the word "anointing," what is the first thing that comes to mind? Allow the group members to provide some responses from their own experiences. Perhaps campaigns, conferences, televangelists, renowned people, etc. come to mind. But: *Who is anointed and who does it?* Let them have a say.

1. Anointing in the Old Testament

The word anointing is widely used by the church today, but it has its origins in the customs of the people of Israel. The Jewish religion, full of symbolism, gave it its maximum splendor.

The Old Testament mentions the anointing of objects and people to consecrate them to God (Genesis 31:13; Exodus 30:25-29; 1 Samuel 16:13; Isaiah 21:5). Exodus 29:1-9 reveals the purpose of anointing and how it was done. Anointing had several characteristics:

   a. The fundamental purpose was to consecrate and dedicate a person for a holy responsibility (vv.1,9).

   b. Anointing was closely tied to the holiness needed to be before Jehovah. In the Old Testament, holiness was related to anointing (consecration), cleanliness, clothing, and sacrifices (vv. 1, 4-7, 10, 15).

   c. Not all people had divine authority to anoint. In this case, Moses did it. Oil was the main element for anointing (v.7).

   d. God granted authority to the person in charge of anointing others (v.1).

   e. When a person was anointed, God gave them some power over certain functions. In this passage, Aaron and his sons would have the perpetual priesthood (v.9).

Anointing denoted divine guidance. Although material elements intervened, the belief was that behind them was the hand of Yahweh and that He was present on the spot. Only anointing supported the fulfillment of an extraordinary commission (Isaiah 61:1; 1 Samuel 16:6-13). The passage from 1 Samuel 16:6-13 offers us the characteristics discussed earlier, but sheds light on others that are important, although specific to this story. Although Samuel was the anointed one of Yahweh and had the anointing of God, he was not exempt from making mistakes regarding the will of God (he looked at the outward appearance of Jesse's sons). But he was ready to hear the voice of God (vv.6-8). God chose the humble, one whom others didn't take into account (v.11). Anointing on God's part guaranteed His presence in the person. The oil was seen as a symbol of Yahweh's Spirit (v.13).

It shouldn't be overlooked that oil was also used as a toiletry item (Ruth 3:3; Amos 6:6). On the other hand, not anointing was a sign of mourning or spiritual searching (2 Samuel 12:19-20; Daniel 10:2-3).

2. Anointing in the New Testament

The New Testament with its New Covenant that God established with His church, modified and changed some Old Testament concepts. Anointing is one of them.

The New Testament begins with the life of Jesus, who received the title of the Anointed One (Luke 4:18; Acts 10:38). The name of Christ was alluding to the divine mission that He was going to fulfill, and it revealed the holiness of God in the person of Jesus. Anointing rested in him, not as the bearer of the presence of God, but rather He was God incarnate, reaching a concept of anointing never seen before or after. The passage from John 1:29-34 makes clear reference to Jesus being anointed by God through the Holy Spirit.

Unlike the Old Testament where the anointing was for certain chosen people; in the New Testament, it was available for all believers, and a person was not needed to make the act official. The Holy Spirit was the one who anointed.

The text that speaks clearer about the term in question is found in 1 John 2:18-29. In it, central truths are manifested that reveal the New Testament meaning of the anointing: (1) It's centered on the presence of the Holy Spirit in the lives of believers. (2) The fruit it produces is a discernment of good and evil, a knowledge of truth and falsehood (vv.20-21,27). (3) Anointing may be lasting in the believers (v.27). (4) It teaches us what we should know, precisely in the spiritual order (vv.20,27).

After Pentecost, the Holy Spirit was present in all who accepted Jesus as their Savior and sincerely sought Him. Having the anointing of the Holy Spirit gives divine authority to preach, testify, cast out demons, heal the sick, in short, everything that was done in the book of Acts. Anointing represents the work that the Holy Spirit does through believers.

In the New Testament, we also find that the disciples anointed the sick, and the sick were healed (Mark 6:13). Later, James recommended it in his letter (James 5:14). In the time of Jesus, visitors were often anointed, as a sign that they were guests of honor (Luke 7:46); bodies were also anointed to prepare them for burial (Mark 14:8, 16:1).

3. The term anointing today

Despite the age of the term, the practice and concept of anointing haven't lost their validity; perhaps today we hear it more than before, but on many occasions it's used incorrectly.

Today, anointing has become an ideal for Christians rather than an experience daily lived in the Holy Spirit. Anointing is considered a privilege only for certain people. A very common expression today is: "So and so is anointed." It's a phrase that's distant from the biblical text, because 1 John 2:20 tells us that we're all anointed if we've really been filled with the Holy Spirit. Anointing is a blessing for all believers who consecrate their lives completely to God, seek to be filled with the Spirit, and live a life that reflects holiness. Anointing is reflected in humility, service, passion for the lost, and desire to make Christ known. There is a real danger when a person is used mightily by God but takes pride and doesn't give glory to Who deserves it, the Holy Spirit (1 Corinthians 12).

John the Baptist was someone who knew his place and diminished himself so that Christ would increase. Only people who are truly anointed can do that: put fame, ambitions, and material goods at the feet of the Lord.

Everything miraculous that happens through the believer is because the Holy Spirit was pleased to do it, but that shouldn't be a reason for pride but rather for humility. The church should focus more on seeing the anointing in the Christian by their behavior than by what they can do.

Anointing isn't achieved by human merit or through a renowned evangelist, but is by divine will for all believers (1 Corinthians 12:1-11). Now the question is: Am I anointed, and do I have the presence of the Holy Spirit in my life? Take time to pray.

Review/Application:

These sentences can be completed while you teach the class, or you can ask them to complete it at the end of the lesson. If so, be sure to make the following points clear:

- In the Old Testament the fundamental purpose of the anointing was: **To consecrate, to dedicate a person or thing to God.**

- The anointing was linked to: **The holiness that should be had before God.**

- In the Old Testament, not all people had divine authority **to anoint.**

- **God** granted authority to the person in charge of anointing others.

- In the New Testament, **oil** is seen as a symbol of the Holy Spirit.

- After Pentecost all who confess Jesus Christ as their savior can receive **the Holy Spirit.**

- In Jesus' time on earth, the sick were anointed to be **healed**, visitors were anointed as a sign of welcome, and bodies were anointed to prepare them for burial.

- What was your definition of anointing before the lesson?

- What is your definition of anointing now?

Challenge:

During the week, interview several leaders, asking them what they believe about God's anointing, and in the next class, bring the answers to share with the class.

Words that affirm

Objective: To understand the meaning of the words hallelujah and amen in the light of the Bible.

Memory Verse: "The twenty-four elders and the four living creatures fell down and worshiped God, who was seated on the throne. And they cried: "Amen, Hallelujah!" Revelation 19:4

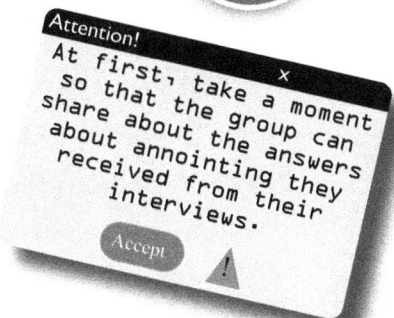

Attention! At first, take a moment so that the group can share about the answers about annointing they received from their interviews.

Accept

Connect | Navigate

Introductory Activity (12-17 years).

- Supplies: A worship song known and commonly sung in church, using the words Hallelujah and Amen.

- Instructions: Sing the selected song together, then ask questions to analyze the song. For example: *Who is this song directed toward? What is the central message? What words are repeated? Would you think of changing them for some other clearer expression? Why? In what other contexts do you use these words?*

Introductory Activity (18-23 years)

- Supplies: Two envelopes with cut out letters. In one envelope place the letters that make up the word "Amen" and in the other envelope the letters that make up the word "Hallelujah." Two sheets of paper, two glue sticks, and two pencils.

- Instructions: Form two groups and give each group an envelope, a sheet of paper, the pencil, and the glue. Ask each group to discover the word that's made from the letters in the envelope and stick them on the sheet and write a definition for it. At the end, each group will give a brief explanation of the definition given.

Connect | Navigate

1. The meaning and use of the word Hallelujah

The word Hallelujah is an exclamation from the Hebrew liturgy which appears in the Psalms and is equivalent to "Praise the Lord."

a. Your grateful people praise you, Hallelujah!

An important part of our praise is gratitude. In the course of our lives, we've experienced different situations, good and bad. If we use Psalm 105 as a parameter, we'll see how God can guide life experiences in our favor. In verses 7 to 24, stormy and uncertain times are summarized for God's people and their leaders, but they served as strength and were tools to see the wonders of God. By being grateful, we can have spiritual eyes that allow us to see divine intervention even in the most difficult moments. Allow time for the group to express why they're grateful to God.

Psalm 105:45 concludes by explaining that for God's children, everything has a purpose. In this case, God wants your past experiences to bring you closer to Him and His Word. The Psalm ends by exclaiming Hallelujah! In this way, the psalmist praised God's name for everything that had happened.

If we're obedient, our whole life will be living praise, not just when we sing or pray. We praise God through radical obedience, recognizing that He is the owner and Lord of our lives.

b. Your redeemed people praise you, Hallelujah!

In Revelation 19:1-6, we read of a cry from heaven, in jubilant praise for the coming of the kingdom of God. In this case it represents a hymn where the heavenly multitude praises God for His just judgment, and for His eternal reign. It's full of celebration and throng (v.1).

In the middle of this celebration, the word Hallelujah appears four times exalting God. This glorious reunion of the church with Christ is announced as "... the marriage of the Lamb..." The church purified by the blood of the Lamb, clothed in fine linen (holiness), will have prepared for this eternal union with Christ (vv.7- 8). Verses 6 through 8 illustrate what it will be like to be in God's presence and heavenly praise: noises, thunder, music, joy, a crowd... Ask: *"Are you ready?"*

2. The meaning and use of the word Amen!

The word "Amen" is a Hebrew word and indicates a strong affirmation or agreement.

a. God's Word confirmed, Amen!

God wants to establish a significant relationship with His children, which entails a pact - union by common agreement and acceptance of His laws. In Deuteronomy 27:14-26, God's people were about to enter the promised land and God stopped them to remind them again of the laws that had been instituted by Him, and exhorted them to complete obedience. God established the laws with His people through His servant Moses, indicating to them that He would seal the acceptance of His laws by saying "Amen" (vv.15-26).

When God speaks, nothing can ever be the same - either we accept His Word or reject it. There will always be a response on our part, and as a result of our response, we're part of a covenant which will mark our present and future.

Every time we say "Amen," we're ratifying a covenant union where we commit ourselves to fulfill our part (obedience), and obedience brings fruit of blessings granted by God, who is faithful to His word. Ask: *"How faithful are you in saying 'Amen' to the word that God has given you?"*

By answering "Amen" to God, we take full responsibility for our commitment. In Jeremiah 11:3-5, God spoke to the prophet reminding that His covenant didn't have an expiration date. That is, from generation to generation, His word doesn't change; and in response to this reminder, the prophet confirmed it with an Amen (v.5).

b. Glory be to God, Amen!

"Amen" appears asserting divine greatness and glory. Romans 1:25 confronts us with the result of having broken the covenant of obedience to God, where man exchanged the glory and image of God for the human image. God doesn't change, it's humans who break the covenant by being unfaithful to God.

In 1 Peter 5:10 we read "... the God of all grace, who called us ...", will save us in affliction, because to Him belongs "... the glory and the empire ..." (5:11). This will be for all eternity what is confirmed at the end of the verse with an "Amen," "So be it; let it be that way; so it shall be" (Adam Clarke's Commentary on 1 Peter).

3. Hallelujah! Amen! These words in the church today

a. Songs

One of the oldest practices of God's people is to musically express worship and praise. Nowadays, worship services which have an important musical content are developed in our churches. Sometimes, we get so focused on the musical level that we forget the content of what we sing. In fact, we use words that lack meaning and expressions that don't convey what God is expecting.

Hallelujah! affirms our intention of exalting God, enhances His greatness, and encourages others to praise Him. Praising God implies our gratitude for His benefits (Psalm 103:1-2).

When we sing amen, it has a broad meaning since we affirm in this way that what we're singing is true in our lives.

b. Prayers

As children (physically or spiritually), we're taught a formal form of prayer, which changes as our relationship with God grows. What generally doesn't change is the closing of the sentence saying Amen! It's evident that we would never contradict ourselves, expressing disbelief at our words. Not saying "amen" would be the same as saying, "Lord, I know you can't do what I ask you to do" or perhaps "Lord, don't believe what I told you before."

One essential ingredient in our prayer is "Hallelujah" (praising God) and the other is "Amen" (reaffirming what we've said and committing ourselves to it).

Review/Application:

Allow time for the students to review the passages studied and fill in the blanks.

1. Psalm 105:45
   - God's purpose for his children is *(Follow his laws and keep his statutes)*
   - Hallelujah! Here encourages to praise God How? *(in obedience)*

2. Psalm 106:1
   - The imperative sense (order) of Hallelujah here is because *(He is good)* Because his love *(endures forever)*

3. Deuteronomy 27:26
   - The Amen of the people of God means *(Commitment to obedience)*

4. Jeremiah 11:5
   - When the prophet said Amen! He confirmed that he was *(True – Faithful)*

5. Romans 1:25
   - According to this passage, when we break the pact of obedience to God, we change *(The truth of God for the lie).*

6. 1 Peter 5:10-11
   - With the Amen! from verse 11, we affirm that *(His glory is eternal)*

Check to see if the group fully understands the meaning of the words hallelujah and amen in the light of the Bible. Point out ways they can develop a deeper relationship with Christ.

Challenge:

This week try to record in writing your expressions of praise to God: In what ways do you praise God, what words do you use and how do these relate to what you've learned in this lesson? Exercise yourself in your spiritual disciplines; start a spiritual journal that records your daily encounters and pacts with God.

The God of covenant

Tabita González y David González • USA

Objective: To understand the meaning of the word covenant and its importance in their relationship with God.

Memory Verse: "This is the covenant I will make with the people of Israel after that time, declares the Lord. I will put my law in their minds and write it on their hearts. I will be their God, and they will be my people." Jeremiah 31:33

Attention!

Before starting the lesson, dedicate a few minutes to help the group see the importance of developing a deeper relationship with Christ.

Accept

Connect / Navigate

Introductory Activity (12-17 years).

- Supplies: Blue and yellow balloons, yarn, scarves, a blank sheet of paper, and pencil or pen.

- Instructions: Form two groups, one will be the yellow team and the other the blue team. Distribute two balloons of the group's color to each person and ask them to tie one on each hand and cover their eyes with the scarf. Give the signal for the battle to begin, The battle will consist of bursting as many of the opposing team's balloons in two minutes. The team that pops the most balloons will win and must draw up a cease-of-war pact (use the blank sheet of paper). In the pact, it should be clear that the winning team agrees not to attack the losing team any more, but in return, the losing team must comply with the conditions that it establishes. A representative from each team will sign the agreement.

  In some cases, as in war, one of the parties involved takes advantage of the other. In the particular case of divine covenants, God sought the benefit of His children.

Introductory Activity (18-23 years).

- Supplies: Candy, leaves and pencils.

- Instructions: Divide into two groups, women and men. Ask the following question: *When a couple marries, what are the promises or vows they make to each other?*

  The activity is for each team to make a list of wedding promises/vows in two minutes, seeking to be as original and creative as possible. The team with the longest and most creative list wins.

  When time is up, each team will read the vows they wrote. Give the winning team a prize.

Connect / Navigate

The word "covenant" sounds a bit formal to us, and we don't normally use it. We generally hear it in reference to the agreements that one nation signs with another or governments with others of similar importance. In other cases, we've heard it in a negative way, for example, when one talks about people who make a pact or covenant with the devil. Whatever the context used, we don't think of covenant as something that's part of our life. But when analyzing the meaning of this word, also known as an alliance or agreement, we'll see that in our day-to-day lives, we live according to many covenants to which we're bound.

A covenant is an agreement between two or more people that requires a reciprocity of benefits and obligations, the breaking of which normally generates negative consequences. More often than we think, we make covenants with the people around us.

Of all the covenants that we know of, perhaps some of the clearest examples are the marriage covenant, the citizenship covenants through which we have the obligation to obey the laws of the country, pacts between friends, with educational centers, etc. Ask about the types of covenants the group members acknowledge having in their lives (as students, members of a church, between friends, etc.).

1. God established covenants with humans

Throughout history, we see that God established covenants that always sought the good of humanity and that involved a personal relationship with Him - a relationship of obedience and blessing.

Read Jeremiah 31:31-33. Then talk with the group about phrases or ideas that draw their attention in the text you read. Write what group members say on the board for reference.

The text for this session speaks of a new covenant that God would establish with human beings. To understand this new covenant, we have to look back a bit. Since Genesis, God has established covenants with humans. With Adam as the representative of all humanity, God began by establishing a covenant of obedience and the reward of life (Genesis 2:17), but that covenant was broken and death reached the heart and life of humans. As we can see, it wasn't God who broke the covenant, but people. However, and despite the decision made by Adam and Eve, God continued firm in His commitment to bless humanity. For this reason, He provided ways to reestablish the broken relationship (Genesis 3:15). A little later in the book of Genesis, we see that God established a covenant with Noah (Genesis 6:18) to save his family and thus preserve mankind. As in the first covenant, faith and obedience were key. Noah would have to keep his faith in God for the promises to be fulfilled. At the end of the flood, Noah, his family, and the animals were able to be saved. There, God made another covenant with Noah and sealed it with a visible sign called a rainbow. God promised never to destroy living things again through another worldwide flood (Genesis 9:11).

Later in history, God established a covenant with Abraham. In this covenant, where faith and obedience were also key, God promised Abraham a descendant, the possession of a land, and the reconciliation of people with God. The sign of this covenant was male circumcision (Genesis 17:10).

Many years later, God confirmed this covenant with the nation of Israel, liberating them from Egypt through Moses and gave the people the tablets of the Law. For the first time, human beings would have a covenant written by God himself. The same covenant continued in progression and was renewed with David, to whom God promised that from his descendants, the Savior, promised to Israel and to all humanity, would be born.

2. Passing to new covenant

This original covenant and the progression of covenants that followed, were interrupted again and again. This helps us understand that God doesn't force us but wants the agreement of the people involved. Sadly, once the first covenant was broken, the sinful nature of mankind led them to break covenant after covenant. But God's grace and love for humanity made possible a new and better covenant, a covenant of redemption that nothing could break and that would be sealed in people's hearts (Hebrews 8:8-13).

However, it was necessary to prepare mankind, and that's why God chose a people and established a progression of covenants. These covenants were intended to reconcile people with God. But an internal action would be necessary so that people would change their behavior. One of the characteristics of the old covenant was an endless system of sacrifices and offerings so that people could be reconciled with God. But in the new covenant, it wouldn't depend on the repetition of sacrifices. The new covenant would offer complete forgiveness based on the unique sacrifice of Jesus Christ. The very Son of God, the promised Messiah, announced by the prophets, would make it possible for us to have communion with the Father, without mediators or the need for continuous animal sacrifices (1 Timothy 2:5).

3. The new covenant

By studying each of the covenants that God has made with people, we find a common element: God's love. God loves us, and the purpose of his covenant is to allow us to relate to Him as His children (1 John 3:1).

In the new covenant, it's no longer necessary to shed the blood of animals for the forgiveness of sins because Christ, the perfect Lamb, shed His blood once and for all (Hebrews 9:13-14). God seals His promise of salvation and eternal life, giving the Holy Spirit to dwell in our hearts, guide us into all truth, and work in our lives so that we become more and more like Christ. He wants to make a covenant with each person, but everyone must recognize that they're a sinner and repent of their sins. The new covenant offers complete forgiveness based on the shedding of the blood of Jesus Christ, who reconciles us with the Father, and through this reconciliation, we have the opportunity to know Him personally. May God work in our hearts as He wants, may we love Him with all our being and be obedient to the rules that help us maintain a dynamic relationship with Him. The reward? Eternal life with God!

Review/Application:

- What is the difference between the old covenant and the new covenant?

- Think about and write why you think a new covenant was needed, in which Jesus' sacrifice was a vital part.

- Read the following Bible passages and find the names of some people who made a covenant with God, write the corresponding name, and briefly describe what the covenant they had with God consisted of:
  ◊ Genesis 2:15-17
  ◊ Genesis 8:20-22, 9:11-13
  ◊ Genesis 12:1-3
  ◊ Genesis 26:1-5
  ◊ Exodus 19:3-6
  ◊ 1 Samuel 1:9-11
  ◊ John 3:16

Guide the group to a deeper commitment and effort to complete their side of the covenant. Be sure they understand the meaning of the word covenant and its importance in their relationship with God.

Challenge:

We enjoy the blessings of the new covenant through the sacrifice of Jesus. God offers you eternal life with Him. What are you willing to offer?

Write a list of five specific things you need to give to God, but you've been struggling to do so, but today you're willing to give them to Him. Think about this during the week and share in the next class how it went if you feel comfortable.

God's Presence

Objective: To understand the meaning of the presence of God in the light of the Bible.

Memory Verse: "You make known to me the path of life; you will fill me with joy in your presence, with eternal pleasures at your right hand." Psalm 16:11

Attention! Give time for students who want to talk about the five specific things they gave to God after the last class. Accept

Connect | Navigate

Introductory Activity (12-17 years).

- Supplies: Tools used in a particular trade, for example, carpenter: A hammer, a handsaw, etc. A box or bag where tools can be placed so that they aren't seen.

- Directions: Divide into two groups. Ask one person to go out of the room and hand him/ her the box or bag with the tools. Then ask the person to come in and tell the groups to guess the person's trade. Each group will be shown one tool per turn, the first group to guess the profession wins.

  Say: "Just as tools reveal someone's trade, the fruit of the Spirit reveals the presence of God in the life of the believer."

Introductory Activity (18-23 years).

- Supplies: Posters that say: The presence of God makes me dance, the presence of God makes me sing, the presence of God makes me fall. Write different actions that denote the presence of God, be sure to make a sign that says: The presence of God makes me change. The more posters you have, the better.

- Instructions: Fill the entire room with posters and allow each person to decide on just one, and explain why they chose that option.

  Lead them to reflect, that although in all options God can manifest Himself, because He is sovereign. The first thing that God does and He continues to do in the life of every believer is to transform and change us.

Connect | Navigate

1. The presence of God in the Old Testament

The presence of God has been evident to humans since creation to the present day. Although He is the same God, worshiped by the people of Israel and the church today, His manifestation to humans has not always been the same.

In Genesis 1 and 2, the presence of God is highlighted in a visible and audible way for the person who interacted with God in a direct way. Later, in the patriarchal age until Joseph, men like Abraham, Isaac, and Jacob received direct communication from God (Genesis 3-50). God's presence was audible, phrases like "the Lord appeared to..." are common (Genesis 12:7; 17:1; 26:2). God manifested Himself to give instructions and promises, to commission and make His will known to His people.

In Exodus, God manifested His presence by speaking through inanimate objects like a bush (Exodus 3:2-7) and sending plagues before Pharaoh (Exodus 7:14-11:10). This was a stage where miracles of all kinds abounded, and the people recognized the great power of God.

On the journey through the desert, His presence became visible with a pillar of cloud during the day and of fire at night (Exodus 13:21-22). The manifestation of God in the tabernacle through the priests in the most holy place was extremely important. Then, there was the ark of the covenant, signifying God's presence with them (Exodus 25:22).

In the time of the judges and the prophets, God manifested His presence through chosen servants such as: Othniel, Deborah, Gideon, Samuel, Elijah, and Elisha. Appearances by theophanies or the angel of Yahweh were common during this time (Judges 13:3). The experience of Elijah recorded in 1 Kings 19:1-18 is vital in illustrating the practical meaning of God's presence.

In the times of the Monarchs and even the pre-exilic prophets, the presence of God was reflected in the temple and limited to the nation of Israel. The temple played an important role in the Jewish community, it was given a central place in the worship of God and the manifestation of Him. Although the priesthood existed, the prophets were regarded as the mouthpiece of God. God's presence was contained in His Word, which was aimed at producing change in people. It often was a word of judgment; it didn't make the person feel good but rather tried to persuade them to repentance, to change their behavior. In the times of the prophets, the presence of God manifested in the same way.

The exile was a difficult period for Israel because they no longer had a temple. This was a time that served to renew concepts about the presence of God. They understood that God was not limited to Israel. They were able to experience God's presence in a foreign nation. A new form of Judaism began, where the temple was replaced by the synagogue. In this time period of the exile, God manifested Himself through visions that the prophets had. Many of them had apocalyptic content pointing to the future restoration of the people of Israel (Lamentations, Daniel, etc.).

In the post-exilic stage, the temple was rebuilt and it became again the place where God poured out His presence, where the people heard the voice of God.

Throughout the Old Testament the Holy Spirit came and went, was not continually present with the people, but performed certain functions.

2. The presence of God in the New Testament

In the New Testament period, God's presence was made tangible through the coming of His Son into the world. The Gospels bear witness to His life (Matthew, Mark, Luke and John). God became incarnate in the person of Jesus and dwelt among men - He was a real and direct presence. After the ascension of Jesus, (Mark, 16:19-20, Luke 24:50-53) the presence of God was manifested through the Holy Spirit which continues to this day.

The book of Acts contains a large number of stories that show how God revealed Himself through the Third Person of the Trinity. The Jews were able to experience the presence of God in a different way as well as the Gentiles, as happened at Pentecost (Acts 2). It was a time when miracles abounded, people were perplexed by the wonders of God, since the mere presence of God produced repentance and genuine change in their lives. In Peter's first sermon, about three thousand people were converted to the Lord (Acts 2:41).

The presence of God, more than making people happy, produced changes. Rather than leaving them alone, He stirred in them and commissioned them to preach the gospel. In the time that the book of Acts was written, God's presence was not limited to the people of Israel or to special places. In Paul's letters, a very revolutionary thought is seen: He refers to the body as a temple of the Holy Spirit since God doesn't dwell in temples but in the person. The apostle wrestled with Jewish concepts about the manifestation of God in the temple (1 Corinthians 6:19-20). In the New Testament, the presence of God is manifested through the Holy Spirit in people's hearts.

3. The presence of God for us today

The presence of God in the church today is understood in various ways. When we refer to the presence of God, we're not talking about the manifestation of God in a place, at a time, with one or several specific people; but we're referring to the real experience that's reflected in the life of each Christian.

Some churches have fallen into emotionalism, lowering the presence of God to what you feel in a worship service and not in consecrated lives separated from sin.

Many believers claim to be "touched by God" during a church service, but their way of behaving at home, at work, and in their relational life with others doesn't reflect that presence of God. There are many churches currently that try to touch people's emotions to simulate the presence of God. Their purpose is to make the believer feel good inside the church, but that doesn't produce spiritual changes and remains only a mere emotion.

As human beings, we dislike confrontation; we're afraid of change; but when God is present, He confronts our life of sin and changes everything that hinders our relationship with Him. That's why the presence of God, more than excites us, revolutionizes our life. Its impact goes beyond a moment. Those believers who live in His presence reflect the fruit of the Spirit in their life (Galatians 5:22-23). Having the presence of God doesn't give us pride or arrogance. On the contrary, it makes us humble because when we look at God, we feel infinitely small; and when we look at our brothers and sisters in Christ, we esteem them as superior to ourselves (Philippians 2:3).

Although it's good to talk about the ways in which God has made Himself known to people throughout history, the most important thing is to ask ourselves: "Do I really feel the presence of God in my life? Do I know God because I have been taught about Him, because it's something beautiful, or because I have really entered into His presence and His presence is continuous in my life?" The answers to these questions will define many things for us. It's time that we stop talking about the experiences that others have had and start talking about our own, which are the result of a relationship with God. Let us remember what the psalmist said: "... In His presence there's fullness of joy ..." (Psalm 16:11).

Review/Application:

Ask the students to answer and complete the following questions:

1. Make a list of the ways God manifested his presence in the Old Testament. *Some forms were visible, direct, and audible through angels in the temple.*

2. Ask him to write in what ways God manifested his presence in the New Testament. *God manifested his presence in the coming of Christ into the world, the coming of the Holy Spirit, in genuine changes in people, repentance and miracles.*

3. Why is the presence of God not just emotionalism? *Because emotionalism is temporary.*

4. Explain how the presence of God is manifested in the life of the believer. *It manifests itself in change of life, repentance and the fruit of the Holy Spirit.*

5. Is your desire to enjoy the presence of God in your life? Why?

Challenge:

Seek more earnestly the presence of God in the coming week. In the next class, discuss what God is doing in your life.

What will you offer?

Attention!
Ask for testimonies from the group members who are living closer to God and having a more intimate relationship with Him.
Accept

Objective: To understand the significance of an offering in light of the Bible.

Memory Verse: "Remember this: Whoever sows sparingly will also reap sparingly, and whoever sows generously will also reap generously. Each of you should give what you have decided in your heart to give, not reluctantly or under compulsion, for God loves a cheerful giver." 2 Corinthians 9:6-7

Connect / Navigate

Introductory Activity (12-17 years).

- Supplies: Cans or small boxes, glue, papers of different colors and textures, and markers.

- Directions: Encourage the group members to make a personal offering box. After decorating them to their liking, ask them what an offering box is for.

   Then talk with them about how we use money, what we invest in, and how much we set aside for God from everything we gain.

   Encourage the group that after studying the lesson, they can have this offering box to set aside their weekly offerings to God.

Introductory Activity (18-23 years).

- Supplies: Sheet of paper, pencils, calculators.

- Directions: Give each person a sheet of paper and ask each one to make three columns. One column for "income," another column for "expenses" and the last one for "balance."

   Encourage the group to write on the sheet (privately) their personal budget. At this age, most young adults work or manage their own money. Once each one of them has written the income they have, the fixed expenses and the balance, lead them to reflect on the needs that arise in each one. Then ask how many on their expenses list put God/tithe/offerings.

Connect / Navigate

A Dictionary of the Bible & Christian Doctrine in Everyday English (Eby, et al, 2004) notes:

An offering is a gift given as an act of worship to God. Offerings in the Old Testament were sacrifices given to the priests in the temple. These could be animals, doves, grain or other gifts.

- There were many kinds of offerings in the worship of Israel. Some offerings were to show that the givers were sorry for their transgressions. Other offerings were to show that they had given themselves to God completely. Others were to give thanks for all that God had done for His people.

- The prophets warned the people of Israel that God didn't want only offerings. He wanted His people truly to love, obey and serve Him.

- Jesus Christ gave Himself as an offering to God to provide salvation for everyone (Romans 3:21-26; Galatians 2:19-20; Philippians 2:5-11 and Hebrews 10:5-18).

- Believers should offer themselves as "living sacrifices" to God (Romans 12:1-2). They do this by giving themselves completely to Him and living for Him.

- Obedience to God in daily living is the offering that pleases Him most (Romans 15:15-19). This obedience includes giving money to help support the preaching of the Gospel (Philippians 4:14-18). Offerings today usually refer to such gifts of money.

(Genesis 4:3-5; Exodus 24:5; 25:2; 35:22; Leviticus 1:2-14; Nehemiah 10:37; 13:5 and Malachi 3:8)

1. Offerings in the Old Testament

The first biblical mention of "offering" is in Genesis 4:3-4, where the children of Adam and Eve voluntarily offered the fruit of their labor to God.

From this story, we can extract that the detail of Cain's offering doesn't give any indication of being something special, only a formality of "complying" with God. However, verse 4 details that Abel's offering was "of the best," the first-born and the fattest of his animals, which God looked upon with pleasure. God was not surprised by Abel's offering, but by his generous heart and his faith in giving. For this reason, in the book of Hebrews 11:4, he is mentioned among the heroes of the faith.

God doesn't need our offering; what He seeks is that when we give, we have an attitude of gratitude and recognition that everything is His (1 Chronicles 29:14).

There are terms linked to offering in the Old Testament; the offering itself was not an independent practice, but part of a ceremony instituted by God.

Old Testament worshippers offered sacrifices. These were practices carried out in numerous people groups from very remote times. Many sacrificed animals, although some performed human sacrifices.

God's plan of salvation was instituted from the moment man sinned. Leviticus 1-5 gives a very detailed description of the forms of sacrifice offered to God for purification and forgiveness of sins. The priest was in charge of receiving the offerings of the people, according to the forms instituted by God. Whether they were animals or fruits of the field, they had to be according to the characteristics indicated (Example: Leviticus 1:1-3).

God indicated to the people that it was necessary to seek God's forgiveness through a sacrificial act. Later, it would be His own Son Jesus Christ who would give Himself once and for all for us, granting forgiveness of sins (John 3:16).

Another term used for the offering is a grain (food) offering. This, unlike sacrifice, refers to the idea of a gift made to Yahweh, given as an offering. The grain offerings instituted in the law of Moses are: Offering of fine flour (Leviticus 2:1-4); a pouring of wine (Leviticus 23:13); first fruits of the crops (Leviticus 23:10).

It's a fact that the Lord pours out His blessings in response to consecration (Malachi 3:7-10). The offerings and sacrifices that Israel was to offer pointed to the fact that they belonged to God. Believers today must remember this fact and recognize that everything they have has been given to them by God. Thus, they'll have a powerful motive to honor God with all their resources and possessions. An accurate statement is that even more important than the method of giving is why we're giving.

2. Offerings in the New Testament

A. Offerings to God

In Mark 12:41-44, we can see the act of formal offering in the temple. There were different areas in the temple. The situation related in this passage takes place in the so-called "Court of the women" where thirteen trumpet-shaped boxes were found called "the trumpets." These were designed to receive the offerings and were where contributors declared the amount of their donation and purpose. Jesus was present at this scene, watching the crowd and their offerings.

While many gave large offerings, a widow gave two of the smallest coins of money available (two copper coins). On this occasion, Jesus downplayed the big offerings of the rich, recognizing that it isn't the amount we give that impacts God, but the attitude of the heart. The genuine offering for God implies sacrifice, not what is left over, but what actually costs something, and implies not keeping anything for ourselves, but making a total surrender. This way of giving creates a greater dependence on God.

An offering must be a voluntary act that one offers in the form of thanks, recognition and worship to God. We don't move God with these acts, but He seeks those who worship in spirit and in truth (John 4:24). True worshipers give their best because they do it from the heart and for God, not to be seen by others.

B. Offerings to the saints

In 1 Corinthians 16:1, the apostle Paul distinguishes this type of offering from the others previously taught, and here it refers to a special collection. No amount or percentage is mentioned; it was only indicated that it would be according to how God had given to each one.

We won't focus on the administration or details by the Apostle Paul. These indications of verse 2 were due to a strategy that facilitated the end, according to the income of each one. The important thing here is once again the attitude of the heart of the giver, this time thinking of the brothers and sisters in the faith who would be recipients of this gift who were going through a difficult time.

As important as giving is, so is the good administration of the gifts collected. Verse 4 indicates the responsibility that they needed to have so that the offerings arrived to the recipient and the initial purpose was fulfilled.

3. Offerings today

God presents himself as someone who doesn't need our money or material goods, but someone who expects to see our attitude of gratitude and dependence. God wants to see us surrendered to Him, recognizing that He is the giver of all things. God longs for us to offer our whole lives, all that we are and have, into His hands.

Currently, there's a saying of sowing and reaping that refers to the offerings and what we receive from the Lord, respectively. Giving isn't an investment or a business deal that we make with God. We shouldn't think of an offering as an exchange where we give to God to receive the benefits from Him in return. This isn't so. God, in His great mercy, gives us everything we need, knowing what the right measure is (Proverbs 30:8-9). We must offer without expecting anything in return since God gave us salvation through His Son. What more can we ask for?

But the wonderful thing is that God isn't in debt to anyone. The more we give, the more we see God's mercy, like the widow experienced with the prophet Elijah (1 Kings 17:8-16). When she gave, she never lacked food in her home again.

What do you have in your hands to give to God? When we give (sow) for the kingdom of God, we're extending God's compassion to people, who in turn may be drawn to His gift of salvation as a result of what we have offered (Matthew 6:19-21).

Review/Application:

Allow time for the students to answer the following questions personally:

* What does God expect of his children when they give? **The offering must be a voluntary act that one offers in the form of thanks, recognition and adoration to God.**

* Why offerings?

* What does the account in Mark 12:41-44 teach you? **Jesus minimized the large offerings of the rich, recognizing that it is not the amount we give that impacts God, but the attitude of the heart.**

* What are your current giving practices?

* Do you think you need to change something after what you studied today?

Find out if the group understands the significance of an offering in light of the Bible. Help the group to be thankful for all their blessings and to give with joy.

Challenge:

Think this week about setting aside a voluntary percentage of the money you manage for your offerings. When you give your offerings in the worship service, remember everything that God did to save you, and give it with joy as an act of worship to the one who gave everything for you.

The gift of God

Objective: To understand the significance of grace in light of the Bible.

Memory Verse: "But you offer forgiveness, that we might learn to fear you." Psalm 130:4b (NLT)

Attention!
Start the session by asking for volunteers who want to share their experience of giving an offering as an act of thanksgiving.

Accept

Connect | Navigate

Introductory Activity (12-17 years).

- Supplies: Pencils and a "magic box" template for each person.

- Instructions: Distribute the "magic box" templates and pencils to the group members and give them instructions to solve it and as soon as they ask for help, offer it to them.

  Help them out if they ask for it.

Magic box template:

Magic Box

Magic Box

8	1	6
3	5	7
4	9	2

The "magic box" should be filled in as follows:

1. They should write the numbers from 1 to 9, without repeating numbers, in the "magic box".

2. Each line of the table (the horizontals, the verticals and even the diagonals) should equal 15, when adding the three digits.

There isn't only one right way to solve the puzzle; but one key is that at the center of this box should be the number 5 (It's in the middle of the requested numbers and, therefore, the one that causes 'balance' in the box.)

Sometimes, God wants to accomplish something through us, and we think we can't. But it doesn't occur to us to ask Him for help.

Introductory Activity (18-23 years).

- Supplies: Pencils and a number puzzle template.

- Instructions: Distribute the number puzzles and pencils to the group, and give them directions to solve the puzzles. Only help those who ask you for it.

  If someone finishes before everyone else, let them help others if they ask for it.

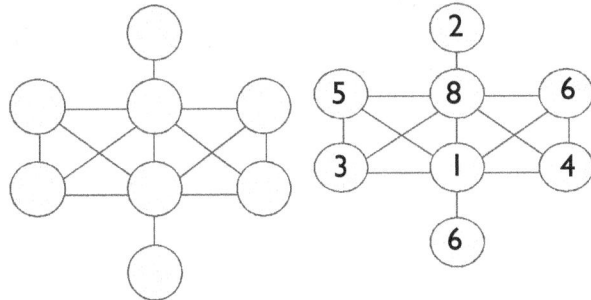

The number puzzle should be filled in as follows:

1. They should write the numbers from 1 to 8 in the circles, without repeating any.

2. The numbers shouldn't "connect" with others that precede or follow them (5 cannot "connect" with 4 or 6).

3. The winner is whoever can distribute all the numbers without getting "stuck".

There isn't only one way to solve the puzzle, but one key is that in the two circles in the center must be the number 1 (which is the only one that has no antecedent number) and the number eight (which is the only one that doesn't have a consequent number in this exercise).

Sometimes things that seem difficult aren't difficult with God's help.

Connect | Navigate

How many stories do we read in the Bible about people who accomplished the impossible?

King David (2 Samuel 11-12), who being chosen by God to rule, committed the sin of adultery; yet when he asked for forgiveness, God granted it (Psalm 51).

Rahab was a prostitute and she saved her life and that of her family because she asked the people of Israel for help (Joshua 2).

Sometimes things seem difficult in the beginning, but we can achieve them with help from God. In these stories, we saw these people accomplish the impossible because they asked for help.

1. Divine grace

God is love. That means He's always willing to hear our prayers, and every time we call upon Him, He responds (Psalm 37:5).

The Bible states that God forgives us every time we ask Him for forgiveness with all our hearts. And that action of God, that wonderful act of divine justice of "giving us what we don't deserve," we call grace; and grace is a gift.

Furthermore, we believe there's a journey of grace. We believe in the saving grace of God that He will never deny us His forgiveness and deliverance if we honestly cry out to Him. However, we see that God's grace comes to us even before we seek it. In His great love, God seeks us. Did you ever notice before you became a Christian that God kept you from something bad?

When we come to know God and enter into a relationship with Him, His grace continues to manifest itself in our life, and in all of our affairs, the simple and the complex, the ordinary and the extraordinary, the permanent and the circumstantial. The grace of God is being manifested in our daily activities (in housework, on the way to work, when we eat or sleep) and in those unusual matters when we don't know why something happens. By God's grace, we mature as Christians. God's grace helps us come to a place of full surrender to Him, so He can entirely sanctify us.

2. Real stories of divine grace

(The names of the people are changed, but the stories are real.)

"Mike had been a rebellious young man. From the time he was a child, he knew that Jesus loved him. One morning, after leaving a party where he drank a lot of alcohol, he crashed his car. The car was rendered useless and he was on the verge of death. In the hospital, he remembers that he silently said a very simple prayer: "Lord Jesus, forgive my sins and deliver me from death." That was it.

Within a few days Mike was healed. Upon leaving the hospital, his relatives told him that the doctors were amazed by the incredible miracle that had happened. But he, calmly and sincerely, for the first time in his life, opened his heart and said: "This was not an incredible miracle; it's only God's answer to the prayer of my heart."

"When Pamela saw the results of the medical studies that had been carried out three months before, she couldn't resist anymore: She bowed her head, burst into tears and the only thing that occurred to her was to say to God: "If you heal me from this disease, I will dedicate my life to serving you." She had visited three clinics, and all three gave her the same result: HIV positive. It isn't worth delving into the cause of her illness, suffice it to say that she was a promiscuous woman.

But an honest prayer from her heart was enough for God. And today, just a few years after everything that happened, she preaches the gospel of Jesus Christ inside and outside of her community, wearing a smile on her face and the three certificates from the same medical clinics, only now with the diagnosis: HIV negative".

God's grace is the response of His love to us, in spite of our imperfections, our sins. He loves us. We don't have any credentials to make us righteous before Him, but He loves us. We don't have a perfect record or great qualities, but He loves us (Psalm 130:3-4).

3. We're instruments of divine grace

Jesus manifested the grace of God the Father throughout His life. That grace is with us, and God calls us to be His instruments. But do we manifest the grace of God in our life? Do we forgive people even when they don't deserve forgiveness? Do we restore a sinful person or do we condemn them?

God's Word is always challenging our comfort, both in daily life and in our ministries in the church. Are we people who imitate Christ, sharing God's grace in forgiveness and restoration? Are we sharing our journey of grace with others?

One way to know if we're manifesting the grace of God in our congregation is by reviewing our church activities. Do we have ministries to those in need in our society, those who most need the wonderful grace of God, or do we cater to our church members who already know and live in that grace? Do we have a system to win other young people to Christ, or do we have services and meetings just for those who already attend church? One of our responsibilities as Christians is to "give what we've received from the Lord" (Matthew 10:8b). Why deprive people of that "amazing grace" that continues to seek to save sinners?

Let's be encouraged to be instruments of God's grace! Let's enjoy that grace and strive to live it, sharing it with all the people around us!

Review/Application:

Ask them to briefly write down the most important moment in their life when they clearly saw the grace of God.

Then tell them to draw two pictures: one that shows what they were before, and one that shows what they are now by the grace of God, and share their pictures with the class and explain them.

End with a prayer of thanks for the grace of God in their lives and invite them to commit to living and sharing that grace with all who need it.

Challenge:

Take some time this week to write down those times in your life when you palpably noticed the grace of God. Then think about what might have happened if you had not decided for Christ. Thank God for all that He has given you by His grace.

God bless you!

Objective: To understand the meaning of the term "blessing" in light of the Bible.

Memory Verse: "I will make you into a great nation, and I will bless you; I will make your name great, and you will be a blessing." Genesis 12:2

Attention!
Ask if anyone will share about the times in their life when God's grace was very real to them, and the difference that made.
Accept

Connect | Navigate

Introductory Activity (12-17 years).

- Supplies: Sheets of paper, pens, pencils, whiteboard, and markers.

- Instructions: Divide the group into three. Give each group a sheet of paper and a pen, and choose a secretary to take notes.

  Ask the group to list all the words they know related to the word "blessing," whether by verb conjugation, by family of words, or by their meaning.

  After the group work is finished, the secretaries will share the list of words and write a new list on the board without repeating any words. The teacher can use the results as an introduction to the lesson.

Introductory Activity (18-23 years).

- Supplies: White board or sheet of paper, markers.

- Directions: Encourage discussion by asking the following questions:

  ◊ Is the word "blessing" a familiar term?

  ◊ When do we use it?

  ◊ How can you define the action of "blessing"?

  After discussing this, divide the group into three teams (depending on the number of people you can form more or fewer teams). Ask each group to come up with a definition of the word "blessing."

  When finished, copy or stick the definitions of each team on the board and use this as initial content to address the lessons topic.

Connect | Navigate

The word blessing appears in the Bible from the beginning in the form of an action on the behalf of God, with which He seals His creation in a special way. If we look at Genesis 1:22, 28 and 2:3, we can find that God blessed all living beings and also blessed the day that He designated for rest.

In all cases, it's God who grants blessing (or special grace) to others, and in this way, the person is positively affected as a result of this divine action. When some things or some people are blessed by God, they have the possibility to bless others. Ultimately, we're "blessed to bless."

1. Blessing in the Old Testament

In all cases, God shows Himself to be a just God, who desires well-being for His creation and wants to bless humanity (Proverbs 10:22).

A. A blessed people

Genesis 12 recounts the beginnings of a people that God separated through a man named Abraham, son of Terah, who lived in Ur of the Chaldeans, a place given to idolatry (Joshua 24:2-3). In this context, God called Abraham with a definite purpose, to form through him a great nation, a people chosen by God. They were called the "people of God." God sent Abraham to other lands to test his obedience and turn him away from idolatry (Genesis 12:1). God promised Abraham a great family and blessing. This was a special grace, a prosperous favor, a promise of permanent protection and assistance in response to his faith (Genesis 12:2a). In this blessing, God promised that Abraham would be a blessing to others (Genesis 12:2b). God's blessing promised to extend for generations (Genesis 12:3).

B. A promised blessing

Over the years, the promise of a great family for Abraham was fulfilled and that family became the people of Israel. After the passage of many generations, going through various stages such as slavery, the pilgrimage through the desert and the arrival in the promised land, the people of God knew the importance of obedience. God was clear with them and gave them strict laws (for example, the Ten Commandments) so that they would turn away from evil and be blessed. God's blessing had not changed, God was still the same, but the people weren't like Abraham, obedient and full of faith in God.

Deuteronomy 28:1-14 presents a list that God gave to His people, renewing His promise of blessing as a result of obedience. For this the people had to do the following: Know the Word of God, Obey the Word of God, Not have any other gods (vv.1, 9, 14).

God was going to bless them (vv.1-14) as a nation and as a city (vv.1-3):

- To His descendants and general economy (vv. 4-5, 8, 11-12).
- In their daily activities (v.6).
- He would free them from those who wanted to harm them (v.7).
- Others would respect them (v.10).
- They would have spiritual authority (v.13).

In these verses, all areas of our lives are represented. *Can you see God's blessing in your life? In what areas? Do you feel that you're not enjoying this blessing? What could you do about it?*

C. Blessing vs. curse

Remaining with divine blessing, we feel so comfortable that we forget that there are also consequences for disobedience. Curse is a word that we don't like, but in Deuteronomy 28:15, we find God's justice over sin as well. People always demand a blessing, but forget their part in this agreement.

Psalm 62:4 demonstrates how human passions can lead us to lose the integrity of our heart. Blessing can just be another word in our vocabulary if it isn't accompanied by a right heart in the eyes of God. Once again, God confronts us with ourselves. Blessings carry a weight of glory, as long as the Holy Spirit dwells in our lives.

2. The concept of blessing in the New Testament

The concept of blessing is the same throughout the Bible—a God full of love and mercy who wants to favor His children, seeking to strengthen His personal relationship with them.

The repeated disobedience of his chosen people led God to renew His covenants with them. But they again and again failed Him by breaking the covenant, sinning, and straying from His ways. The question is: Has the blessing of God ended? No! But a new time of hope for all has arrived, the fulfillment of the promise of eternal salvation.

A. The blessing extends

Galatians 3:13-14 tells us that God, through His Son, removed the consequence of sin from us. The blessing that God promised remains effective and contextual. In Jesus Christ, the blessing given to Abraham extends to us. God's blessing expands and recreates in the person of the Holy Spirit and is a promise for those who believe.

B. A spiritual blessing

In Ephesians 1:3, the apostle Paul emphasized interesting aspects of the blessing. First of all, we bless God. The Greek term "eulogetos" "is a compound word composed of "eu," which means "well," and "logetos," which means "speaking". Literally, the Greek word carries the idea of "speaking well". What Paul was saying is: "We praise God, we say good words about Him." Only God "is worthy of being blessed because He is genuine and constant in character and action"(Beacon Biblical Commentary, Volume 9. Beacon Hill Press of Kansas City, 1969).

Secondly, we receive blessing from God, He has "blessed us with all spiritual blessings." God always wants to bless us, He wants to give us all His blessing. We're the ones who limit God's spiritual blessings in our lives when we're not obedient or lack faith. We shouldn't limit ourselves to material things, because the greatest blessing given by God is salvation.

Third, Paul mentions that the blessing received from God comes from the heavenly places. It certainly elevates us to another level, a Kingdom that draws closer to humanity through Jesus Christ Himself—a place where we, who have been saved by faith in Jesus Christ, belong.

3. The concept of blessing today

Is "God bless you" a catchphrase that we use randomly or a phrase with the weight of glory? It's common today to hear the expression "God bless you" in different areas. Before it was almost exclusive to Christians, but today it's popular in use. It gives the impression that we get along well with the person by saying this. Ask: *"Do you think this is a phrase to take lightly?"* We must remember that we cannot give something that we don't have. How much spiritual blessing is there in you? Has the Lord blessed you with all His spiritual blessing? It's time to receive God's blessing with faith and obedience; it's time to bless others and share God's grace. We do it by word and action. We're blessed to be a blessing, just like Abraham.

Review/Application:

Allow time for the students to fill in the blanks (here in italics).

1. **Abraham's** selection was for the purpose of creating **God's people**.

2. God blessed **Abraham** to be a **blessing**.

3. If I am **blessed** by God, I can bless **others**.

4. Blessing is the fruit of **obedience** and **faith**.

5. The curse is the fruit of **disobedience**.

6. To bless God is to **honor** him and give him **glory**.

7. God's blessing is that which **enriches**, and does not add **sadness** with it (Proverbs 10:22).

Challenge:

This week, challenge yourself to find practical, everyday ways to recognize God's blessings and be a blessing to others in turn.

You don't have to do weird things. Every morning take time with God, consecrate your day and be attentive to enjoy what He will do in you and through you. In the next class, share how God blessed you, thanking him for his favors, and you will bless your classmates, giving living testimony of His divine work in you.

+/- 10?

Objective: To understand the importance of tithing in the life of a Christian, which is a good indicator of their relationship with God.

Memory Verse: "...and of all that you give me I will give you a tenth." Genesis 28:22

Attention!
Welcome the group by saying "God bless you!" and chat with them about how God has blessed them in the past week. Encourage them to pass on that blessing to others.

Accept

Connect · Navigate

Introductory Activity (12-17 years).

- Supplies: White sheets of paper cut into rectangles that simulate money, pencils

- Instructions: Give your group members 10 "bills". On each one they'll write something they have to buy (set a value for the bills according to the needs of your group, 10, 100, 1000). You should have more bills in your hands and tell them that if they need more money, you can give them more.

  When they have written down what they would buy with their money, take time to share with the group how they might spend their money.

  Listen carefully to how many people set aside their tithe for the Lord before spending on something else. Congratulate those who have taken this aspect into account and if no one did, start the lesson.

Introductory Activity (18-23 years).

- Supplies: Sheets of paper and pencils

- Directions: Ask your group to list from one to ten according to their priorities of how they spend or use the salary from their jobs. In case they don't work, ask them to imagine how they would spend their salary.

  Compare the answers together, and notice how many took tithing into account. Congratulate the ones who set aside their tithe, and if nobody did, start the lesson.

Connect · Navigate

Tithing has been a popular topic when it comes to stewardship in the church. Just as we talk about dedicating gifts, caring for the environment, tithing is a fundamental aspect in the life of the Christian. Talking about tithing is talking about our relationship with God; it's an act of gratitude and love for God who has given us everything.

Talking about tithing is very common; we're familiar with the envelopes that are on some boards in churches and are common and have been mentioned so often that at this point we don't even have to mention them. But what does tithing mean? What does the Bible say about it? Keep in mind that it isn't only about money, it goes beyond a mere 10 percent.

1. The origin of tithing

In Leviticus 27:30-34, we find the laws about tithing that God established, which had to be observed to the letter. The Bible says in Deuteronomy 14:22-23 what should be tithed.

But in Genesis 14:17-20 and 28:12-22, He gives us examples of who tithed, not out of following the law, but rather out of an act of commitment and loyalty to God.

Comment on the situations that the characters lived through. Ask the group to compare what the practice of tithing was like in each of the cases.

Abraham: He tithed when he returned from a war, in gratitude for his victory (Genesis 14:17-20).

Jacob: After a dream, he promised to tithe as gratitude for all that God promised to give him. He also erected an altar, which indicates that it was an act of thanksgiving, adoration, and homage to God (Genesis 28:12-22).

The teaching of these two characters is that the motive for their tithe went beyond obeying a law—it was an act of devotion to God.

2. Jesus and tithing

In the New Testament, we find that Jesus didn't come to bypass or change the law but to fulfill it (Matthew 5:17). Since tithing is part of the law, how did Jesus interpret the law of tithing? Read Matthew 23:23 and Luke 11:42. Then ask the group to share their understanding of these passages.

When Jesus spoke on the subject, He did so in the form of an accusation towards the Pharisees and interpreters of the law. We must understand that Jesus didn't accuse them for not giving, because if we read well, the Pharisees didn't fail and perhaps gave more than they were required to give. So why was Jesus accusing them? Let's look at the passage.

We could say that they tithed the minimum. We know that rue, mint, dill, and cumin, are very small vegetables that weren't necessary to tithe and yet they were careful to tithe them.

But what was behind all this? As we read it, it becomes clear to us that hypocrisy had taken hold of their hearts and that they had stopped doing what was truly necessary.

They had stopped practicing justice, mercy, and love. The detail of this accusation was related to the attitude of the heart of these people. They were complying very well with what the law said, but they were neglecting the most important commandment to "love your neighbor as yourself." Jesus was teaching them that they should tithe, but this was no excuse to stop doing good to others.

3. Tithing: A response of love or a law

One day, a member from the church approached the Pastor and made a comment about a question: "Pastor", he said, "a friend asked me why I tithe in this church since I'm not yet a member I don't have the obligation to do so."

The Pastor replied: " It's true you aren't obliged to do so, but something I do assure you, that when you have tithed, God has blessed you." The brother was left thinking and he had no choice but to confirm what the Pastor told him. And so far he has faithfully given.

When we accept Christ as our Savior, we declare that all of our life and everything we have is His. God doesn't need what we have. He wants our faithfulness. On the other hand, we may be concerned with quantity, and what God cares about is attitude.

Just as we surrender our lives at the altar of the Lord, so everything we have must be surrendered to Him. Our tithe is only a part of what we possess, and we give it to God in worship. By giving our tithe, we're declaring that Jesus is Lord of everything, even material things. Also, by giving to the Lord, we're supporting His work and showing our love for it.

Many times, young people think that they don't have an obligation to tithe because many of them aren't employed or don't have a fixed income. Another reason for not tithing is since their parents do it, they excuse themselves from tithing. Some go to the other extreme and don't tithe because they have the idea that the church could misuse those resources.

And although there are some groups and friends who want to make us stop this practice, we must defend it based on the principle of love for God, who is the absolute owner of everything we possess.

Make two teams in your group. Each team should discuss and come to a conclusion regarding the following questions:

- *According to Malachi 3:8-9, what do people who don't tithe become?* **They become thieves.**
- *Who should tithe?* **Anyone who receives money, whether it be a little or a lot.**
- *According to Malachi 3:10, what does God promise to those who tithe?* **He promises overflowing blessings.**

Let's ask God for a willing and grateful heart that can give much more than just our tithe.

Review/Application:

Allow time for the students to answer the following questions, and then discuss them as a group.

- What are the similarities that you find in the tithe of Abraham (Genesis 14:17-20) and Jacob (Genesis 28:12-22)? **Abraham tithed in gratitude for the victory won. Jacob out of gratitude for what God would give him.**

- What is the relationship between the altar and the tithe? **When we put something on the altar, as in this case the tithe, it's to consecrate it, as worship and gratitude to God.**

- Do you believe that failure to tithe is a sin according to Malachi 3:8-9? **It is a sin because according to Malachi, not tithing is stealing from God.**

- Have you ever neglected to tithe? Why?

- Do you know how tithes are used in the Church of the Nazarene? **To support the pastor of the church and to fulfill the great commission.**

Be sure the confirm that the group understands the importance of tithing in the life of a Christian, which is a good indicator of their relationship with God.

Challenge:

God gives you the opportunity to tithe. If you still don't do it, you can, together with your group and your teacher, form an accountability team. Although it's something very personal, you can remind each other of it every Sunday, as well as praying for each other. Choose a discreet method as a signal.

Church titles

Objective: To understand the different ecclesiastical titles in light of the Bible.

Memory Verse "...and whoever wants to be first must be your slave—just as the Son of Man did not come to be served, but to serve, and to give his life as a ransom for many." Matthew 20:27-28

Attention!
Continue to talk about the importance of tithing. If someone tithed for the first time, congratulate them! Encourage everyone to tithe.

Accept

Connect | Navigate

Introductory Activity (12-17 years).

- Materials: Blackboard or three sheets of thick paper and markers.

- Directions: Draw the following shapes at home and post them in front of the class. Or draw them on the board before the students arrive.

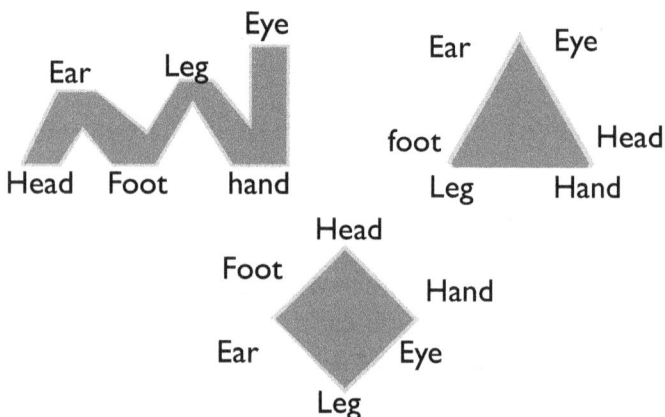

Eye
Ear Leg
Head Foot hand

Ear Eye
foot Head
Leg Hand

Head
Foot
Hand
Ear Eye
Leg

Ask the class to indicate which figure best describes the importance of these body parts and take a moment for a brief discussion about it. Then ask can you live without some of these parts?

Although you can live without any of these body parts, none is more important than another; God endowed us with an anatomical harmony where all parts complement each other. In the same way, the Christian body needs the gifts and ministries given by the Holy Spirit to develop in harmony.

Introductory Activity (18-23 years).

- Supplies: Strips of cardboard or white paper, markers, and masking tape.

- Instructions: On the strips of paper write all the body systems (nervous system, digestive system, muscular system, circulatory system, etc.).

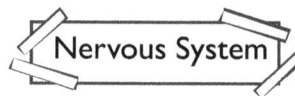

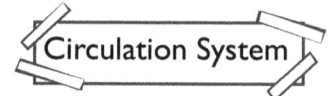

Nervous System | Circulation System

On the day of the session, begin by distributing to the group a strip of paper or cardboard (per person or in pairs) and tell them to stick it on the blackboard or wall, one above the other by priority based on the statement: "This system is the most important because…. " Once they have stuck the pieces of paper on the wall or blackboard, lead a brief discussion asking if they were placed correctly.

The correct answer is actually that they should all be placed in a line equally or in a circle. No system is more important than the other, even though they have different functions. That's why biblically this is the figure that's used to talk about ministries. It isn't about hierarchies, but about functions or tasks that lead others to know God and to serve.

Many of us know or have heard words like "priest," "deacon," "prophet," "apostle," "teacher," "evangelist," "chaplain," among other ministry or church titles. Perhaps we've heard or been part of discussions where they discuss what one or another religious group understands or believes about this. Today, we'll look at some passages from the Bible to find light in the midst of so much discussion.

1. Ecclesiastical Titles in the Church of the Nazarene

The Church of the Nazarene, when speaking of ministry, affirms that "all believers are called to minister to all people" (Manual of the Church of the Nazarene 2017-2021, paragraph 500). This means all of us saved by Christ have the ministry of proclaiming what He has done in us. However, the church also recognizes that some are specially called by God to exercise the ministry in a more official and public way. Based on Scripture and experience, we see that God calls some people a preaching ministry but calls others to ministries that aren't specifically to preaching.

Elder: "The Church of the Nazarene recognizes only one order of the preaching ministry, that of elder.

It also recognizes that the member of the clergy may serve the church in various capacities. (Ephesians 4:11–12) The church recognizes the following roles of service in which a district assembly may place an elder, deacon, or, as circumstances warrant, a licensed minister: pastor, evangelist, missionary, teacher, administrator, chaplain, and special service." (Manual of the Church of the Nazarene 2017-2021, paragraph 504)

505. The roles of ministry are as follows:

506. **Administrator.** The administrator is an elder or a deacon either elected by the General Assembly as a general official; or a member of the clergy elected or employed to serve in the general church. An administrator may also be an elder elected by the district assembly as district superintendent; or a member of the clergy elected or employed as his or her primary assignment in the service of a district. Such person is an assigned minister.

507. **Chaplain.** The chaplain is an ordained minister who feels divinely led to specialized ministry in military, institutional, or industrial chaplaincy. All ministers seeking to serve in chaplaincy must be approved by their district superintendent. An ordained minister serving in chaplaincy as his or her primary assignment shall be an assigned minister, and shall report annually to the district assembly and give due regard to the advice and counsel of the district superintendent and the District Advisory Board. The chaplain may receive fellowship members into the Church of the Nazarene in consultation with an officially organized Church of the Nazarene, administer the sacraments in harmony with the Manual, give pastoral care, comfort the sorrowing, reprove and encourage and seek by all means the conversion of sinners, sanctification of believers, and the upbuilding of the people of God in the most holy faith. (519, 538.9, 538.13)

508. **Deaconess.** A woman who is a member of the Church of the Nazarene and believes that she is divinely led to engage in ministering to the sick and the needy, comforting the sorrowing, and doing other works of Christian benevolence, and who has given evidence in her life of ability, grace, and usefulness, and who was in the years preceding 1985 licensed or consecrated as a deaconess shall continue in such standing. However, those women called to active and assigned ministry but not called to preach shall complete the requirements for ordination to the order of deacon. Women desiring a credential for compassionate ministries may pursue the requirements for lay minister. (113.9, 503.2-503.9)

509. **Educator.** The educator is an elder, deacon, or licensed minister employed to serve on the administrative staff or faculty of one of the educational institutions of the Church of the Nazarene. The district shall designate such a person as an educator for their ministry assignment.

510. **Evangelist.** The elder or licensed minister who is an evangelist is one devoted to traveling and preaching the gospel, and who is authorized by the church to promote revivals and to spread the gospel of Jesus Christ abroad in the land. The Church of the Nazarene recognizes three levels of itinerant evangelism to which a district assembly may assign ministers: registered evangelist, commissioned evangelist, and tenured evangelist. An evangelist who dedicates time to evangelism, outside his or her local church as his or her primary assignment and who doesn't sustain a retired relationship with the church or any of its departments or institutions, shall be an assigned minister.

2. Ecclesiastical titles today

Today, there are ecclesial titles such as "apostle," "prophet," "priest," and "elder." In some countries, only a few people have been singled out with such titles so they assume authority over everyone else. The problem with this stems from transforming these ecclesial titles into misunderstood hierarchies. Basically, it's the idea that the world gives success or fame to a leader, this being the exercise of power to obtain the greatest or the best.

As we see, one of the great problems with people is the power that comes from the hierarchy. Since ancient times, humans have wanted to exercise dominion or power over everything (Genesis 11:1-4). If we go back to the Bible this comes from God who gave us the ability to exercise power from the moment of creation (Genesis 1:26). However, we really exercise power when we do it in community and for the common good in the Kingdom. Many times, we lose sight of this and are intoxicated by the power that we can exercise as individuals, however the correct meaning of power in the kingdom of God is that which we exercise as a community for a common good.

In the church, power shouldn't be exercised for an individual's good but for the good of the community (Philippians 2:3-4), and if we want to be greater, we must be a servant (Matthew 20:26-28).

3. Biblical Ecclesiastical titles

In Ephesians 4:11, Paul gives a series of ecclesiastical titles that give an idea of how the church was organized in the early years. Most scholars agree that here the apostle was not trying to give an exhaustive list of ministries within the church, but a reference to the development that the organization had up to that time. Many of these responsibilities weren't confined to a particular place but were done by itinerant ministers. Some of these titles were apostles, prophets, evangelists and pastor/teachers.

Apostles: To be considered an apostle, at least two requirements were needed (1) To be sent by Jesus, (2) to have witnessed the resurrection ... hence Paul's argument when defending his apostolate (1 Corinthians 15:7-9). The apostle spoke with Jesus after His resurrection and was sent by Him (Acts 9:17; 26:12-18). A Dictionary of the Bible & Christian Doctrine in Everyday English (Eby, et al, 2004) notes:

a. An apostle was a special kind of minister. The risen Christ called certain people to be apostles. Their mission was to preach so that people would become disciples of Jesus Christ.

b. Therefore, apostles were a type of missionary. They included Paul, the disciples of Jesus, and a few others.

Prophets: "He who speaks instead of another." All true Christian believers are to be prophets. It isn't predicting the future, but calling attention to God's message and announcing what will happen if God isn't obeyed. Eby, et al (2004) note:

a. A prophet is one who speaks for God. A prophet delivers the message of God to the people.

b. A false prophet is a person whose claim to speak for God is a lie.

c. There were many prophets in the Old Testament. Some were called "former prophets" and some "latter prophets". The former prophets included Abraham, Moses, Samuel, Elijah and Elisha. The latter prophets were the writing prophets.

d. The writing prophets were those for whom books of the Old Testament are named. These prophets are divided into the Major and the Minor Prophets.

e. The Major Prophets were Isaiah, Jeremiah (including his Lamentations), Ezekiel and Daniel.

f. The Minor Prophets were Hosea, Joel, Amos, Obadiah, Jonah, Micah, Nahum, Habakkuk, Zephaniah, Haggai, Zechariah and Malachi.

g. There were also prophets in the Early Christian Church. (Deuteronomy 18:15, 18, 20, 22; Judges 6:8; 1 Samuel 3:20; Jeremiah 1:5; 5:31; Amos 2:11-12; Matthew 1:22; Acts 13:1; 1 Corinthians 12:28 and Ephesians 4:11)

Evangelists: These are itinerant preachers (Acts 21:8; 2 Timothy 4:5). Eby, et al (2004) note:

a. An evangelist is a person who preaches the gospel to other people. The evangelist tries to win converts to Christ. "Evangelist" comes from a Greek word meaning "a messenger of the good news".

b. All Christians should help tell the gospel to those who haven't heard it. They're evangelists or witnesses when they do this.

c. Some Christians have been called to preach the gospel as evangelists (Ephesians 4:11).

Pastors - Teachers: It's a double office, explaining the Christian faith to converts and feeding the Lord's flock. Eby, et al (2004) note:

a. A pastor is a Christian minister who leads a congregation.

b. The word "pastor" comes from the Greek word that means "shepherd" or "one who leads sheep".

c. A pastor leads a congregation in worship, evangelism, service and spiritual growth. A pastor acts as a shepherd by counseling, comforting and caring for the people. Pastors in the New Testament Church were also called bishops. (Jeremiah 3:15; John 21:15-17; Ephesians 4:11; 1 Timothy 3:1-2 and 1 Peter 5:4)

Now, to close this point, we must emphasize that the objective of the titles mentioned here isn't to highlight their importance but to present them as gifts of the Spirit so that "speaking the truth in love, we'll grow to become in every respect the mature body of Him who is the Head, that is, Christ." (Ephesians 4:15)

Review/Application:

Some ministries in the church.

Vertical

1. Their calling and ministry allow them to minister with a lot of melody **(Music Minister)**.

3. Serves in military, civil and industrial institutions **(Chaplain)**.

4. Serves in a Christian educational institution **(Teacher)**.

Horizontal

2. Serve cross-culturally **(Missionary)**.

5. Travel preaching the gospel **(Evangelist)**.

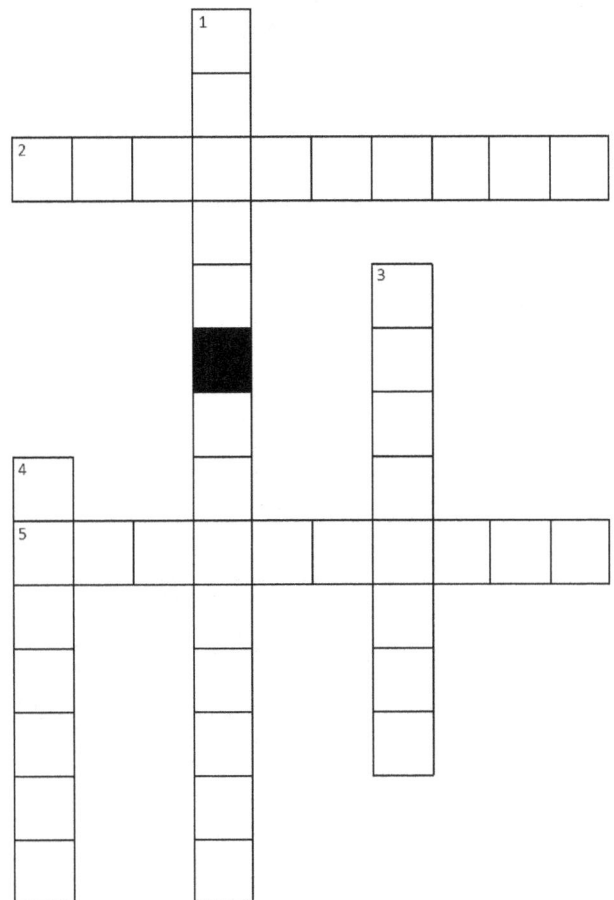

Challenge:

We invite you to reflect on your abilities and the gifts that God has given you and think about how you can use them in the work of your local church. A good start would be to choose a prayer partner today, a person with whom you can spend the next three or four weeks in prayer. Perhaps you will discover a new gift in your life.

What a celebration!

Objective: To understand the significance of this celebration and the importance of this event in the fulfillment of the prophecies of the Savior.

Memory Verse: "Say to Daughter Zion, 'See, your king comes to you, gentle and riding on a donkey, and on a colt, the foal of a donkey.'" Matthew 21:5

Attention! Remember to start your session asking the group if they have been praying that God would help them discover their gifts.

Accept

Connect — Navigate

Introductory Activity (12-17 years).

- Supplies: Paper and pencil for each person. Whiteboard and markers.

- Instructions: Present the following situation to the group. The President of your country is coming for a brief visit to your town and your group is chosen to organize the reception. Have them write ideas about what they could do. At the end write on the board the ideas presented and make a plan, from transportation, accommodation, to tourist attractions, etc.

  Share with the group how Jesus was received in the city of Jerusalem on that special Sunday, known today as Palm Sunday. Tell them about how everything was designed and planned by God so that this moment would be meaningful in the life and ministry of Jesus and also of the people who received Him.

Introductory Activity (18-23 years).

- Supplies: Whiteboard and markers.

- Instructions: Together with your group choose something that deserves to be commemorated in your country, city or church. It can be a fictitious moment of something that's longed for or an important event in the history of the country, city or in the life of one of the group members.

  Once the event has been chosen, discuss with the group how they should prepare and celebrate the event.

  Then talk with the group about the celebration of Palm Sunday. This was a great celebration for Jesus as King and Savior. Every detail of what happened was part of the great divine plan to give a Savior to the world.

Connect — Navigate

Unforgettable! A triumphal entry! After winning on penalties against Italy in the 1994 soccer world cup, the Brazilian team returned home as the winners. In a large open car, the players paraded through the streets of Brazil. Thousands of people gathered, shouting joyfully to greet their heroes. Television channels interrupted their usual programming to broadcast that historic moment in the life of the nation. It would be very difficult for someone not to notice what was happening on the streets. It wasn't just any moment!

In almost all countries, when there's an occasion of great celebration, people take to the streets to celebrate together. More than two thousand years ago, in a historic event, people took to the streets of Jerusalem to celebrate. Read Matthew 21:1-11.

1. The entrance to Jerusalem

From the 10th chapter of Matthew, Jesus began to instruct His disciples about what was to take place in Jerusalem. His arrival in that city, the center of the religious life of the Jewish people, triggered a succession of events that culminated in his death.

In less than a week after his entry into Jerusalem, Jesus was betrayed and crucified as if He were a criminal. There, He faced the most painful and crucial moment of His life and ministry. At that time, opposition to Jesus from the Jewish leaders was great. Surely, entering Jerusalem, the most important city for the Jews, posed a threat to the leaders of the people. It was a great risk; despite being aware of this, to fulfill the divine plan for humanity, Jesus did it. He could have chosen a calmer entrance, perhaps hidden from the people, especially the religious leaders who constantly hunted Him, but instead of avoiding it, Jesus made a triumphal entrance in full view of everyone.

In the passage we read, we can see the reaction of the crowds to the arrival of the King. They were full joy and gladness, and there was a great euphoria in the streets of Jerusalem. With their cloaks and palms, the people decorated and adorned the path through which the King would pass. We see the reason for this reaction in Luke 19:37. There it says: "... the whole crowd ... began to praise God with loud voices for all the wonders they had seen." There were people who had walked with and met Jesus, people who had seen His miracles: the multiplication of the loaves, healing the sick, casting out demons and forgiveness of sins. People had seen and experienced how Jesus had changed lives.

Now He was approaching the city of Jerusalem, a city where previously the great kings had ruled, where religious life was carried out, and which was a symbol of the very presence of God. In their hearts was the great hope that He was the promised Messiah, the King who would deliver the people. It was a great cause for joy—the King, the Messiah, had arrived in Jerusalem!

Stop and ask the group about a time of great celebration they have had in the city, in their country, or in their own lives. Ask if any of them went out to celebrate with the people. In case they haven't experienced or cannot remember something like this in your area, ask them about celebrations they have seen on the news.

Today, it's difficult to find politicians who really treat their people well. It's more common to see people take to the streets to march, protest and strike because of the bad treatment they have received instead of recognizing the good work of their representatives. But in Jerusalem, this was not the case; the voices, the clapping and the greetings were in recognition of Jesus, the awaited Messiah, who had done much good for the people.

2. The prophecy fulfilled

Despite the greatness of the moment, everything was very simple. Generally, when kings or important people in our society make their parades through the streets, they do it with glamor and brilliance. At that time, we would have expected the arrival of Jesus in a chariot drawn by mighty horses or even by the people themselves. But Jesus' entry didn't match the Jews' expectations. He chose to enter with humility rather than with human pride and glory. In truth, being the Master, His humility was not uncommon. He had already left His glory, making Himself similar to His creation. Simplicity was His way of life; His arrival on a donkey revealed a very important fact about himself, and one that the crowd could safely identify.

The way He arrived showed the fulfillment of Zechariah's prophecy about the Messiah (Zechariah 9:9). Entering Jerusalem mounted on a donkey was proof that He was the Savior, promised by God to rescue His people and the whole world.

The Jews lived under great pressure from the Romans. Despite being allowed their religious practices, they weren't considered citizens, they had no political rights, nor an indigenous governor to intercede on their behalf. The people longed for the arrival of the promised king who would free them from oppression. If Jesus had come to Jerusalem in a different way than He did, this would only be a celebration for someone who had done good to the people. But by choosing a donkey, He put the seal of the fulfillment of the promise: Jesus was the Messiah promised by God to His people.

3. What does this story tell us today?

For those of us who have truly believed in Jesus, we know that the reign He came to establish was far beyond a political reign for a nation. Jesus came to build a greater kingdom, an everlasting kingdom in the hearts of human beings. This is the kingdom of God, which you and I are part of. Back then, the people went out into the streets praising God, bringing palms and leaving their own cloaks so that the path that Jesus passed on would be a path worthy of a King.

The arrival of Jesus in our lives should be a similar celebration. It should certainly be something to celebrate on a daily basis. On Palm Sunday, we remember this celebration that occurred more than two thousand years ago in the city of Jerusalem. But today, like the people who received Jesus back then, in our hearts there's gratitude for the blessings and eternal life that we've received from Him.

Review/Application:

Divide the class into two or more groups, and divide the questions between the teams to answer. After giving them time to answer, ask them to share their answers with everyone. Below we write possible answers.

1. How do you think the disciples felt about obeying Jesus' instruction? What does this teach us about obedience? *A little strange or perhaps confident that the word that Jesus had announced would be fulfilled. That teaches us that we must be obedient to what Jesus asks of us.*

2. Why do you think Jesus said to them, "And if someone says something to you, answer him, 'The Lord needs them, but then he will return them'"? *Because Jesus knew what would happen and wanted nothing to prevent the task from being accomplished.*

3. What does the attitude of the crowd, described in verse 8, show us about the attitude we should have toward Jesus? *That we should honor Jesus with what we have.*

4. What did the fulfillment of the prophecy of verse 5 mean? *That Jesus was truly the promised messiah.*

5. What does the prophecy tell us about the person of Jesus for us today? *He was a humble person.*

6. Do you think that all those who received Jesus at the entrance to Jerusalem believed in Him? What different kinds of people do you think were in the crowd? *There were people who really believed in Jesus as the son of God. In the place were Pharisees who were looking to catch him and people who were only there for the miracles he performed.*

Encourage the group to make changes in their lives to honor Jesus. Be sure they understand the significance of this celebration and the importance of this event in the fulfillment of the prophecies of the Savior.

Challenge:

Since our lives is the place where Jesus lives, how can we make it a place worthy of a King? During the week, think of areas that you must change so that your life is that worthy place.

To live again

Objective: To understand the importance of the resurrection for our salvation.

Memory Verse: "...even though we were dead because of our sins, he gave us life when he raised Christ from the dead. (It's only by God's grace that you have been saved!) For he raised us from the dead along with Christ..." Ephesians 2:5-6a NLT

Attention! Ask for volunteers to share about the areas of their lives that they have changed so that their lives are places worthy of King Jesus.

Accept

Connect | Navigate

Introductory Activity (12-17 years).

- Supplies: Whiteboard and markers/blackboard and chalk.

- Instructions: To begin the conversation about the importance of the resurrection, it's necessary to understand the concept of death and its consequences. If appropriate for your group, ask your group to share about someone they know who has passed away.

  According to what they say, write on the board a list of feelings that a person experiences during that circumstance.

  It would be helpful to have a story ready in case the group doesn't have one.

Introductory Activity (18-23 years).

- Supplies: Whiteboard and markers or blackboard and chalk, paper and pens.

- Instructions: Separate into two or more groups and ask them to write a definition of "death," and some characteristics and consequences of this word (For example: Death is the absence of life, where vital signs stop working; a dead person doesn't eat, or drink, or communicate with the environment.) Write on the board what they say. Be sensitive when they share their answers, and be ready to comfort anyone who for some reason has gone through this experience with a loved one recently.

Connect | Navigate

From very early in school, we're taught that the cycle of life to be birth, growth, reproduction, and death. It's in this last phase that we stop being "living physical beings." Death is a natural part of the human journey, but despite that, many people live with a certain fear or anxiety produced by the idea that one day they'll stop being in this world.

Our life here on earth is an opportunity to learn about two kinds of death: physical death and spiritual death.

1. Mary before the tomb

Read John 20:1-10. In verse 1, it says that Mary Magdalene went to the tomb, where the body of Jesus was. She was one of the women forgiven by Jesus and who followed Him throughout His ministry on earth. We can be sure that she was very saddened by the death of the one who had taught and helped her so much.

Verse 1 also gives us interesting details about this first discovery of Jesus' resurrection. The verse says that "The first day of the week ... the morning while it's still dark." As we read these details carefully, we realize that Mary Magdalene was the first person to realize the wonderful news that Jesus had risen because she was in the right place, at the right time.

In the Jewish tradition then, it was strictly forbidden to do any kind of work on the Sabbath. Mary obeyed the law and kept the day of rest, but on the first day of the week, she wasn't lazy; she got up very early and went to see the body of her teacher.

In Luke 24:1, we read that the women carried "… the aromatic spices that they had prepared…." These aromatic spices were ointments that were prepared to care for, and maintain as well as possible, a deceased body. It's interesting to note the love that motivated Mary Magdalene to care for the Lord Jesus even after His death. She wasn't distracted by any other details or personal problems, but rather, she worked diligently to serve Jesus. Mary Magdalene didn't let laziness nor her deep sadness keep her from experiencing God's blessing. She knew what was necessary and she did it. What an example she is to us!

Her diligence enabled her to receive the first disclosure of Christ's resurrection. Finally, we read in John 20:2 that Mary Magdalene was not paralyzed by the discovery in the tomb. Despite her great surprise and confusion, she ran to tell her friends that Jesus was no longer in the tomb..

2. The disciples at the tomb

Mary Magdalene "ran" and told two of the disciples about the disappearance of Jesus' body. As an important detail, the passage expresses exactly who the two disciples were: Simon Peter and another who is mentioned as "the one whom Jesus loved." It's understood that "the one whom Jesus loved" or "the beloved disciple" was John (John 21:20).

If we continue reading the passage, we see that both disciples, like Mary Magdalene, left without hesitation or waiting, to verify what had been said for themselves.

The account mentions that John arrived before Peter simply because he "ran faster" (John 20: 4). When John received the news, he ran to fast to see all the evidence. This would be vital information for his life, especially because it was in relation to Jesus.

Although John arrived at the tomb first, it was Peter who "entered" first without knowing what he would find inside. In Peter, we see an attitude of courage. He wasn't willing to let anything get in the way of him knowing more about what had happened to Jesus. Both Mary Magdalene's attitude of diligence and Peter's attitude of courage should identify us as Christians.

John 20:6-7 tells us that John and Peter found the linen cloth in which the body of Jesus was wrapped, and the shroud that had been placed on his head, rolled up in a separate place. Note that if Jesus' body had been stolen, as some critics have wanted to mention or the leaders of the time themselves wanted to use to explain, these things wouldn't have been found in such order or they wouldn't even have been found because they would have taken everything.

Finally, verse 8 explains that "the other disciple also entered, saw and believed." The responses of Peter and John were clear and decisive. They went when they were called, and they saw with their own eyes the evidence that Jesus lived again, just as He had said he would do before His death (Luke 9:22 and Luke 18:33).

3. Us at the tomb

John 20:10 says, "And the disciples returned to their own place." It's very likely that the disciples immediately began to tell their friends and family about what they had experienced at the tomb. The resurrection of Jesus had changed their lives. They were no longer sad or confused … Jesus was alive! Death had not succeeded in separating them from their Teacher.

At the beginning of the lesson, we discussed two very important concepts: spiritual death and physical death. Physical death is the absence of life in our human body, when our heart stops beating, and our brain stops functioning. We can no longer experience the things of life in this world, like a hug, a feeling of love, or a smile. In a parallel way, spiritual death is that situation in which our soul is dead, and we cannot experience the love, presence and blessings of God.

People can be physically alive; their hearts can beat, they can walk, eat, and be with us here on earth. But at the same time, they might be spiritually dead; that is, not enjoying a full life, or a relationship with God. When people die physically without experiencing salvation, they die eternally and are separated from the presence of God.

Christians will experience physical death, but thanks to the resurrection of Jesus, we won't experience spiritual death. When we have spiritual life, we can receive and feel God's perfect love and seek God's direction to live a full life. This spiritual life allows us to talk to God, express our feelings, thoughts, and above all, experience His unique presence which fills us with His peace. In 1 Corinthians 15:20-22, Paul gives us the confidence that even though Adam sinned, and we all deserve to die, through the resurrection of Jesus, we can all be resurrected (1 Corinthians 6:14). This means that our spiritual life will have no end—it will be eternal in the presence of God.

To end the lesson, take a moment to reflect with the group: *"Has Jesus transformed your life? If He hasn't, will you allow Him to transform you today? Will you share what God did in your life with other people?"*

Review/Application:

Ask the class to find the following passages in their Bibles, and after reading them, write what they teach about Jesus' resurrection, and how it relates to their resurrection. They can include what they have learned in today's lesson.

Then have them share their answers with the rest of the class.

- Luke 9:22: **Jesus spoke of his resurrection.**

- Luke 18: 32-33: **Jesus announced his resurrection.**

- 1 Corinthians 6:14: **God's power will be able to resurrect us too.**

- 1 Corinthians 15:20-22: **The resurrection of Jesus gives us hope of eternal life.**

- Colossians 2:12: **God's power raises us from our spiritual death.**

- Colossians 3:1: **Once we are resurrected, we should seek to do what pleases God.**

Challenge:

God's priority is that you have the opportunity to "live again," and in that life, fully enjoy His presence and perfect love for you.

During the week, write a prayer expressing your gratitude and love to God. You have to know that you can thank God every day for your new life in Christ! He loves to hear your voice speaking to him each day. Share it with the class the next time you meet.

Super Power

Objective: To understand that to have a truly victorious life, they need to be filled with the Holy Spirit.

Memory Verse: "But you will receive power when the Holy Spirit comes on you" Acts 1:8a

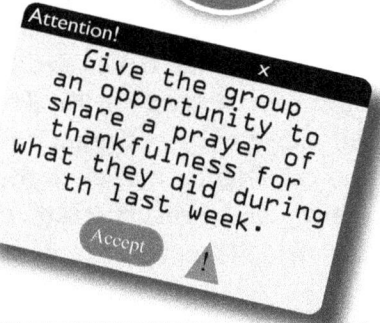

Attention!
Give the group an opportunity to share a prayer of thankfulness for what they did during th last week.
Accept

Connect | Navigate

Introductory Activity (12-17 years).

- Supplies: Masking tape or chalk and rope.

- Directions: Divide into two groups. With the chalk or masking tape, mark a dividing line on the floor. Then each group will take one end of the rope. When you indicate, each group should begin to pull the rope to their side. (Tug of War) The group that is pulled to the opposite side of the dividing line will lose.

    Then brainstorm and write on the board the reasons why one group won and the other lost. Conclude by explaining that this is a test of strength and that the strongest group won..

Introductory Activity (18-23 years).

- Supplies: A small table and two chairs.

- Instructions: Divide the group into smaller groups with the same number of participants. Taking turns, have one member of each group arm wrestle members of other groups. The contestants must each sit on their chair, join the right hand with that of the opponent and their elbow must be touching the table. Each one must try to defeat the other only with arm strength, without lifting their elbow from the table. Whoever manages to bend the opponent's arm to the opposite side wins. The group with the most winning members will be the winner. At the end, they must analyze why one group won and what the other needed to do to win.

    The determining factor in this activity is the force exerted on the other person.

Connect | Navigate

We all sometimes encounter critical moments in which we don't know what to do or feel. We think that our actions aren't correct or that we're not strong enough. Today, through the lives of the disciples, we'll discover who can help us.

1. A life without power

Begin by reading Acts 2:1-13. There are people who are characterized by their negative attitudes, and for fear that their attitude will affect us, we avoid being near them. Negative attitudes are the fruit of what is in the heart. Let's look at some examples.

Selfishness: In Mark 10:37, we find two brothers who thought of obtaining personal benefit because of their relationship with Jesus. Ask your group for their opinion on this passage and ask: *"Can you share some examples of this attitude today?"*

Fear: Many times we can consider ourselves brave until a difficult situation scares us. In Mark 14:50 and 14:54, we find Jesus' disciples who, when faced with the possibility of being arrested just as their teacher was, preferred to flee. *Have you ever been afraid to tell others that you are a Christian?*

Anger: Angry people are those who don't know how to control their anger and react without reasoning about what they're doing or the consequences of their actions. In John 18:10, we find Peter experiencing a feeling of anger that motivated him to attack another person, trying to do justice in the situation. *Have you ever lost self-control?*

Cowardice: Sometimes we're surprised by our own reactions, right? The same man who at one point drew his sword to defend his teacher, hours later, denied Jesus (Mark 14:66-72). *Have you ever openly or covertly with your actions denied Jesus?*

Isn't it true that our reactions aren't always the best? Isn't it true that our attitudes then embarrass us? What's happening to us? Why are we like this? What do we need to be different and act correctly through appropriate attitudes no matter the circumstances?

2. An explosive power

In life, we experience disappointments, frustrations, fears, disappointments, dissatisfaction, unhappiness, etc. We're all exposed in one way or another to having moments of difficulty. What can we do? Will there be any solution?

When Jesus said goodbye to His disciples before ascending to heaven, He promised them that the day would come when they would receive power. Power for what? The power that Jesus promised wouldn't change their circumstances, but it would help them face the difficulties that would come. On that occasion, Jesus' followers showed this characteristic: after the resurrection of Christ they obeyed Jesus' command to stay together and pray in search of God's direction for their lives (Acts 1:4, 12- 14).

As they united in prayer, God manifested Himself in an extraordinary, supernatural way (Acts 2:2-4). It was the manifestation of God's presence! Jesus' promise had been fulfilled! Yes, the Lord Jesus fulfilled His promise to fill them with the power of the Holy Spirit.

The visible form of the filling of the Holy Spirit was the appearance of something like tongues of fire which settled on each one of them. They also began to speak in other languages according to what the Spirit gave them.

The people who came to Jerusalem to celebrate the Feast of Pentecost were amazed at that supernatural event, never seen before. They didn't understand what was happening, but the interesting thing was that although many of them were of different nationalities, each one heard the message about God's love in their own language. The disciples received the filling of the Holy Spirit, and it was noticeable to their community. The coming of the Holy Spirit produces changes that can be noticed.

3. A life with super powers

Bearing witness to faith in Christ can cause different reactions in people. In some, it produces recognition and credibility, and in others rejection and mockery, and this has happened since the beginning of Christianity.

After the coming of the Holy Spirit, this situation no longer hurt the hearts of the disciples. They gave evidence of a radical change in their attitudes and humanity, and they experienced the power to bear witness to Christ fearlessly and boldly.

Another interesting example is that of Peter, who was once angry and cowardly, then stood up with great courage in the midst of the crowd of onlookers to deliver a powerful speech about the love of Jesus Christ (Acts 2:14-40). Later, when he was arrested and forbidden to speak of Jesus, he wasn't intimidated, but on the contrary, he continued to give a courageous testimony (Acts 4:20).

The book of Acts tells how the believers, even when they were persecuted, didn't stop speaking boldly about the love of Christ. They were no longer selfish, nor did they cower, because their hearts were filled with the power of the Holy Spirit. This power made them brave and gave them the strength, the security they needed, not only to face problems, but to do God's will.

If we feel that our life is empty, unsatisfied and sad, we must recognize that we need, as did the disciples, God to enable us to face the difficulties of life. Ask the group: *"How are you doing today? Maybe you're dissatisfied with yourself, perhaps you don't like your family, possibly you don't know if you should please your friends, or maybe you can't stand your school anymore. You need to fully surrender yourself to God and cry out to Him for the baptism with the Holy Spirit. It's what you need for greater power to obey God, to enjoy the Christian life, and to love others."*

The Bible says that if people, being evil, know how to give good gifts to their children, how much more will the heavenly Father give the Holy Spirit to those who ask Him (Luke 11:13).

Review/Application:

Give the students some time to answer the following questions, or if you wish, they can answer them during the class. And then discuss the answers as a group.

1. Why were the disciples selfish, fearful, angry and cowardly? **Because they had not received the Holy Spirit.**

2. What did Jesus promise his followers (Acts 1:8)? **That they would receive power when they were filled with the Holy Spirit and would be his witnesses.**

3. Where were the disciples gathered on the day of the Feast of Pentecost? **In Jerusalem, on the top floor of a house.**

4. What were the Christians doing in that house? **They were gathered together, praying and waiting.**

5. How was the coming of the Holy Spirit manifested? **The coming of the Holy Spirit was manifested with a loud sound like a strong wind, with tongues like fire spreading over the heads of each one and gave them the power to speak in other languages.**

6. What changes occurred in the disciples as a result of receiving the Holy Spirit? **The disciples, who were previously selfish, fearful, angry and cowardly, became courageous preachers of the gospel of Jesus Christ.**

7. What are the areas of your life that aren't satisfying?

8. What do you need to enjoy life with Christ? **The coming of the Holy Spirit on me.**

Challenge:

This week, thank God for the changes he's made in your life. And pray that his Holy Spirit will continue to strengthen your weak areas. Don't stop giving testimony of what the Lord continues to do in your life.

What are we celebrating?

Objective: To understand the significance of the celebration of Christmas.

Memory Verse: "She will give birth to a son, and you are to give him the name Jesus, because he will save his people from their sins." Matthew 1:21

Attention!
Start the session by asking your group if during the week they thought about the changes that the Holy Spirit is doing in them.
Accept

Connect | Navigate

Introductory Activity (12-17 years) .

- Supplies: A cardboard box, wrapping paper, a large bow, a large sheet of paper (or cardboard) rolled up as parchment, marker, and a pencil.

- Instructions: On the large sheet of paper (or card) write the Bible verses Isaiah 7:14 and 9:6-7. Roll the sheet like parchment and put it in the cardboard box and close it. Decorate the cardboard box in advance with wrapping paper and put a big bow on it. Bring it to this session, and place it in the center of the room before your group arrives.

At the beginning of the session, tell them that it's a Christmas present for them. Ask your group what they would like to see in it. Let them participate freely and be careful not to make fun of any of the answers. Don't comment as they give their answers.

After a while, select one of your group members to open the gift box, remove the contents, and read what the scroll says. Then ask the group if that's what they expected to find in the box and how they feel about it.

Tell them that during this session, they'll understand what the best gift they can give or receive is this Christmas.

Introductory Activity (18-23 years) .

- Supplies: Sheets of paper, pencils or pens.

- Instructions: Distribute the sheets of paper to your group and give each person a pencil or pen. Tell them to write what in their opinion would be the best gift they could receive this Christmas and why. Give them a few minutes to reply. Then ask several volunteers to share their responses and explain why they asked for that gift. Don't comment or rate any of the gifts they ask for as good or bad.

Explain that Christmas is certainly about a gift and that in this session they'll see what God's gift to humanity is.

This activity will make your group reflect on the reality that we often forget about Jesus Christ when we think of Christmas gifts. Start the session by keeping in mind the wonderful gift of salvation that God gave us by sending Jesus into the world.

Connect | Navigate

Every year as December approaches, in many place, shops are filled with lights and Christmas decorations. Some promote sales. Television begins to broadcast Christmas-themed advertising. Some show families sitting around the tree opening gifts bought in this or that place, or sitting at the table laughing and enjoying a delicious dinner with food from a particular brand.

Yet there are some people who experience loneliness, and those who haven't seen each other for a long time, look forward to a reunion or a reconciliation. Christmas, for many, is a time to be happy, spend time with the family, give gifts, but nothing more. However, what do Christians really celebrate at Christmas?

Ask for volunteers in the group to read Isaiah 7:14; 9:6-7, and Matthew 1:18-24. You might also ask one adult to dress as the prophet Isaiah and another to dress as an angel and each recite their portion of Scripture. Ask if the group knows what those Bible verses are referring to.

1. Immanuel: God with us

Isaiah prophesied about the birth of Jesus in 700 B.C. He prophesied in Judah, although his prophecies also reached the northern kingdom, Israel. Part of his prophecies included the theme of the Messiah. These prophecies were fulfilled at the birth of Jesus. Isaiah spoke of a virgin or maiden who would give birth to a son, and there are several interpretations of who that woman would be and the child that she would have. But Matthew 1:23 quotes the prophet indicating that the angel's words to Mary were the fulfillment of that ancient prophecy mentioned in Isaiah 7:14.

"Immanuel" is a word of Hebrew origin that means "God with us." The child that would be born (and of whom Isaiah had spoken), would be given a name that indicated that God was with His people. The presence of God Himself would be in the child.

In Matthew 1:21, the angel of God spoke to Joseph that the child to be born of Mary would be named Jesus. This is because He would fulfill a special purpose: to save His people. Save them from what? Israel was no longer at war, although it did suffer under the control of the Romans. Would this child come to save them from Roman oppression? Many hoped so.

However, God's divine plan, orchestrated many centuries back as shown in Genesis 3:15, just after the disobedience of Adam and Eve, had its culmination in the birth of this child named Jesus.

After the fall of Adam and Eve, the human race lived separated from God, without that communion that they had enjoyed from their creation. But this little one who would be born indicated that God was with the people and that His plan to restore mankind and save it from sin would be fulfilled. With this birth was God's gift of salvation for humanity. It was the beginning of what centuries later the world is celebrating at Christmas.

2. Four titles for a baby

When a baby is born, the first thing parents are usually asked is what name they'll give the baby. The name Jesus was given long before His birth (Isaiah 7:14). And close to the date of His birth, the angel told Joseph that he should call Him Jesus, or "Savior," because He would save the people.

This child had four other names or titles, something usual in the proclamation of kings, an indication of the nature of this child. The names would be the following (Isaiah 9:6):

- "Wonderful counselor": He will be extraordinary and His advice will be wise and unique since He will be omniscient (all knowing).

- "Mighty God": This name refers to God's attribute of His omnipotence (all powerful). Let's remember that Jesus would have the presence of the Holy Spirit and He would also be God.

- To speak of the "Everlasting Father" is to speak of the omnipresence of God (He is everywhere). "Designating someone as 'the father of' is the Hebrew and Arabic way of saying that he is properly the source of the thing designated as his attribute... he's everywhere since "there is no point in time or space in which he isn't present "(Beacon Bible Commentary, volume IV. Beacon Hill Press of Kansas City, 1969).

- Most writers agree that "Prince of peace" refers to the Messiah's rule of peace and justice. In Hebrew, peace means well-being, prosperity, health, something complete, solid, and not just the lack of war.

Ask your group if they know of any other names that have been given to Jesus and on what occasions they were used.

3. The Gift

The first part of Isaiah 9:6 says, "For to us a child is born, to us a son is given." Which son? The Son of the Most High (Luke 1:32), Immanuel, God with us (Matthew 1:23). This is the greatest and best gift we could ever receive, a gift heralded and expected for centuries.

It's important to note that at the center of Christmas is the birth of Jesus. God Himself gave us His Son so that we could once again have that communion that man lost in the fall described in Genesis 3. We no longer have to live in darkness. The lights that decorate shops at Christmas time are nothing compared to "That true light, which enlightens every man" (John 1:9). That light is Jesus and He came for each one of us.

The gifts we buy have no comparison with the gift of God. There's no more expensive gift than the one God has given us. And there's no one else who can give us the wonderful gift of salvation. If the festivities don't focus on Jesus, what is done at Christmas doesn't make sense.

Ask your group to share some experiences in which they attended Christmas gatherings in the homes of non-Christian people and to explain what they're like and what they do. What is the difference between these gatherings and the Christian gatherings at Christmas? Ask for concrete examples.

Review/Application:

Noor and Sahid are two brothers who come from Yemen as an exchange students at a university in your city. The Christmas period is approaching and they don't understand why all the fuss with the lights, the tree, the dinner and the presents. They found out you're a Christian and come to ask you what Christmas is. Knowing that they come from a Muslim culture where they don't celebrate Christmas, how would you answer them?

Break into groups to discuss what you would say to Noor and Sahid. (Their answers should include some points like what is provided below)

1. What's Christmas? **Christmas is the celebration of the birth of Jesus, the Son of God.**

2. What's special about this birth unlike others? **His birth was announced many years ago by the prophets and was fulfilled when a virgin gave birth to a boy. Furthermore, this child would bring salvation to humanity.**

3. Why was the name chosen for that child? **This child was named Jesus, which means "savior" because he came to save the world from its sins.**

4. What's the connection with the fact of giving gifts at Christmas? **God showed us his love by giving the gift of His son. We give gifts to others as a way of showing our love to them.**

Challenge:

Do a little poll with your friends about what they think is the meaning of Christmas. Record their answers. Compare them with what the Bible says. Meditate on this and then write down what you believe. Share your answers during the next class.

Something new!

Objective: To understand that God wants to do something new in their lives in the coming new year.

Memory Verse: "Forget the former things; do not dwell on the past. See, I am doing a new thing! Now it springs up; do you not perceive it?" Isaiah 43:18-19a

Attention! Start the session by giving the group the opportunity to share the meaning of Christmas that they have discovered.

Accept

Connect | Navigate

Introductory Activity (12-17 years).

- Instructions: Ask about anything the group has done wrong in the past and what the consequence was. For example, I didn't make the bed when my mother asked me to, and consequently she didn't let me be with my friends for several days. The goal is to help the group understand that every action has a consequence.

Introductory Activity (18-23 years).

- Instructions: Ask the group about two or three things they did last year but don't want to repeat next year: things that were done but that ended badly or had bad consequences. For example, I dropped out of school, I didn't do my homework, I wasn't faithful to the Lord, etc.

Connect | Navigate

On some occasions, some people start walking and get so distracted listening to music or talking on the phone, that when they realize it, they have already walked more than they should have, and they're far from home. And they wonder, "How did I get here?"

Something very similar happens to people when December arrives. Suddenly, they feel like the year is ending so quickly that they didn't even realize what they experienced. And when December arrives, they need to sit down, analyze and think, how did we get here? This will help them reflect on what they've experienced; (failures, victories, mistakes, disappointments, triumphs) and reflect on improvements they would like to make in the future. But also, it can help them focus - if they want to get anywhere, they have to keep walking!

1. What has been: What have I learned?

"Have you experienced so much for nothing? Surely it was not in vain, was it?" (Galatians 3:4 NLT).

What we've experienced would be of no use to us if we cannot learn from it. Therefore, we need to start the new year taking into account what has happened and what we can learn. It will be up to us to make sure that the experiences of the past year haven't been in vain, and we can take something from it that helps us improve our future.

When we're young, we may feel so dynamic and self-sufficient that we don't think the following three aspects are important:

- Plan better and measure the consequences: Many times, we make the mistake of making decisions without thinking and without measuring the consequences (Proverbs 27:12). Was it raining when Noah started building the ark? No! But he heard the voice of God and began to plan the construction of the ark. In fact, it took him over 120 years to build. If we fail to plan, we're planning to fail!

- Heed advice: Another mistake is that we don't listen to the advice of others (Proverbs 15:22). We must learn to seek, listen, and analyze advice. Why don't we like to listen to advice?

Perhaps because we think we don't need it, or we think we know everything, or that it's better to learn it along the way (Proverbs 12:15). The advice of those who have already gone through what we're going through can be useful to us. It's wise to listen to the advice of others!

- Do not give up: It's very easy to get discouraged and give up when something doesn't go well or when there's "opposition." This shows that we're not persistent enough (Proverbs 24:10). When something goes wrong or when we fail at something, it's time to evaluate and change things or start over. Very few get what they want on the first try. Many times we give up just when we're about to get there. At school, math is difficult for some people. But if one day they determine to have the attitude "I like it," although it may continue to be difficult but they don't give up, they can finish the year with a good grade in the class. Let's not give up!

2. What will begin: What do I have in my hands?

We have a lot of experience. Many times we're not aware of it, but at the end of each year, we have, in many aspects of our lives, more experience than we had the previous year. Let's use it!

It's important to think about failures, victories, blessings, losses, etc. of the year that has just ended. Then we must analyze what's really left. Exactly! We're left with the experience of what has been lived. Today, you have much more experience than yesterday and much more experience than last year.

So let's start this year using the experience we've gained. To paraphrase what Galatians 3:4 says, "Are you going to waste such great experiences?" Let's hope not! God wants us to use our life experiences to grow. There are different experiences to consider:

- Educational experiences: We have more knowledge than last year. Let's not waste it, or miss out on opportunities to study (school, university, church, etc.).

- Spiritual experiences: we've grown and matured in faith. We've participated in the church, youth services, retreats, camps, etc. If we take advantage of every moment with God and His Word, we must have learned something new. Although we have times where we socialize, we must also take advantage of the opportunities in which God wants to speak to us.

- Family experiences: The relationship and responsibilities at home. Let's take care of our family life. Remember that this is part of training and growth.

- Painful experiences: God uses the difficult experiences in our lives to shape our character. Loss due to death, loss of friends, economic loss, loss of job, etc.

In the year that is to begin, we must be determined to initiate each project and goal using the experience acquired in the past year. If we've had failures, now we have the wisdom to avoid them. If we've gone from victory to victory, we have the experience of continuing on the same path. Whatever we start, let's do it with what we have ... experience.

3. What will come: What will we do?

God wants to do something new in every young person in the coming year. Something never seen before. Something special. Something that cannot and shouldn't be lost. But to get there:

- Don't limit God: Even our limited imagination limits God's work in our lives. Sometimes, the limit of what God wants to do is our own mind. The words of Isaiah 43:18-19 were written many years before they were fulfilled. Isaiah was prophesying to a people who would soon be in captivity, far from their land. God wanted them to know that when they cried out for deliverance, God would give them something new. The people of Israel could expect God to work with them as He had in the past. And although the past was wonderful, God wanted to do something even more extraordinary! (Isaiah 43:16-21).

The same thing happens with us. By thinking that God has to act in a certain way, according to our reasoning, we're limiting what He plans to do with us. God is going to do something new through young people who don't limit Him with their thoughts, imagination, and dreams. God wants to do something new, but He won't do it if we continue to put confidence in our limitations. Let's allow God to put His dreams in us!

- Trust God: It's important to trust God and not our own strength. In Luke 18, we see that Jesus was talking to the rich young man, and those who heard Jesus' response said, "Who then can be saved?" It's impossible! And Jesus answered them, "What is impossible with men is possible with God" (Luke 18:24-27).

  When we stop trusting in God and start trusting in our own strength, knowledge, and abilities, we're headed for defeat or a waste of resources.

- Act in faith: Faith is essential if we want to undertake something new. We need faith for the new year since we're going to enter new, unexplored territory. We don't know what God has in mind for us, but if we want to let God do something completely new in our lives, we must have faith.

Jesus said in Matthew 9:29, "Because of your faith, it will happen." This is a simple phrase, but very powerful. This new year, God wants to do something special in your life, don't limit Him with your doubts, trust only in Him and take each step in faith, and He will surely do the rest. He's already doing it!

Review/Application:

Ask the students to answer the following questions. Discuss if they feel comfortable sharing.

1. What have I learned from my mistakes this last year?
2. What expectations do I have for the new year?
3. What three goals do I want to achieve in the next year?
4. What things from the past that don't help me should I let go of?

Challenge:

Answer the following questions and save them.

- What are your expectations for this new year?
- What do you expect from God this new year?
- What do you expect of yourself this new year?

Review the questions and their answers throughout the year and you'll see how you're progressing.